Television Economics

For James Nelson Rosse

Contents

List of Figures

List of Tables

Preface

The material in this book is intended to be accessible to the general reader interested in television policy in the United States. In writing for such an audience, we have tried to translate the economic jargon of our analytical material into reasonably plain English. There are two dangers in this. The first is that the result may turn out to seem merely tedious to the lay reader and terribly fuzzy to the professional economist. The second danger is that there may be an insufficiently clear distinction between those results and conclusions which are based on "hard" analysis, and those other conclusions (absolutely unavoidable in policy work) which are based on casual analysis, or "armchair price theory." We hope that this difficulty has been alleviated, at least, by our division of the book into two parts, the first emphasizing theory and analysis, the second policy. Throughout both parts of the book, we hope, there are new ideas and significant extensions of old ideas that will be of interest to the professional economist. We ask these readers to take account of our attempt to make the material accessible to others. We have tried diligently to separate and label (but not to eliminate) those policy conclusions which have not been derived from rigorous analysis.

This book came into being when we realized that we had thought and written so much about television that all the pieces could be fit together and form a coherent whole. It is our hope that the content of this book will be of assistance to students of the television industry in their research, and more important, to policy-makers and their advisors in seeking better answers to the great issues of mass-communication regulation in the United States. It is our view that economic analysis is indispensible to this latter task, although we are not so lacking in humility as to regard it as sufficient.

We are grateful to Professor James Nelson Rosse of Stanford University, to whom this volume is dedicated, who has served unstintingly as a mentor to each of us in turn, and who has stimulated so much of our thinking and training in this endeavor.

Grateful acknowledgement is due to various institutions for financial and other support in the past, support that led to the development of many of the ideas contained here. These institutions include the National Science Foundation, the White House Office of Telecommunications Policy, the Brookings Institution, the Hoover Institution on War, Revolution and Peace, and the J.F. Kennedy School of Government of Harvard University.

We are indebted to the editors of *Public Policy* and to the Office of Telecommunications Policy for permission to revise and use materials originally published by them.

It is impossible to list all of the many individuals who have helped us in discussing and criticizing our work, but special mention must be made of Stanley

Besen, Henry Goldberg, Bridger Mitchell, and A. Michael Spence. We are also indebted to Robert Crandall, Donald Dunn, Roger Noll, Marc Roberts, and Tom Whitehead for their comments and assistance.

Mrs. Marianna Scherrer was an excellent and patient typist.

Finally, we would like to gratefully acknowledge the support of our wives, Jo, Patricia, and Ricky, in seeing us through this project.

Television Economics

Part I:
Economics of Television
Program Markets

1 Introduction

Organization

Glamour and social influence not withstanding, television is a business. Television performance is influenced by the economic incentives facing owners, managers, customers, suppliers, and employees, and by the structure of its markets. It is quixotic to hope to "improve" the performance of this or any other industry without first understanding the economic motivations of the people who participate in it. We do not deny for a moment that noneconomic goals and values are important in this industry. Nevertheless, policy debate about television too often ignores precisely those economic factors which can shed the most light on the merits of alternative policies, or which most plausibly explain existing behavior.

As the reader will shortly discover, the economics of television markets are usually subtle and complex, and a good deal of research remains to be done before they can be fully understood. There are no short and easy answers to the question of how to make the television business serve the public better, but there are certainly many answers that are misleading, and that if pursued will lead to frustration and disillusionment. We hope that readers of this book will be better prepared to work out for themselves some satisfying solutions to the terribly important questions of television policy and performance.

The present chapter will set out a general framework for economic analysis of television markets, together with some technical and historical background, and a short discussion of the authors' prejudices. The rest of Part I is made up of three more or less self-contained essays. Chapter 2 deals with the program-supply market, arguing that it is one in which competition and entry play an important role, and that the supply of programs is quite responsive to changes in the demand for them. In Chapter 3 we explore the problem of program choice by stations (and networks) under various parametric conditions regarding advertiser demand, viewer preferences, and market structure. The goal of this chapter is to examine the effect of market structure on viewer satisfaction. Chapter 4 is devoted to an analysis of the role and behavior of television networks. The major contribution of Chapter 4 is a model of oligopolistic rivalry among the networks, and its implications for program quality. Chapter 4 also contains a discussion of the network-affiliate relationship. These three chapters provide the basis for the policy oriented chapters in Part II. The first of these, Chapter 5, asks whether it is possible to improve the performance of the television industry by alterations in market structure or regulatory policy within the present limited television spectrum allocation. We are concerned here with such questions as localism, new networks, and pay TV. Chapter 6 is concerned with cable television, and the opportunities and problems raised by this new medium of "unlimited" channels. This discussion supports the recommendations of the Cabinet Committee on Cable Communications. Chapter 7 examines the public-ownership alternative to commercial television. This chapter is devoted principally to a discussion of the structure of decision-making in public television, and to the question of funding levels. Finally, Chapter 8 is devoted to a *potpourri* of public-policy issues not considered in earlier chapters, such as license renewal, the fairness doctrine, and newspaper-TV cross-ownership.

We do not claim to have treated every aspect of television markets in this book. Some issues are treated peripherally. Among the topics not considered in great detail are advertising economics (Backman [25],[a] Simon [505]); the question of copyright economics and exclusivity (Chazen and Ross [119]); sports (Horowitz [256]); news, daytime, and public-affairs programming (Mayer [352], Epstein [178]); the political and social effects of program content (Schramm [493]); the politics of broadcast regulation (Krasnow and Longley [311]); and spectrum-allocation reform. Many of these issues are, however, touched on briefly in passing, and the bibliography contains references to the more significant works in these areas.

Basic Economics of Television

The first and most serious mistake that an analyst of the television industry can make is to assume that TV stations are in business to produce programs. They are not. TV stations are in the business of producing *audiences*. These audiences, or means of access to them, are sold to advertisers. The product of a TV station is measured in dimensions of people and time. The price of the product is quoted in dollars per thousand viewers per minute of commercial time.

It is often said that TV stations are interested in maximizing audience size, but this is an oversimplification. First, advertisers are interested not merely in the size of an audience, but in its characteristics. In the trade these audience characteristics are called "demographics," and refer to the age, sex, and income composition of the audience. Thus, some audiences of given size are more valuable than others. Second, a TV station may be able to maximize its audience only at prohibitive program cost. If TV station managers are rational business-men, as their stockholders have every right to expect them to be, they will be interested in maximizing the difference between advertising revenue and costs, and this difference is of course profit. Thus, while it is certainly true that TV stations are interested in achieving as large an audience as possible for any given

[a]Numbers in brackets refer to items in the bibliography.

program expenditure, we should not expect to find stations seeking to obtain an indefinitely large audience regardless of the cost.

Why is it that television stations sell access to audiences instead of programs? Is this not a rather peculiar economic situation, if not a serious moral issue? One reason that stations sell audiences, of course, is that most stations are unable to collect from viewers directly. Not only is it technically difficult and expensive to scramble signals, for instance, or to collect money from coin boxes on TV sets, but it is actually *illegal* to charge viewers for most TV programs under current FCC rules. (The FCC's more significant rules and regulations for television can be found in the back of any issue of *Broadcasting Yearbook*.) A more fundamental reason for the sale of audiences to advertisers is that audiences are valuable to advertisers. Audiences that pay something to receive messages (as with magazines and newspapers) are often more valuable to advertisers than those generated by free messages, since it is clear that the audience is in fact interested. Even if it were as easy to collect for TV programs as it is for magazines or movies, there would almost certainly still be "commercials" of one kind or another presented with many programs. Doubtless these commercials would have to be of greater value to consumers than those we see now. (We will return to this issue in Chapter 3.)

To the extent that there is competition among stations and between TV stations and other media, individual TV stations have little choice but to attempt to maximize long-run profits. This does not mean that they are not "good citizens" interested in public-interest objectives. But they are engaged in a business, and have responsibilities to stockholders that cannot be disregarded.

If broadcasters really try to maximize profits, how can we explain the presence of TV programs that clearly do not draw audiences as large as those which could be obtained with the same expenditure? Such programs include public affairs, documentaries, presidential speeches, congressional hearings, and religious programs. It is true that the owners of the station can choose to "give up" otherwise attainable profits in order to do public service programming. To the extent that they do so, they may simply be deciding on one of many ways in which to spend their incomes. But a more plausible explanation of such programming lies in regulation. TV stations operate under three-year federal licenses, which can in theory be revoked if the FCC finds that a station has not been operating in the "public interest." (For an overview of the license renewal process, see Goldberg [223], Krasnow and Longley [311] and Chapter 8 of this book. While TV licenses are seldom revoked, the threat is nevertheless a real one.) This license is a valuable asset, for reasons to be discussed below, and is not lightly risked. The FCC associates certain kinds of programs (namely, those listed above) with performance in the public interest. Minority groups have successfully demanded such programs as the price of their support for license renewal. If it appears to the licensee that this price is less than the cost of legal services plus the risk of license revocation times the value of the license, then the station will acquiesce.

The economic motivation of TV stations is taken for granted in this book. We assume that licensees are engaged in attempting to maximize long-run profits, taking due account of regulation, the behavior of their competitors, risk-avoidance, and so on. This paradigm of economic behavior is, we feel, useful in understanding television markets, and equally useful in making conditional policy statements. (A conditional policy statement is one that says, "Provided you want to reach *that* particular goal *this* is the best way to do it.")

The economic motivation of TV stations is fundamental to this book in a "positive" (descriptive, analytical) sense. The normative implications of this assumption are really outside the scope of our work, except in Chapter 7. That is, we do not regard it as inherently either "bad" or "good" that TV stations seek profits, but merely examine the consequences of this motivation in the light of industry structure and regulatory constraints. It is impossible to understand the behavior of the industry or the consequences of alternative policies without accepting this fundamental premise. Many present policies are ineffective or perverse precisely because they ignore the fact that broadcasting is a business. Policy-makers of course are free to make broadcasting into a nonbusiness activity, either by subsidization (as with U.S. public broadcasting), or through state monopoly, as in many European and communist countries. But with the exception of Chapter 7, we shall limit our analysis to commercial television.

Television: A Profile of the Players

While TV stations are the backbone of our commercial broadcasting system, there are many other groups and institutions that are important to it. Most prominent are the networks, which act as agents or brokers on behalf of local stations both in selling audiences and in acquiring programs. These and other players are the cast of this book. Their interactions are sometimes strange and complex, but never uninteresting. Figure 1-1 provides some overview of the crowded scene, but it is a very simplified view indeed, as the following chapters will show.

Stations

There are about 900 television stations in the United States. Of these, 220 are educational or public-broadcasting stations and 680 are commercial stations. Stations can be broken down into VHF and UHF categories, and into those which are and are not affiliated with a network (see Table 1-1).

Network-affiliated commercial stations, in addition to being the largest single group in terms of numbers, revenues, and profits, attract by far the most viewers, and are thus most influential (see Table 1-2). UHF stations in general

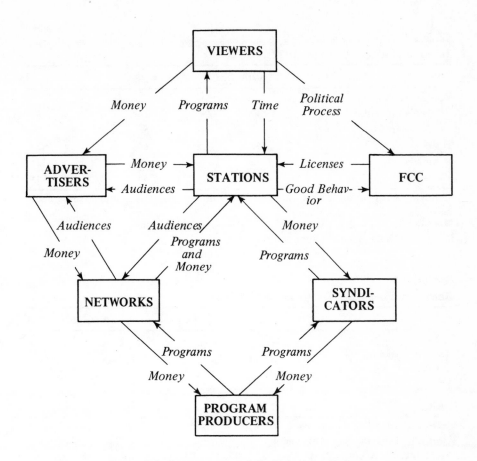

Figure 1-1. Organization of the Television Industry

and independent UHF stations in particular are something of a pathological case, the dimensions of which will be discussed in Chapter 5. Educational stations will be treated in Chapter 7.

Networks

There are three fulltime national commercial television networks, and a number of parttime special networks, such as the Hughes Sports Network. The networks serve as brokers or intermediaries between local stations and both advertisers and program suppliers. The three commercial networks are perhaps the most important single part of the television industry. The economics of network behavior and of the network-affiliate relationship are treated in Chapter 4.

Table 1-1
Television Stations by Type, 1972

	VHF	UHF	Total
Commercial stations:			
Network Affiliated[a]	428	110	538
Independent[a]	33	53	86
Total Commercial[a]	461	163	624
Noncommercial	130	91	221
Total[b]	620	264	884

[a]Excludes part-year stations, satellite stations, and stations with annual revenues under $25,000.
[b]Includes stations with under $25,000 in time sales not included above.
Source: Federal Communications Commission data.

Table 1-2
Television Finances, 1972 (millions of dollars)

	Revenues[b]	Expenses	Profits Before Tax
3 TV networks	1271	1160	111
15 O & O stations[a]	327	225	102
475 Other VHF stations	1396	1041	355
173 UHF stations	185	201	(16)
Totals	3179	2627	552

[a]Stations owned and operated by the networks.
[b]Net, after commissions and discounts.
Note: Includes stations with less than $25,000 in time sales, in contrast to Table 1-1.
Source: Federal Communications Commission data.

Viewers

There are now about 66 million American households with at least one TV set. Of these, about 37 million homes have color sets. The average household is said to spend about seven hours per day watching television. Great care must be exercised, however, in dealing with viewer data based on ratings or audience surveys. Methods of measurement in this area are subject to errors, which may be very large. There is an extensive discussion in Chapters 3 and 4 of viewer behavior patterns.

Advertisers

Television is only one of many ways in which advertisers can communicate their messages. In fact, TV advertising is not as important in total advertising expenditure as one might imagine. Television accounts for only about 17 percent of all advertising expenditure (see Table 1-3).

There are three distinct television advertising markets. The first is national advertising, in which advertisers seeking to reach the entire national audience have a choice between TV networks and magazines, among the media. This advertising is sold at a very high price (upwards of $50,000 per commercial minute in prime time) because it reaches the very largest audiences that can be obtained through any medium, but it is also sold at a relatively low price per viewer (about 2¢ per viewing home per hour) because it is not very selective.

National advertisers can reach *selective* local audiences by purchasing time directly from local TV stations. This is called the national spot market. Advertisers who engage in this market have a choice among TV stations, radio stations, newspapers, and regional editions of national magazines.

Finally, there is local advertising, or time bought by firms with only local sales. Such advertising is not very important for television, probably because most local advertising carries a high proportion of information relative to persuasion, a job for which the television medium is relatively ill suited, and for which local newspapers are quite efficient. (For background on advertising, see Barton [51], Doyle [166], Johnson [271], Simon [505].)

National spot advertising is distinguished from local advertising by the identity of the buyers. In the national spot market, big advertisers deal with local station representatives and buy time on the basis of published "rate cards." In the local market, local merchants deal directly with the station, and as with newspapers, many transactions take place at unpublished prices.

Table 1-3
Advertising Expenditures, 1971

	Billions of Dollars	Percent of Total
Television - Total	3.6	17
Network	1.6	8
National spot	1.2	5
Local	0.8	4
Newspapers	6.2	30
Magazines	1.4	7
Radio	1.4	7
Direct mail	3.0	15
Other	5.0	24
Total	20.6	100

Note: These data differ from those in Table 1-2 by the amount spent by advertisers directly on program and commercial production, plus agency commissions.

Source: Derived from data prepared for *Advertising Age* by McCann-Erickson, Inc., and used with permission.

The Competition

The television industry is in competition for advertising with other industries, notably radio broadcasting, newspapers, magazines, and more recently, cable television. Each of these media offers special advantages to certain types of advertisers, depending on the nature of their product, the amount and kind of information that is customarily transmitted in their advertisements, and the geographical dispersion and identifiability of their potential customers. There are some advertisers for whom television is entirely unsuitable, and others for whom it is indispensable. But most advertisers can substitute one medium for another in response to changes in prices of advertising time or space and the relative productivities of the media. Thus, competition between TV stations or networks and other media may be nearly as important in the long run as competition among TV stations.

Since advertising demand is a function of audience size, the media also compete for audiences, and in particular for those special audiences which are most valuable to advertisers. This kind of competition is very important indeed within the television industry, but perhaps less important in the short run on an intermedia level. In the long run, of course, intermedia competition for audiences is terribly important. The growth and success of television has caused important losses in newspaper readership, mass magazine circulation, radio listening, and especially movie theater attendance. Cable television promises today to "fragment" the television audience similarly.

The Regulators

Television would be a more ordinary business if it were not for the fact that it makes use of the electromagnetic spectrum to transmit its signals. The broadcast spectrum in the United States was nationalized by an act of Congress in 1927, and ever since has been allocated by a Federal regulatory commission. TV stations now use the spectrum under a renewable three-year license from the Federal Communications Commission. The licensing power of the FCC is exercised in such a way that virtually all of the activities of TV stations, except advertising prices, are directly regulated. Even advertising prices are indirectly regulated by virtue of the FCC's power to control entry and the number of competitors. This regulation is in some part an historical accident, since use of the spectrum is not essential to the television business. TV signals can be, and increasingly are, carried on wires. In discussing television regulation, it is well to remember that the organic statutes of communication regulation were enacted in the days of radio, long before television was a practical commercial business. There are many excellent works on the history of broadcast regulation, which excuse us from an extensive discussion of that subject here (see Barnow [43],

Herring and Gross [251], Coase [130], [131], Minasian [363]). Instead, we will concentrate on a few important economic implications of regulation.

Only a relatively small part of the usable electromagnetic spectrum is used for commercial broadcasting. Such services as police, fire, and military communication systems, radar, taxicab radios, microwave systems, and citizens' band radios all use the spectrum, and their users are constantly clamoring before the FCC for more spectrum. Since the FCC is charged with allocating the spectrum in the "public interest," it is faced with the difficult task of allocating an economic resource without the usual market signals from prices. The spectrum probably could be bought and sold as private property rights (Coase [130], DeVany [160]). If it were, and if the property rights were sufficiently well defined, so that significant interference problems were avoided, we could be better assured that it was utilized in the most productive manner. As it is, we have no such assurance. That portion of the spectrum allocated to television is, from an economic point of view, of arbitrary size. There is a relative scarcity of VHF-TV licenses, leading to economic rents—profits in excess of those required to keep the stations in business—which accrue to the holders of licenses (see Levin [328], Greenberg [234], Webbink [607]). Lord Thompson of Fleet once characterized a TV license as a "license to print money." In competitive industries, entry by new firms takes place until excess profits are reduced to zero, and only sufficient profits are earned to return the market price of capital and other inputs. In television, FCC decisions about spectrum allocation have prevented entry from reducing VHF profits in this way. Consequently, a TV license is a valuable asset, for which its holders are willing to pay a considerable price in the market. Licensees are also willing to pay a considerable price to do things that satisfy the regulatory objectives of the Commission and potential challengers at license-renewal time. It is worth noting that there is an active market in these licenses, and even firms that specialize in brokerage of TV and radio stations. Permission for such sales must be obtained from the FCC, but the transfer process is usually pro forma.

The relationship between excess profits due to the scarcity of licenses and the ability of the FCC to require licensees to perform costly public-service functions was first recognized not by the Commission but by a court (*Carroll v. FCC* 258 F. 2nd 440, 1959; see Posner [449]). The so-called Carroll Doctrine now requires the Commission to take into account the economic impact on TV stations of its entry policies, in order to preserve an appropriate level of public service programming. The issue in *Carroll* was the ability of an existing station to do public-service programming if it were faced by new competition through an FCC grant of a new license in its market. This concept also provides the principal judicial rationale for FCC regulation of cable television. That is, the FCC's jurisdiction over cable is due to the potential ability of cable to compete away TV station profits and thus affect their ability to do public service programming (see *Midwest Video* [361]).

It is generally valid to say that the FCC has been uncomfortable with the notion that its policies have economic implications, and indeed with the notion that broadcasting is a business. The quasi-official view of broadcasting at the FCC has been that broadcasters are public-spirited citizens, fiduciaries of the public, who are unfortunately obliged to sell advertising in order to defray expenses of operation. The responsibility of broadcasters is, officially, to the viewing public, and not to shareholders. This unrealistic view is the source not only of much ineffective policy, but of two considerable evils. The first is that broadcasters take advantage of the public-interest myth to promote a variety of protectionist policies, motivated in fact by economic self-interest. The second evil is that the public at large is misled in its perception of the role and function of broadcasting in America. It does not follow, necessarily, that because broadcasting *is* a business, it therefore ought to be a business. But it does follow that so long as it is a business, regulators and the public should recognize that fact and explore its implications for policy.

Perhaps the most significant event in the history of television regulation was the creation of an artificial scarcity of VHF-TV licenses. The effect of this policy has been to create a system of powerful vested interests, which continue to stand in the path of reform and change—particularly change involving increased competition and viewer choice. We shall meet this problem time and again in the following pages. One obvious possibility for dealing with it is to increase the number of channels, a policy that would meet with perhaps insuperable political opposition from the industry. Another possibility is for the government to use the market mechanism, rather than fiat, to allocate the spectrum among competing users. Although we shall mention this possibility from time to time, it too is likely to be politically infeasible, and we do not place great emphasis upon it.

Competition, Economic Efficiency, and the First Amendment

In analyzing television markets in the following chapters we admit two prejudices, and the reader is entitled to be informed of this fact. The first concerns economic efficiency; and the reader is warned that "economic efficiency" has a different meaning than technical or business efficiency in the colloquial sense. As economists, we are concerned with the functioning of markets, and in this case with the functioning of television markets. We shall be concerned when these markets are inefficient. There are several different ways in which a market can be inefficient. One is a consistent failure by firms to minimize the cost of producing whatever output they choose to produce (or, equivalently, a failure to maximize output with given resources). Another is a failure to produce the type and quantity of output that would maximize consumer welfare. A third is the presence of constraints, usually inspired by government, which prevent the sale of certain products or services or the very existence of a market in these services. Generally speaking, markets that are competitive tend to be efficient, whereas markets characterized by significant monopoly power tend not to be efficient. (We leave aside "natural" monopolies—firms that for one reason or another can achieve minimum cost only by serving 100 percent of the market. As we shall see in Chapter 6, cable-television firms have this characteristic in a local area.) In a market like the television market, where consumers do not pay directly for the services they consume, it is often difficult to make strong statements about the relative efficiency of alternative market structures. We shall encounter this problem often in this book.

Our second prejudice is that we take the spirit of the First Amendment as given.[b] By this we mean, first, that government intrusion in the television medium is to be avoided, and second, that monopoly in the medium is undesirable. (See the discussion in Chapter 8 on the fairness doctrine.) In many important respects television now occupies the constitutional role that the newspaper business did in the eighteenth and nineteenth centuries. Whether it is as well suited to perform this role is another question. We shall take these objectives as good ones, ones to be valued highly in communications policy. Where we think that there are conflicts between economic efficiency and the spirit of the First Amendment we shall point these out, but on the whole these goals are complementary; frequently in pursuing one we can more nearly attain the other.

We recognize, of course, that the present structure of broadcast regulation, predicated though it is on similar objectives, seems to reach diametrically opposing conclusions. That is, the government has created broadcasters with monopoly power, obliged them to exercise control over program content, and then proceeded to regulate their exercise of that power more or less directly. This approach seems to us to be simply wrong. It probably grew out of a series of judicial and legislative decisions taken in ignorance or awe of new technology, rather than through a conscious rejection of the antipaternalistic ethic of the First Amendment. Nevertheless, there are many who would argue that television is inherently "different" from the other media—more powerful, influential, or insidious—and that this McLuhanesque difference justifies or compels government regulation, regardless of the structure of the medium. Such people put television regulation in the same category as safe food and drug laws. We want to make it plain that our argument with this approach is philosophical (and logical) but not "economic," and as such must simply be taken as a prejudice of ours in

---

[b]We say "spirit" because we are not lawyers. The words in the First Amendment may seem perfectly clear to the layman: "Congress shall make no law . . . abridging the freedom of speech, or of the press. . . ." But we know enough of the law to recognize that these words have not been interpreted to say what they seem to mean on the surface.

the present context, rather than an area in which we have some special claim to expertise.

A common rejoinder to excessively sanctimonious dicta concerning the constitutional role of the press is to point to the actual content of the media and to ask whether it is worthy of constitutional protection. While the network news may have some element of virtue in the "marketplace of ideas," *I Love Lucy* has little obvious relationship to high libertarian ideals. Indeed, most of television is entertainment, not "ideas" in any very direct constitutional sense. Is the dichotomy between entertainment and news (or opinion) a valuable one for policy purposes? This is dangerous ground for two reasons. First, some "entertainment" contains politically sensitive content. Second, it is not clear in what way the consumption of ideas and information is to be distinguished from the consumption of entertainment. Ideas and information are often consumed because they are packaged in an entertaining way.

Another point worth making is that much of the content of that common whipping boy, the commercial, consists of information, and sometimes valuable information. TV commercials typically contain less "straight" information than newspaper want ads or print media space advertising, but they contain some. The role of television, as with any other medium, is to broadcast information, because information is a commodity in demand. Television entertainment programming is very popular partly because it is free, and partly because it packages information in a very engaging way. That the content of the information is often trivial or banal is not of any particular moment from the constitutional point of view. Most newspaper content is, from some perspective, almost equally banal or trivial or wrong or misleading. The point is that the role of the media is to provide conduits for the flow of information and expression in society, and that the content or packaging of that information is a separable issue from the degree of efficiency and freedom with which the media themselves operate. This is true even though one cannot deny Innis's (and McLuhan's) dictum that the "medium is the message." Surely the economic structure and the technology of the media condition the nature, content, and effect of messages. But this is precisely what is meant by the relationship of media structure to efficiency and freedom, since efficiency and freedom are concepts associated (by us) more closely with messages than with media or conduits. It comes down to this: we seek that structure of the television medium which is most competitive and which generates the greatest possible degree of freedom, from the point of view of the production and consumption of ideas and information. This distinction becomes particularly important when there are trade-offs between the efficiency of information production or consumption and the distribution of that information, or when freedom for producers and consumers of information can be augmented only at the expense of the owners of the media.

The Notion of a "Public Good"

Television has a peculiar characteristic that we shall encounter from time to time in the following pages—the notion of a "public good." It is important because it puts certain limitations on our ability to associate "competition" with "economic efficiency"—an association that is normally made quite directly. There are two kinds of goods or commodities—"private" and "public." The distinction has nothing to do with who provides the good—a "private" good can be produced by the government. A pure private good or commodity is one whose cost of production is related to the number of people who consume it; it is a good which, if consumed by one person, is no longer available for someone else. A slice of bread is a good example of a pure private good. A pure "public" good, on the other hand, is one whose cost of production is independent of the number of people who consume it; more precisely, one person's consumption of such a good does not reduce the quantity available to other people. The standard example of a pure public good is national defense or national security.

Most goods have some elements of "privateness" and some elements of "publicness." Motion pictures and books, for instance, exhibit this dual property. Their content is a public good, but they are delivered to customers in the form of a private good. The conditions for efficient allocation of a *pure* public or a *pure* private good have been known for some time, and the two sets of conditions are markedly different. In particular, there is reason to believe that a decentralized competitive private market system will not produce an adequate supply of pure public goods. Private production of such a good sometimes requires monopoly power for its producer (protection of that producer from entry or competition); it may also require the existence of "exclusion devices," or mechanisms for denying the public good to nonpaying consumers. "Free riders" are a common problem with public goods. The public-good elements in toll roads, sports exhibitions, concerts, and the like will suggest the kind of difficulty this implies. Finally, even a monopoly producer of a public good from which free riders can be easily excluded may not produce enough of the public good unless he is also able to practice price discrimination among his customers. The reason for this should be clear: Since it costs nothing to supply an extant public good to any given consumer, it is inefficient to exclude any consumer who values the good at any positive level. Any uniform price will exclude all consumers whose value for the good lies between zero and that price. Given the need for the producer to receive at least enough revenue to cover his costs (thereby excluding the uniform price of zero), no uniform price is efficient. Therefore, efficiency requires that each consumer be charged a price that is no greater than the value he places on the public good. A similar argument can be constructed to demonstrate that the producer must charge each consumer no *less* than his valuation of the good, or else the producer will not be able to produce the right quality or level of the public good.

What does all this have to do with television? A great deal. Both television programs and the electromagnetic signals that carry them are public goods—indeed, very nearly pure public goods!

Once a TV *program* has been produced, the cost of production is independent of the number of people who will eventually see it. (On the other hand, the production cost may very well determine, at least partly, how many people will *want* to see it.) The program, whether on tape or film, remains available and unchanged no matter how many viewers see it.

If the program is *broadcast*, the broadcast itself is a public good, at least within the geographical area of the signal. The receipt of the signal does not reduce the quantity of the signal available to others. In this respect a TV broadcast is unique. Most entertainment (while itself heavily infected with "publicness") is "delivered" to the consumer in or through a private good—a book, a magazine, a ringside seat, a theater chair, etc. But television has a public good as its delivery mechanism, and not just a public good, but also great difficulty in excluding nonpayers. If the over-the-air television business were run on a viewer subscription basis, in other words, the transactions costs of collecting from viewers for the broadcasts would be high.

The public-good problem in television makes it very difficult to say things about the efficiency implications of alternative market structures. We shall return to this problem many times in the pages that follow, and especially in Chapter 3.

2

The Supply of Programming

Introduction

Chapter 1 noted that television is a business whose product is audiences. Broadcasters use programs to attract audiences, which the stations and networks sell to advertisers. This programming is acquired by stations largely from the three commercial networks and the syndication market.

Who produces this programming? Is control vested with the networks, or a few movie producers? Or is there a large number of diverse producers of programs? Are the costs of producing programs so high and the risks so great that entry into the industry is difficult? These and related questions of structure and cost are important. Public policy, aimed at altering the content of commercial television, cannot blindly ignore the industry that creates these programs. For this reason we shall analyze the program production industry in some detail. This examination will provide a foundation for the following chapters on broadcaster behavior and public policy.

This chapter uses existing public information[a] to describe the economic organization of the industry that supplies television programs to stations through the syndication market and the networks. (We are concerned primarily with prime-time entertainment and syndicated programming. Daytime programs, news, sports, and public affairs are not discussed in this chapter. Those interested should read Mayer [352], Chapters 5-8.) Our analysis suggests that the supply of programming to the networks is very competitive, in the sense of monopolistic competition.[b] This conclusion is based on the following four characteristics of the supply to the networks: the fact that the networks themselves distribute the programs to their affiliates; the existence of a well-developed rental market for the factors of production; the viability of a

---

[a]This chapter is based on data from several sources. The trade journals (*Television, Broadcasting,* and *Variety*) provided background material. Much of the unfootnoted text in the following sections represents our own interpretation of that trade literature. The Little [335], [336], Land [317], and OTP [599] reports were the sources of nearly all the "hard" data. A.D. Little Co. prepared its reports on behalf of the networks. Herman Land Associates prepared its report for the National Association of Broadcasters. Because of the vested interests that supported the production of these reports, their data, sources, and definitions should be studied carefully. Before reusing those data, we strongly encourage the reader to read the originals.

[b]"Monopolistic competition" describes an industry where a very large number of producers sell differentiated products that are readily substitutable. If entry is not restricted, competition among such producers ensures that no producer will earn profits in excess of a "normal" rate of return on his capital and skill.

17

wide range of firm types and sizes; and the ease of entry for new producers. The syndication market appears to be less competitive, but it is not monopolistic. The difference between syndication and the supply to the networks arises, in part, because the syndicators distribute their programs to stations, while producers who "package" programs for the networks do not.

The subsequent sections will develop these conclusions more fully. The following section describes the role of distribution economies in the supply of a public good such as television programs. (See the discussion of public goods on pp. 15-16.) The next section deals with the structure of the supply of programs to the networks, and the final section examines the syndication market, which supplies most of the nonnetwork programming to stations. The appendix contains a discussion of network and syndication program costs, and the relationship between costs and revenues in prime time.

Role of Distribution Economies

Given the prevalence of distribution economies, there is a tendency for television program markets to be oligopolistic in structure. These economies arise primarily from the public-good character of programs (see Chapter 1).

The public-good character of a program causes economies in distribution within a market and across markets. Once the decision to display a program has been made, the profit-maximizing audience size is all of the local viewing public. (This also assumes that the power, capital equipment, and tower of the station are fixed.) Within any market, one viewer's decision to see a program does not interfere with another person's viewing the same program, and consequently the cost per viewer declines with the number of viewers. Since revenues increase with audience size, the greater the number of people who view the show, the greater the station profit.

The public-good economies hold across markets as well as within them. As long as there are enough viewers in a market to cover the incremental cost of distributing the program to that market, the larger the audience and the greater the number of markets, the greater the profits of a show. It would be extremely expensive to write, produce, and edit *I Love Lucy* in every one of the hundreds of television markets. By distributing each episode, broadcasters spread the original cost of the programs and avoid replication costs.

Historically, program distribution has taken two forms—networking and syndication.[c] Networking not only spreads costs over a large audience, it attempts to minimize the number of distribution links between the distributor

---

[c]In the early 1920s radio stations began to share programs on a barter basis, a primitive form of syndication. RCA created the National Broadcasting Corporation in 1926. NBC, the first permanent network, began operations in 1927 (Mayer [352] p. 12).

and the stations by simultaneously broadcasting programs to affiliates.[d] Syndication, however, requires that copies be returned to the distributor in order to check the films for wear. As the closing section of this chapter notes, the use of syndication entails higher distribution costs than networking.

In addition, most stations cannot afford to produce local shows of quality comparable to network and syndicated fare, because the cost per viewer would exceed the likely advertising revenue per viewer. Local stations appear to use local origination only if local tastes diverge significantly from national tastes, or to satisfy FCC requirements for locally originated programs. Recent station behavior indicates that stations prefer network and syndicated programs to local programs. During prime time (7-11 PM) in 1968 network affiliates broadcast on average 1.4 hours *per week* of local fare. In the same period independents televised only an average of 5.6 hours per week of local shows in prime time. The relative profitability of network versus syndicated programs may be inferred from the fact that the average network affiliates broadcast only 3.4 hours per week of syndicated programs in prime time (Little [336], pp. 192, 200, as corrected).

Programming Supply to the Networks

The industry that supplies programs to the networks is monopolistically competitive. The economies that are inherent in distributing television programs do not directly affect the supply of programs to the networks, because the networks themselves distribute the programs to affiliates. Given the absence of supplier economies of distribution three other aspects of the market indicate that it is competitive. These factors are the existence and viability of a wide range of packager firm sizes and types; the ease of entry by new packagers; and the existence of a well-developed rental market for film inputs in Hollywood. We will examine each of these in turn. But first, it is necessary to describe the evolution of the present structure of network-supplier relationships, in order to understand why the networks are much more instrumental in making programming decisions than are advertisers and packagers.

The pattern of program supply through the networks has changed significantly over the past fifteen years. In the late fifties, many advertisers actually financed their own programs. Advertisers supplied about one-third of the entertainment series to the networks; this proportion fell to 3 percent by 1968. By 1968, the networks were acquiring the program rights directly from

[d]A network can exploit transaction economies both in advertising and in program distribution. If there are X stations and Y national advertisers, there must be X times Y contracts written in the absence of networks or collective station representation. If the X stations affiliate with a network, then there are X+Y contracts. For realistic values of X and Y, networking cuts costs.

independent packagers for 80 percent of the regularly scheduled series hours (Little [336], p. 1). This shift away from advertiser program provision enhanced the networks' control of programming decisions.

There were four major causes of the shift from advertiser-supplied to packager-supplied series. First, the rising cost of network time outpaced the budgets of many advertisers. Gross time charges and the cost of a half-hour or hour series episode exceeded the budgets of nearly 88 percent of the advertisers by 1964 (Little [335], Vol. II, p. 64).

Second, as the costs of a series grew relative to advertising budgets, advertisers began to spread their messages over a number of different programs in order to decrease their own risks in reaching audiences (Little [336] pp. 17-18, [335], Vol. I, pp. 13-27). The advertisers' gains from being identified with a particular program were more than offset by the danger of having all their advertising eggs in one program basket. (The logic is the same as that of stock portfolio managers who spread risks by purchasing a number of different stocks.)

Third, the networks had incentives to do their own programming. Television audiences are more likely to watch a program if they have watched the preceding one or plan to watch the succeeding one. If the networks plan the whole evening schedule they can take advantage of this "adjacency" effect. Advertisers supplying their own programs would fail to take this consideration into full account.

Finally, the networks assumed the responsibility of acquiring programs as a result of the quiz-show scandal, for which the Congress and the FCC held the networks partially responsible. To relieve this public pressure, the networks assumed almost complete control of program acquisition.

Thus it has evolved that the networks bear the principal responsibility for program selection. Network control extends even into the development stage. In the spring of each year the network program departments begin program projects for the season eighteen months away. As the departments develop program ideas with packagers, weaker ideas are dropped at various stages between the detailed outline stage (which may cost a few thousand dollars) and the pilot (which may cost several hundred thousand). By late fall the original hundred or more ideas have been cut to twenty pilot projects. On the basis of the pilot programs, the likely advertiser response, and the response expected from the other networks, the network selects the new programs for the fall schedule. (For a more extensive discussion, see James Aubrey's statement in FCC [193], pp. 217-18.)

Concentration and Hollywood Production

In the late fifties and early sixties the supply of programming to the networks changed, for technological reasons. The networks started to rely on filmed rather than taped episodes. This change occurred, in large part, because films could be more easily reused. Early television had not used film because films ran at twenty-four frames per second while television used thirty (Mayer [352], pp. 18-19, 81-87). The development of the telecine chain in the fifties removed this limitation. The kinescope versions of taped shows (film taken from television screens) were inferior to film because of graininess. On the other hand, films could be edited, could be shipped abroad for foreign consumption and reused in the summer for repeats. The disappearance of advertiser-supplied programs meant that the networks did not have to rely on one advertiser to display an episode twice; instead, a new advertiser could be found. By the early 1960s packagers used film for three-fourths of prime-time series (Little [335], Vol. II p. 17). (The switch from tape to film was not permanent, however. The development of easily edited video tape in the late 1960s has led to an increase in the number of taped shows.) Finally, the decline in movie audiences (because of television) meant that excess film studio capacity was available for television film production. Production moved from New York to the West Coast.

With their long-established positions in movie production, one would expect the major studios to dominate the supply of television series. As Table 2-1 indicates, the studios do have the largest portion of program sales, but their dominance is weak. As a group their joint share of prime-time series between 1964 and 1974 varied in the range of 26 to 51 percent. Individual studio shares tended to be small, less than 10 percent, and volatile. The only substantial share is Universal's, in the early 1970s, and its share may be deceptive because of the large number of joint ventures between Universal and small packagers. Universal may receive credit in Table 2-1 for programs that were effectively controlled by the smaller packager in the joint venture (see Table 2-16). The volatile market shares are in large part the result of packagers' having to win slots in the television schedules controlled by the networks.

Traditional "friendships" between packagers and networks are obscured in the aggregated data of Table 2-1. These friendships probably reduce information costs and uncertainties involved in the selection of new shows. The phenomenon is somewhat similar to more stable subcontractor relationships in other industries, such as construction. Historically the pattern of these friendship ties has been MGM and Revue-MCA-Universal with NBC, Screen Gems and Twentieth Century Fox with ABC, and small packagers with CBS.

The use of movies in prime time means that the major studios' share of prime time is greater than indicated in Table 2-1. (Unfortunately, there were no consistent data available on movie origin from which to develop more accurate estimates of market shares.) Since 1961, when NBC introduced motion pictures into prime time, movies have taken up an increasing portion of the networks' evening schedule. As Tables 2-2 and 2-3 indicate, average movie hours per week rose from two hours in 1961 to twelve in 1971, and accounted for 37 percent of network prime-time entertainment purchases by 1971.

Table 2-1
Market Shares of Prime-Time Series Sales

Packager/Year	1964-65	1965-66	1966-67	1967-68	1970-71	1971-72	1972-73	1973-74
Universal (incl. Revue, MCA)	14	11	11	5	13	22	19	22
Warner Bros.	1	3	1	1	0	3	7	6
Paramount (incl. Plautus)	3	0	2	0	10	12	9	10
Screen Gems	3	6	7	5	7	4	5	5
MGM	6	5	7	7	2	3	3	5
United Artists	2	3	2	0	0	0	0	0
20th Century Fox	4	9	12	8	4	4	3	4
Others	66	62	56	74	64	53	54	49
Totals[a]	100	100	100	100	100	100	100	100

[a]Individual shares may not add up to 100 percent, due to rounding.

Source: Appendix, Table 2-16.

Table 2-2
Network Prime-Time Movie Programming (hours per week)

Year	ABC	CBS	NBC	Three Network Aggregate
1961	–	–	2	2
1962	2	–	2	4
1963	–	–	4	4
1964	2	–	4	6
1965	2	2	4	8
1966	2	4	4	10
1967	4	4	4	12
1968	4	4	6	14
1969	2[a]	4	6	12
1970	2[a]	4	6	12
1971	2[a]	4	6	12

[a]During the football season ABC displayed "Monday Night Football." After the season was over, ABC inserted movies into that time slot.
Source: Little [336], p. 16 for 1961-68. *OTP Report* [599], Appendix Table 5 for 1969-71.

Table 2-3
Weekly Prime-Time Entertainment Sales (thousands of dollars)

Season	Nonmovies	Movies	Total
1964-65	8,222	782	9,004
1965-66	9,033	1,210	10,243
1966-67	9,922	1,900	11,822
1967-68	10,719	3,900	14,619
1970-71	11,910	4,825	16,735
1971-72	9,316	5,500	14,816
1972-73	10,090	4,900	14,990
1973-74	10,313	4,617	14,930

Source: Appendix, Table 2-16.

Rental and Labor Markets

Hollywood program production provides an example of intense specialization of firms and suppliers of inputs in an industry that is geographically concentrated. This specialization occurs because localization facilitates, through low transportation and transaction costs, the development of rental markets for inputs to production. Fixed costs associated with lumpy, indivisible inputs (such as sound stages) need not be carried fully by the individual firm. A small producer can rent a sound stage and pay only for the time that he uses it. The rental market spreads the cost of the inputs over a number of producers. This is particularly important where small producers are creating pilot programs in the hope of selling a series to the network.

The Hollywood rental market permits a great deal of specialization in the functions performed by different firms. Firms can specialize in renting inputs, in various subprocesses such as film processing, in production, or in any combination of these. The smooth functioning of a rental market makes it possible for the industry to fully exploit economies of scale. For a theoretical discussion of how this division of labor works, see Stigler [532]. The existence of a rental market depends critically upon the stability and elasticity of the supply of labor and other inputs. If rental prices are stable and rented factors are abundant at these prices, then the packager rents the inputs only if he sells his program. If the rental market is unstable and the supply curve of factors is significantly upward sloping, then it may pay a firm to own the inputs as a precaution against fluctuations in the rental price.

The market conditions for the viability of a rental market exist in Hollywood. There has been an ample stock of studios left by shrinking movie production. Craft and talent unions can not find work for all their members. In addition, the marked seasonality of production makes the cost of year-round employment prohibitive for packagers.

The unions in Hollywood are a balkanized patchwork of craft and talent unions. Craft unions are demarcated by production-related jobs—cameraman, editor, propman, etc. Talent unions represent actors, writers, and producers. Each union so jealously guards its jurisdiction that only a propman may move a prop, no matter how light the piece or short the distance. Similarly, a gardener must be used, even though plants may be plastic. This featherbedding creates significant labor indivisibilities. Instead of one production worker performing several small tasks, in film production several people each do a small job. To the extent that these craft unions have fixed union wages and rigid job descriptions, the nontalent expenses of network shows are probably quite rigid. Unfortunately any economies of joint series production, to mitigate these indivisibilities, are probably of limited advantage due to the elaborate set of work rules and the diseconomies of coordination and supervision across series.

The roles of talent and craft unions have changed over the past two decades. When movie production was the life blood of Hollywood, the unions performed two functions: pay and fringe-benefit protection, and accreditation of who might be employed for specific jobs. Studios maintained their own staffs of talent and production workers, handling fluctuations in production through temporary hiring. But television reduced movie audiences drastically, so much so that television-related production (television programs and commercials) began to dominate Hollywood income (see Table 2-4). As a result, studios decreased their permanent staff because of the high cost of maintaining labor through the

Table 2-4
Screen Actors' Guild Earnings (millions of dollars)

Year	Television	Movies	Commercials	Total
1962	28	–	–	74
1964	31	–	–	84
1966	41	24	41	105
1968	36	25	52	113
1970	34	18	61	114
1971	34	21	59	114

Note: Only the first $100,000 of income per actor year are reported. Earnings from non-SAG sources excluded.

Source: *OTP Report*, [599], Appendix Table 16.

TV off season. (With the present level of network reruns, the original episodes are produced in less than a year. Most production occurs during the summer and fall. The remainder of the year is the off season.) Unions now perform a hiring-hall function similar to that of the longshoremen and construction unions.

The decline in movie production in Hollywood has had adverse effects on the unions and their members. Unemployment rates have been high. As Table 2-5 indicates, unemployed individuals claiming the film industry as their profession have had higher unemployment rates than the U.S. civilian labor force. This higher rate occurs during the production season (October) as well as the off season. The Screen Actors Guild has claimed that 85 percent of its members are unemployed *in* film production (OTP Report [599] p. 25). As Table 2-6 indicates, craft union rates and talent (actors and writers) union wage floors have barely kept pace with inflation in the Los Angeles-Long Beach metropolitan area. Union members have apparently not been able to receive real wage increases commensurate with productivity increases in the rest of the economy. This is what one would expect in an industry with high unemployment as it slowly works off its excess labor force. As the legacy of the movie years is diminished, one would still expect to see some unemployment in Hollywood because it is a glamour industry. (Baumol and Bowen [54] have argued that the glamour industry character of the New York stage has caused its chronic unemployment levels.) With a significant amount of "runaway" (overseas) production, the unions are in a weak bargaining position. The combination of high union unemployment and unions with little bargaining power suggests that the supply of talent and craft workers is fairly elastic.[e]

[e]Supply is elastic if there is an abundance of the product available at the existing price. Technically, a supply or demand curve is elastic if a proportional change in the quantity supplied or demanded leads to a less than proportional change in its price. If there is no change at all in the price, the curve is said to be perfectly elastic.

Table 2-5
Unemployment Rates in Hollywood (in percent)

Year	Film Industry Insured Employees[a]		U.S. Civilian
	April	October	Labor Force
1963	16.9	8.4	5.7
1964	15.1	6.0	5.2
1965	17.0	5.2	4.5
1966	11.1	7.0	3.8
1967	13.5	7.4	3.8
1968	15.0	6.2	3.6
1969	11.0	8.3	3.5
1970	18.4	9.8	4.9
1971	19.3	7.8	5.9

[a]This includes only the Los Angeles-Long Beach Standard Metropolitan Statistical Area.
Source: *OTP Report* [599], p. 25.

The Nature of the Firm

In some industries, firms have similar sizes and structures. However, an examination of the programming industry indicates that there exists neither a typical size nor a typical firm structure in the packager supply to the networks. Some companies rent all inputs in order to produce a network program. Other programs are produced by integrated movie studios with their own sound stages, equipment, and staff. One major movie company, United Artists, has no movie lots or sound stages at all. Until antitrust litigation broke it up, MCA (Revue-Universal) was the major talent agency in Hollywood, as well as a major program packager.[f] Once a middle-rank packager, Desilu now rents its studios and equipment to others. Existing program-firm types vary from integrated companies to companies that simply represent the coalescing of key talent for the production of a single program.

The continued existence of a wide range of firm types and sizes could occur only if average costs were relatively independent of firm size. If average costs were not constant over a wide range, competitive pressures would ensure that firms would produce at a firm size near the minimum average cost point or go out of business.

Of course the size distribution of Hollywood firms might merely reflect varying levels of vertical integration from owning studios through film produc-

[f]MCA had substantial control of Hollywood talent in the 1950s and early 1960s. The Justice Department alleged that MCA used its control to further its market position in supplying programs. This arrangement was terminated by a consent decree in the antitrust action *U.S. v. MCA* (1962), which split the talent agency from the film production division of the firm.

Table 2-6
Selected Hollywood Earning Indices

Year	Los Angeles Consumer Price Index[a] (1)	Craft Wage Rate[b] (2)	Actors' Minimum Wage Rate[b] (3)	Writers' Minimum Wage Rate[b] (4)
1962	100	100	100	100
1963	102	111	100	100
1964	103	111	100	100
1965	106	116	100	100
1966	108	116	100	104
1967	110	121	112	104
1968	115	121	112	116
1969	120	135	120	116
1970	126	135	120	122
1971	131	142	138	122

[a]Los Angeles Consumer Price Index is for the Los Angeles-Long Beach Standard Metropolitan Statistical Area, adjusted so that 1962=100.

[b]Adjusted so that 1962 = 100.

Source: (1) *Handbook of Labor Statistics*, 1973, p. 308.
        (2)-(4) *OTP Report*, [599], Appendix Table 22.

tion.[g] However, the data indicate large size variations at each level of production. Since packagers of varying size and type are viable, this variation indicates that the usual reasons for vertical integration (to maintain a stable source of product, or to capture production or distribution economies) are not significant. In fact the existence of vertically integrated movie companies may be just a historical legacy from the pre-Paramount-decision [557], pre-TV days of Hollywood. Prior to the settlement of the last Paramount antitrust case firms in the film industry were vertically integrated.[h] Companies held long-term contracts with talent, owned large studios, produced movies, and distributed them through

[g]Although the types of firms found in programming supply and their size distribution are not inconsistent with the theories of Coase [129], Stigler [532], and Knight [308], none of these can explain how the size distribution came into existence. If we consider talent and success to be randomly distributed over producing firms, then an explanation can be found in the work of Simon and Bonini [503]. If the probability of popular and successful talent is independent of firm size, then the observed distribution of firm sizes can be generated by a stochastic process. Just as in the Simon and Bonini model, the possibility of new entry into the industry only changes the shape of the distribution, higher rates of entry resulting in fewer relatively large firms. Since entry and exit are common in this industry, the existing low concentration is not inconsistent with the Simon and Bonini explanation.

[h]Also, see *U.S. v. Paramount Pictures*, 66 F. Supp. 323, 70 F. Supp. 53 (S.D.N.Y., 1946), 85 F. Supp. 881 (S.D.N.Y., 1949). For a discussion of antitrust in the film industry, see Whitney [613, Vol. II], pp. 145-95.

their own theater chains. The Paramount case suggests that the movie studios' control over what movies were shown at local theaters created a source of market power that enabled the studios to exclude or damage competitors who did not own theater chains. Today the networks handle the distribution of television programs, and incentives for vertical integration are not very significant for TV program packagers.

Why do the networks purchase programs at all? Why don't they produce all their own programming? This is a difficult question. The networks produce much of their daytime, and all of their news and public affairs programs. (This may merely reflect the need to control the content of the latter programs for regulatory reasons.) Sports programming is displayed by the networks, although the teams organize and play the games themselves. In the past the networks have produced larger portions of their own prime time entertainment series; they produced 24 percent in 1957 as compared to 5 percent in 1968 (Little [336], p. 5). Their own production may have been done for bargaining reasons—to maintain the threat that if program prices diverged from program costs, the networks would produce more programs themselves. The fact that they do not produce all their own programming indicates that the economic advantages of doing so may be limited. We have seen that economies of scale are very unlikely. Thus the networks would not have this incentive to integrate into production. The networks may have failed to take over production (to guarantee a more stable supply or more closely tailored product) in order to *avoid* regulatory and antitrust pressures, or because the present market has done the job adequately.

The Competitiveness of Program Supply to the Networks

The preceding sections have described in some detail the supply of programming to the networks. Two important questions can now be answered: Is the supply of programming competitive? and Is the supply of programs price elastic? The answer to each is Yes.

Industries are frequently oligopolistic, because the economically efficient scale of selling and distributing products to buyers is large relative to the size of the market. These economies can arise from indivisibilities in distribution, from inventory economies, and density-of-outlet phenomena. In broadcasting, the public-good aspect of programs means that once a program is produced the marginal cost of an additional viewer seeing the program is negligible, and the efficient scale for film distribution is quite large. But these distribution economies do not affect the efficient size of a packager supplying programs to the networks, because the networks themselves capture the economic advantages of distribution economies. (This is not necessarily the case for other film products, such as motion pictures and syndicated programs, where distribution is an important function of the firm that produces the product.)

The existence of rental markets in the programming supply industry removes many of the potential sources of firm-specific economies.[i] The division of labor is limited by the extent of the market, rather than by the size of the firm.

Although a rental market solves many of the problems arising from indivisible inputs by allowing many producers to share the inputs' costs, a rental market does not guarantee that the industry will be competitive. Increasing returns to scale in production may still lead to oligopolistic or monopolistic market structures. However, program packagers of small, medium, and large sizes all survive and thrive. This could occur only if average costs were relatively independent of firm size.

Collusive behavior by the larger packagers seems unlikely. If such collusion did exist, it would be short-lived, for four reasons. First, the presence of a rental market facilitates the easy entry of new firms to compete away excess profits. Second, collusive agreements in differentiated product industries are hard to maintain, because it is difficult to distinguish product differentiation from cheating on the agreement (Stigler [531]). Third, the networks can produce their own series if the studios' prices diverge significantly from program costs. Fourth, the combined shares of the six major studios have usually been less than 60 percent. The individual shares are small and quite volatile; sufficiently volatile that the size rank of major firms changes from year to year. Such uncertain market positions provide a very weak basis for cartel behavior.

Based on the existence of rental markets, easy entry, a wide range of firm sizes, and the fact that the networks distribute the product, we conclude that the supply of programming is monopolistically competitive (not perfectly competitive, because programs are not perfect substitutes for one another). Although competition is sufficient to ensure that expected prices reflect costs (expected excess profits are zero), successful series may continue to command higher prices, because of their ability to draw larger-than-average audiences. The appendix to this chapter analyzes this in more detail.

Anyone familiar with the history of the movie industry may feel ill at ease with the conclusion that the supply of filmed programs is competitive. In the 1940s, major studios were successfully prosecuted for antitrust violations by the Justice Department; these prosecutions resulted in the well-known Paramount decision. The studios were accused of using their control of theater chains to monopolize the distribution of movies to the detriment of independent theaters and the public. This suggests that the source of studio market power in the pre-Paramount-decision period arose from economies of scale in distribution and exhibition. The rapid emergence of several independent motion picture producers in the post-Paramount-decision period suggests that the production side of motion pictures is far more competitive.

One usually thinks of a competitive industry as having a highly, if not

---

[i]Larger firms may be more viable if there are economies in advertising or increasing returns to scale. A firm is subject to increasing returns to scale if a proportional increase in output requires less than a proportional increase in input cost. Increasing returns to scale lead to declining average costs as output increases.

perfectly, price-elastic supply curve in the long run; at least, many textbooks treat competitive industries in this way. This need not be the case if the supply of inputs into production is less than perfectly elastic. For example, in the case of programming supply, an upward sloping factor supply curve could arise if popular talent, like land, is in fixed supply, or if the industry has to bid higher and higher amounts to draw inputs from the New York stage or other industries.

For several reasons, fixed or limited supply of good talent does not appear prevalent in the industry at the moment. The marked seasonality of production resulting from the present level of reruns leaves long periods when "popular" talent is not working or must turn to motion-picture production. Thus, if new production took place in the off season, then more programming could be produced without straining capacity unduly. Second, nearly all of the Hollywood unions complain of high unemployment rates (unemployment in their preferred industry, film production, as well as high unemployment in any occupation; see Table 2-5). Third, popularity of talent is largely a marketing phenomenon. A show may be popular due to its particular combination of stars, writers, and others. Over time, the talent may capture part of the success rent of the series. But that does not mean that *individual* talent is a scarce commodity, only that the *combination* was unusually successful. The same talent in slightly different circumstances may have far less audience appeal. The continued appearance of new shows with obscure talent that are highly successful, and the failure of new shows with well-known talent, is futher evidence that it is unpredictable combinations that are scarce, not the underlying talent. Finally, the New York stage does not appear to suffer from a dearth of good talent. Like Hollywood, the New York stage is a glamour industry. For the opportunity to sing or act, people seem willing to tolerate high unemployment rates and seasonal employment. The New York stage appears to have an excess supply of acting talent that could be drawn to Hollywood to participate in *increased* series production (Baumol and Bowen [54]).

This argument may seem unlikely to anyone familiar with program-cost inflation in recent years. Program prices rose nearly 90 percent during the sixties, while union scales and floors rose only 40 to 45 percent (OTP Report [599], appendix table 22). If there had been no increase in the already high level of featherbedding (and there is little or no evidence of a large increase in featherbedding), then the fact that program costs rose faster than input prices in a profit-oriented industry is strong circumstantial evidence of a much less than perfectly elastic supply of programming and of programming talent.

Inflation in the cost of programs appears to be a demand and not a supply phenomenon. During the sixties, the number of hours of network demanded original nonsports nonmovie entertainment actually fell (OTP [599], appendix tables 8, 9, 13). Consequently, program prices increased over a period of declining output. Since there is no evidence of increasing returns to scale in production or of collusive behavior on the part of program producers, increased prices are not the result of shrinking production. In Chapter 4, we will argue that the most plausible explanation of program-price inflation is that the rivalry of the three networks has resulted in their bidding up program "quality" in their continued competition for audiences.

Domestic Syndication

Local television stations can acquire nonnetwork programming by purchasing programs through the syndication market. In syndication, each station can purchase the exclusive rights to a show for the local market. (Recent FCC rules have restricted exclusivity to an area twenty-five miles beyond the city of license. See *Broadcasting*, October 18, 1971, p. 76, and September 3, 1973, p. 34.) The station contracts with a distributor, who may be the original producer of the program. Programs that stations can rent typically are feature films (originally produced for movie theater display), off-network series (previously shown on the networks), and first-run syndicated programs (made specifically for syndication). Because of the small number of independent, nonnetwork affiliated stations, and because of the high clearance rate of network programming by network affiliates, the volume of programming passing through syndication markets is a relatively small and declining part of total programming sales (see Tables 2-7 and 2-8).

Table 2-7
Television Program Expenditures

Year	Network Program Expense (1)	Station Expense on Syndicated Programs (2)	Syn./Net. (2)/(1)
		(millions of dollars)	
1961	449.2	73.0	.162
1962	490.8	101.0	.206
1963	515.9	108.0	.209
1964	579.8	116.0	.194
1965	651.8	120.4	.185
1966	733.9	131.7	.180
1967	798.9	139.2	.175
1968	857.0	157.5	.184
1969	929.7	170.5	.184
1970	973.8	171.7	.176

Sources: Column (1): *Federal Communications Commission Annual Reports.*
(2): 1961-67 *Little Report* [336], p. 109.
1968-70 *Broadcasting* (October 18, 1971), p. 76.

Table 2-8
Nonnetwork Prime-Time TV Programming[a] (hours per week)

Station Type	Year	First-Run	Off-Network	Feature Film	Local[b]	Total
Affiliate	1958	3.00	0.41	1.15	1.74	6.31
	1968	0.73	0.92	1.72	1.40	4.77
Independent	1958	8.55	.71	8.20	6.48	23.94
	1968	7.16	7.27	6.94	5.57	26.94

[a]Average for top 50 markets, 7-11 PM.
[b]Includes some local news programs in the Central Time Zone.
Source: *Little Report* [336], pp. 192, 200 (as corrected).

The mechanics of syndication are as follows: The station rents the program at a negotiated rate determined largely by the size of the market in which the station is located. The contract stipulates the number of episodes purchased—the station is usually allowed to show each episode twice. The station then receives the purchased series in episode batches. After broadcasting the episode, the station returns the films to the syndicator. The syndicator then checks the films for wear before forwarding them to another customer.

The syndication of feature-length films often takes place on a package basis. The station rents a standard set of movies from the distributor. Thus, the station manager may buy some movies that he may not want in order to acquire the ones that he does. (*U.S. v. Loew's* 371 U.S. 38, 52, 1962 and *U.S. v. Paramount* restrict the types of block booking that can occur. For a discussion of the economics of block booking, see Stigler [530].)

The Decline of "First-Run" and Rise of "Off-Network"

Beginning in the early sixties, first-run syndication declined in absolute sales. At the same time sales of off-network series grew. (Tables 2-8 and 2-9 indicate these trends.)

The emergence of off-network was the principal cause of the decline in first-run sales. The switch from kinescope and live network performance to filmed production in the late 1950s created libraries of films that could be rerun on television. These old series flooded the syndication market in the early 1960s. The off-network programs had a competitive advantage over first-run material, for two reasons: First, an off-network series had a proven track record that a new first-run show lacked, making it a safer bet for the station manager; and second, off-network series were less costly. The off-network program only had

Table 2-9
Sales in the Domestic Syndication Market (millions of dollars)

Year	Off-Network	First-Run	Feature Film	Total
1957	7.0	18.0	32.0	57.0
1958	9.0	16.0	44.0	69.0
1959	10.0	20.0	66.0	96.0
1960	10.0	20.0	65.0	95.0
1961	10.0	20.0	43.0	73.0
1962	18.0	12.0	71.0	101.0
1963	28.0	7.0	73.0	108.0
1964	32.0	8.0	76.0	116.0
1965	33.5	9.2	77.7	120.4
1966	36.7	14.0	81.7	131.7
1967	43.1	22.0	74.1	139.2

Source: Little [336], p. 109.

to meet distribution costs and residuals (reuse fees paid to talent); production costs had usually been met on the previous network runs. On the other hand, the first-run show made specifically for syndication had to meet distribution costs plus full production costs of a new show. Production costs of first-run programs tend to exceed the residual costs of off-network series of comparable audience appeal.

The first-run syndication market responded in two ways to the emergence of off-network programming. First, it had to shave production costs to remain competitive. (The appendix to this chapter contains a discussion of the differing costs for network and first-run syndicated programs in the early 1960s.) This cost-cutting may have come at the expense of quality. Second, first-run moved out of the program types dominated by off-network and into music, variety, game, and talk shows (Little [336], pp. 72-75).

A method of showing series known as "stripping" enhanced the position of off-network and reshaped the type of programming demanded by stations. In stripping, a station assigns a program to the same time slot for five days a week, a common practice in daytime programming for years. Independent stations introduced stripping to prime time. Stripping appears to build audiences by developing habits among the television audience. Members of the television industry argue that stripping capitalizes on the fact that personal routines are more often daily than weekly. Therefore, the viewer is more likely to fall into the daily habit of viewing a stripped show than he is to watch a different series each day of the week.

Stripping requires program series with a large number of episodes. A show stripped five days a week should have 130 or more episodes if it is to avoid repetition more than twice a year. Stripping can be done with fewer episodes, but the show's ability to draw audiences appears to decline as the frequency of repeats increases. Consequently, the series that have succeeded in syndication have largely been the programs that were popular on the networks and accumulated a large number of episodes. It is not at all surprising that the "first-run" successes in the late 1960s in the adventure, mystery, and drama categories were foreign-produced series such as *The Saint* and *The Avengers*, which were syndicated by Independent Television Corporation *after their display on the British network*. These were not really "first-run" series.

Concentration in the Syndication Market

It is not surprising that the movie studios and networks dominate syndication. Syndication is largely a second-hand market where old movies and network programs are resold and reused. Small producers in the first-hand market are unlikely to be large enough to sustain their own syndication arms. It would be too costly to have a sales force selling only a few series. Many of the smaller packagers sell the syndication rights to their series to major syndicators. As a result, the major movie studios had about 60 percent of series sales and nearly 80 percent of film syndication sales in the mid-sixties. At that time the networks had about 20 percent of series sales and a negligible portion of feature-film sales. Despite this concentration, several syndicators survived with only 3 to 6 percent of the market, as indicated in the appendix.

Syndication Costs

The costs of a syndicated program differ from those of a network program. Since a syndicated program is not simultaneously video-cast in many markets, it incurs a different set of distribution costs. In addition, off-network syndicated programs must pay residuals (rerun fees) to talent each time an episode is rerun.

Distribution costs are a major portion of syndication expenses. As noted in the appendix, sales and distribution costs appear to have amounted to 25 to 38 percent of all program expenses for first-run syndicated programs in the early sixties. By comparison, network distribution, selling, and administrative costs came to only 12 percent of all expenses (FCC [184], 1960, p. 67).

For many years talent unions opposed the reuse of television programs because they felt that such a practice would diminish the demand for members' talent. The unions were unsuccessful in prohibiting reruns and have accepted the practice, but they have successfully demanded that actors, writers, directors, and musicians be compensated each time a filmed series is rerun. These payments are substantial enough that they constituted one-fourth of 1966 Screen Actors Guild (SAG) members' income (Land [317], p. 90).

Full residuals must be paid when an episode is shown in off-network syndication, even if the episode is shown in only one market. Consequently an episode must be sold in enough markets during each release to cover this substantial fixed charge. Because residual fees are usually high, many series available for off-network syndication are never shown.

Television shows that are taped rather than filmed fall under the jurisdiction of the American Federation of Television and Radio Artists (AFTRA). AFTRA's residual charges used to be significantly higher than SAG's. As a result, many of the older taped programs cannot profitably be released into syndication. Over time, AFTRA's residual charges have moved closer to SAG's and the gap is no longer significant. Accordingly, more taped series are now being produced and will find their way into off-network syndication.

The Competitiveness of Syndication Supply

Is the syndication market competitive? The answer is not wholly clear-cut. The difficulty is that syndicators distribute their programs to stations while suppliers to the network do not. As a result the suppliers in syndication can take advantage of the economies of distributing a product with public-good characteristics. In addition, indivisibilities in the distribution of programs lead to some economies of size in syndication. (E.g., one sales team can promote several series almost as easily as one program.) However, the viability of syndication firms with less than 6 percent of the market seems to indicate that decreasing costs due to indivisibilities are quickly exploited.

Although distribution economies do give rise to a rather concentrated syndication market, one would still expect that individual syndicators would have only limited market power for two reasons. First, the economies are so quickly exploited that a large number of sellers are viable and able to compete prices downward. Second, syndicators cannot raise prices significantly above costs without losing some of their business from network affiliates. We conclude that competitive forces are quite strong in the market for syndicated programs.

Appendix:
Programming Costs and
Revenues

Chapter 2 has examined the industry structure in the production of television programming. Some issues have been deferred to this appendix, which addresses the following questions: How much do prime-time series and pilot programs cost? How does success affect the cost of a series over time? Why do the networks use movies in prime time? What are the costs of syndication to the syndicator and the station? We shall consider each question in turn.

Costs for Network Program Series

An analysis of the production costs of a television series requires an examination of exactly what is being produced. The costs of a pilot film differ from the costs of producing episodes. Film and tape have different production and reuse costs. Returning series are different from new series.

The first major cost of a series is the development cost of a pilot show. Since the pilot is a one-shot demonstration good, the script, acting, etc., are more professionally done than in a regular series episode. Consequently, one would expect the pilot to cost more than the series episode. Pilot costs averaged nearly $200,000 per half hour and $330,000 per hour in 1968—average new episode costs were less than half those amounts, on the order of $87,000 per half hour (see Table 2-10).

Filmed series usually cost more than taped ones, for two reasons. First, the technology of film is more expensive than that for taped or live performances. In part, this reflects increased editing, and therefore quality; until recently, film was more amenable to editing than tape. Costs of film, processing, editing, and related expenses explain much of the differences between tape and film.

Also, AFTRA conventions on tape residuals (reuse fees) were until recently so costly that a show was taped only if there was no anticipation of its being rerun in syndication. The networks and packagers have taped only shows for which they expect to recoup costs in one showing. Therefore, one would expect a lower average quality for taped shows than for filmed shows. For packager-licensed series, Table 2-11 confirms the joint effect of technology and residuals on costs; taped shows have been cheaper. During the 1960s music and variety, along with daytime serials, constituted the major portion of taped shows, while comedies, Westerns, and action-adventure shows tended to fall into the film category.

One would expect that continued programs should cost more than new ones. In Chapter 2, we concluded that the supply of new programs is monopolistically competitive. Consequently, the networks initially should have to pay only the

37

Table 2-10
Pilot and Episode Costs

Year	Average Pilot Cost[a]		Average New Episode Cost[b]	
	1/2 Hr. Pilot	1 Hr. Pilot	1/2 Hr. Episode	1 Hr. Episode
1960	$ 72,200	$136,100	$48,900	$ 94,000
1961	77,900	159,800	50,800	98,500
1962	79,700	164,000	53,200	116,800
1963	78,000	174,900	53,500	121,100
1964	86,700	200,300	61,200	127,000
1965	100,400	233,500	65,500	132,400
1966	127,400	227,100	71,500	145,500
1967	185,300	291,900	75,900	160,900
1968	200,000	329,700	87,100	163,000

Source:

[a]Network-financed, packager-licensed pilots, Little [336], p. 39.
[b]New entertainment series, Little [336], p. 41.

amount necessary to draw resources into pilot and episode production. The amount required is just high enough that the packager expects to earn a fair rate of return on his investment through network and syndication sales.

Packagers of continued successful series develop substantially more bargaining power than new series packagers. When a show first becomes popular, network revenues rise rapidly because of the successful show's larger audience. Consequently the packager of the continued series will begin successfully to bargain for part of the extra profits of success. Table 2-11 provides some confirmation of the rising price that the packager of a successful series charges the networks over time. Noll, Peck, and McGowan [394, pp. 44-49] estimated that each rating point above 15 raises the episode cost by about $1500 per half-hour.

The interaction of this price inflation of a successful series with viewer response in part determines its life span. The series may start with a relatively unknown cast. As the show succeeds, the talent asks for and gets higher salaries. The packager bargains for a share of the show's success rent. Costs to the network spiral upward. At some point the increasing price is high enough that the profitability of the series to the network is less than that of a new series; this is especially likely to occur if the popularity of the show wanes, or if the audience ages to the point that it is no longer valuable to advertisers. At this point the series is cancelled. This is how it is possible for what appears to be a successful series to be cancelled.[a]

---

[a]This argument assumes that as the show wanes in profitability the talent costs do not fall. This assumption seems plausible to us. First, as the show succeeds the talent is identified as popular. This identification raises the opportunity cost of the talent, by making them more valuable in films and other series. Second, the individual talent will be able to capture part of the excess profits of the successful *combination* by threatening to leave if salary is not raised.

Table 2-11
Costs Per Episode of New and Continued Packager Series (dollars)

Year	Film Only 1/2 Hr.	Tape-Live Only 1/2 Hr.	Film Only 1 Hr.	Tape-Live Only 1 Hr.
		New Series		
1960	48,858	–	91,694	–
1961	54,745	50,000	101,090	85,750
1962	55,736	29,000	118,714	101,500
1963	54,378	46,000	118,811	123,419
1964	61,452	–	127,000	–
		Continued Series		
1960	51,919	34,033	93,761	101,338
1961	53,683	37,278	110,396	105,325
1962	56,467	41,706	110,908	109,901
1963	64,277	44,196	134,331	118,669
1964	66,171	42,391	135,313	120,346

Source: Little [335, Vol. II], pp. 70-74.

A particular case provides some substantiation of this hypothesis. Table 2-12 is a breakdown of the expenses for *Bonanza* for the 1959-60 and 1969-70 seasons. The division of costs reflects an industry practice of separating talent (above-the-line) costs from production (below-the-line) costs. Individual contract negotiations determine above-the-line costs (subject to union floors). The technology used and union scales for craft workers determine below-the-line costs. Thus, if anyone can capture the profit of success in such an arrangement, it is the talent and the packager. Talent expenses in *Bonanza* increased 167 percent, while below-the-line costs rose only 47 percent;[b] the below-the-line expenses were very much in line with increases in union minimum wages and costs associated with the switch from black and white to color. The talent-cost inflation is further support for the theory of continued-series-cost inflation.

Movies in Prime Time

The networks have increased their use of movies in prime time in part because the movies can attract larger audiences than series with little increase in network out-of-pocket costs. The networks are able to rent movies that originally cost $1.5 million to produce for a rental fee of $350,000 to $750,000 for two showings. Each showing of a movie can replace two hours of series, which would cost the networks about $400,000. The movie is likely to be a better product

[b]Since NBC produced the program, the possibility of the packager capturing the network rent is removed.

Table 2-12
Cost Per Episode of Bonanza

Item	Season		Percentage Increase
	1959-60	1969-70	
Above-the-line expenses[a]	$ 36,700	$ 98,005	167
Below-the-line expenses[b]	77,300	113,530	47
Total cost	$114,000	$211,535	86

[a]Above-the-line expenses include those for supervision, cast, scripts, music, and miscellaneous talent-related items.

[b]Below-the-line expenses include those for production staff, camera, extras, set operations, electrical items and labor, scenery, sound, makeup, wardrobe, hairdressing, set dressing and props, editing, films, laboratory, titles, opticals, general transportation, sound and stage facilities, locations, payroll fringe benefits, and miscellaneous production items and labor.

Source: *Broadcasting* (September 22, 1969), p. 62. (The article contains a detailed expense breakdown.)

(better talent, script, and production) with greater audience appeal. In the 1972-73 season, the average movie drew approximately 21 percent of television homes (*Broadcasting* [January 4, 1973], p. 42). That share was about five percentage points higher than that of the average new series in the late sixties (Noll, Peck, and McGowan [394], p. 67). Thus, for approximately the same outlay, a network can increase its audience and its revenues by using movies instead of new series.

NBC was the first network to introduce movies in prime time, and the others quickly followed. At first each network programmed a movie opposite the series of its rivals. Later, the networks began to "counter-program" movies against movies to minimize the loss of market shares. (This movie competition is an example of the program rivalry that is predicted in the model of Chapter 3 and is explored in detail in Chapter 4.)

Network Advertising Revenue and Program Cost

As noted earlier, networks and television stations essentially perform a brokerage function. They acquire audiences by broadcasting free shows. They then sell commercial time to advertisers who want access to those audiences. Thus, network and station demand for programming is a derived demand. The interaction of advertising demand, the ability of programming to generate audiences, and the supply of programming jointly determine what programs are broadcast.

First, consider the cost of attracting a single TV home. Due to the structure of network television, the network decision process is heavily influenced by the opportunity cost of national air time. Each network attempts to gain approximately 30 percent of a national prime-time audience for each of its time slots. Of the 66-million homes with TV in the United States, approximately half are tuned in during prime time; there are, however, seasonal variations. Consequently, the network quota is nine million homes. For the purpose of calculating a rough estimate of network prime-time program cost per viewer, let us assume that the 9 million homes will watch an episode in its first run and an additional 6 million will watch its rerun (the 9 versus 6 approximates seasonal audience variation). An average half-hour television series program costs $95,000 for the first showing and $15,000 for the rerun. With these rough estimates of audience and cost, the program cost per home delivered is 0.73¢ per half-hour. Since network expenses for technical, administrative, and selling costs are 12 percent of total *network* expense (*Broadcasting* [August 21, 1972], p. 15), the network cost of a TV home delivered is approximately 0.83¢ per half-hour.

It is also possible to estimate the advertising revenue per viewer. In the late 1960s and early seventies, NBC charged about $2.00 per half-minute commercial per thousand homes tuned in (OTP [599], appendix table 35). With six thirty-second commercials per half-hour under the NAB code, this results in network gross revenue of 1.2¢ per half-hour. However, the networks paid 29.2 percent of their revenue to affiliated stations in compensation and to advertising agencies in commissions (*Broadcasting* [August 21, 1972], p. 15). The resulting *network* net revenue per half-hour per home works out to about 0.85¢.

Cost for Syndicated Programs

The costs of a syndicated program differ from those of a network program. Part of the difference is that syndicated programs are not simultaneously broadcast nationwide, as network programs are. But the costs also differ because off-network programs in syndication must pay residuals to talent.

In order to remain competitive with off-network series and with network fare (for affiliates only), the first-run producer must scrimp on production costs. A network series in 1960 cost about $50,000 per half-hour, compared to $28,000 for the first-run syndication series in Table 2-13. (*Broadcasting* [March 4, 1960], p. 86 reported that an average first-run series episode cost $33,000 to produce.) Compared to the *Bonanza* costs reported in Table 2-12, it is evident that the first-run syndication program in Table 2-13 had lower talent and production costs (and probably had lower audience appeal as well).

Distribution costs are a larger part of total costs for syndicated programs than for network fare. Syndicators are unable to take advantage of simultaneous broadcasting. They also have to check films for wear before sending them to new

Table 2-13
Cost of a First-Run Syndicated Program

Cost of 39 Episodes		$1,077,375
Per episode cost		
Above-the-line[a]	$ 8,850	
Below-the-line	18,775	
Total	$27,625	
1000 Additional Prints		25,000
Advertising and promotion		50,000
Interest		51,857
Selling costs		275,253
Administrative overhead		240,846
Total cost		$1,720,331

[a]Stand-ins and extras included as above-the line expenses.
Source: Bernstein [65], pp. 63-64.

buyers. *Broadcasting* reported the following aggregate costs for an average first-run program in 1960 (March 14, 1960, p. 86):

$1,300,000 for production of 39 episodes
        (standard season length at that time)
   10,000 for extra prints
   30,000 for advertising the series
  400,000 for sales, distribution, etc.

$1,740,000 total costs

The syndicators' costs of distributing the series came to 25 percent in the *Broadcasting* example and 38 percent in the example in Table 2-13. By comparison, the networks spent an average of 12 percent of all their expenses on distribution, selling, and administrative costs (FCC [184], 1960, p. 67).

Full residuals must be paid on the release of an off-network episode, even if the episode is shown in only one market. Consequently, an episode must be sold in enough markets during each release to cover these fixed charges. Noll, Peck, and McGowan calculated that the minimum residual fee for a 1966 half-hour program in off-network would be $3000, which is approximately 30 percent of the actors' original salary ([394], p. 76). As a result, many series available for off-network are never syndicated, because residuals have driven up the break-even point on episodes to the point where they are not profitable.

The cost of a syndicated program to a station depends on the size of the station's market as well as residuals and distribution costs. As Table 2-14

Table 2-14
Average Price Per Broadcast Episode for Syndicated Programs (1968, 6-11 PM)

Episode Length (minutes)	Market Group[a]	First-Run Average Price ($)	Off-Network Average Price ($)
30	1-10	405	320
	11-50	133	115
	51-100	58	51
	101-150	46	36
	over 150	41	38
60	1-10	–	665
	11-50	369	155
	51-100	196	90
	101-150	69	70
	over 150	88	37

[a]Markets are cities ranked in order of descending population.
Source: Little [336], pp. 115-17.

indicates, the larger the market the higher the rental fee; rental fees per half-hour range from about $350 on average in the ten largest markets down to about $40 per half-hour in the smallest markets.

These rental fees are the result of a bargaining process between stations and syndicators. No syndicator is going to rent a program for less than the incremental cost of distributing and selling it to a market; otherwise he will lose money. Similarly, no station will pay more than a program earns in advertising revenue less transmission and other costs. With stations facing several syndicators, the station will not pay an amount so high that its profits from a series are less than with the next best deal it can come to with another syndicator. Similarly, no syndicator will settle for a fee less than he can get by selling the program to another local station in the same market. (Territorial exclusivity prevents the syndicator from selling the same program to two stations in the same market.) The result of this bargaining process is as follows: First, in small markets (with a small number of stations and small potential audiences), the rental fee will be close to the incremental cost of serving the market; and second, in large markets (with more stations and larger audiences), syndicators can capture more of the larger revenue pie. The result is higher prices in larger markets.

The following four tables are sources for many of the comments in the chapter. We present them here so that readers can study them in some detail. Table 2-15 describes the packagers' shares of the supply to the networks from 1960 to 1964. Table 2-16 provides these data for the 1964-65 through 1973-74 seasons. Tables 2-17 and 2-18 contain the market shares of the domestic syndication market for 1964 and 1967.

Table 2-15
Packager Entertainment Sales, 1960-64[a] (percentage share of market)

Packager		1960	1961	1962	1963	1964
A.	Major movie companies					
	Revue (Universal, MCA)	6.1	9.9	11.1	7.8	7.7
	Warner Bros.	13.1	10.5	6.3	1.6	1.6
	Paramount[b]	0.2	0.2	0.2	0.7	6.6
	Plautus[b]	–	1.7	3.6	3.9	–
	Screen Gems	5.9	6.5	9.9	4.5	4.4
	MGM	1.7	3.6	4.8	11.2	7.8
	United Artists	2.0	1.1	3.1	2.1	5.5
	20th Century Fox	4.0	7.1	3.0	2.7	6.0
B.	Other packagers					
	Four Star	6.8	3.8	3.7	0.7	2.3
	Goodson-Todman	2.1	2.1	2.7	4.5	2.0
	Desilu	4.0	1.5	3.0	2.9	0.7
	Garry Moore	3.6	2.7	2.7	1.8	0.4
	Sullivan Prods.	2.1	1.9	2.1	2.1	2.4
	Bing Crosby	–	1.7	1.0	3.3	4.2
	Walt Disney	1.9	1.8	1.8	1.9	2.1
	Roncom	2.0	2.1	2.0	1.3	1.7
	Shamley	1.2	1.1	1.9	1.8	1.5
	Red Skelton	0.9	0.9	1.4	1.9	2.0
	Dena	–	–	–	3.1	3.2
	Peekskill	–	–	2.0	2.1	2.0
	Others	42.4	39.8	33.7	38.1	35.9
Addenda:	Number of "other" packagers	52	51	50	48	45
	Total series sales (million $)	212	235	241	252	262

[a]Based on November Composite Week, 1960-64, regularly scheduled advertiser-supplied and packager-licensed entertainment series.
[b]Plautus was a part of Paramount after 1963.
Source: Little [335, Vol. II], pp. 99-105.

45

Table 2-16
Weekly Packager Prime-Time Entertainment Sales

Packager	1964-65	1965-66	1966-67	1967-68	1970-71	1971-72	1972-73	1973-74
I. Nonmovie entertainment								
Market shares[a] %								
A. Major movie companies								
Universal (incl. Revue, MCA)	14	11	11	5	13	22	19	22
Warner Bros	2	3	1	1	0	3	7	6
Paramount (incl. Plautus)	3	0	2	0	10	12	9	10
Screen Gems	3	6	7	5	7	4	5	5
MGM (incl. MGM Arena)	6	5	7	7	2	3	3	5
United Artists	2	3	2	0	0	0	0	0
20th Century Fox	4	9	12	8	4	4	3	4
B. Networks[b]								
ABC[c]	1	2	0	1	5	7	6	6
CBS	5	7	4	5	1	0	4	2
NBC	3	2	3	4	2	2	4	2
C. Minor packagers								
Four Star	3	4	1	0	0	0	0	0
Desilu	1	1	4	6	0	0	0	0
Quinn Martin	2	3	2	2	3	4	5	6
Mark VII	0	0	0	0	0	3	1	2
Others[d]	50	44	44	56	52	36	33	31

Table 2-16 (cont.)

Packager		1964-65	1965-66	1966-67	1967-68	1970-71	1971-72	1972-73	1973-74
D. Subtotals[e]	%	100	100	100	100	100	100	100	100
	$000	8222	9033	9922	10719	11910	9316	10090	10313
II. Movies (various sources)[f]	$000	782	1210	1900	3900	4825	5500	4900	4617
III. Total[g]	$000	9004	10243	11822	14619	16735	14816	14990	14930

[a]Assumes that control of all joint ventures is evenly split among all the partners, unless more detailed information was available. On the other hand, if joint ventures had been assigned to major companies, Universal's 1973-74 share would have been 25.00% (instead of 21.80%); and others' would have been 27.33% (instead of 30.51%), in 1973-74.

[b]Includes regularly scheduled prime-time news series.

[c]1970-74 figures are inflated because only ABC Sports figures were available for Monday night. After the football season, ABC displayed movies on Monday night.

[d]Includes minor packagers of the 1960-64 period and new entrants.

[e]Individual shares may not add to 100 percent, due to rounding.

[f]"Made for Television" anthologies of the Columbo-McMillan and Wife-McCloud-Hec Ramsey variety are not treated as movies, but are included in section I of this table. They appear to bear a closer resemblance to series than to the display of varied theatrical movies.

[g]The sales drop in 1971-72 is the result of the prime time access rule, which limited network programming to three hours per night.

Source: Based on estimated program costs in *Television* and *Broadcasting* before each season. All specials and replacements are effectively excluded.

Table 2-17
Shares of Domestic Syndication Market, 1964

| Distributor | Percentage Share | | |
	TV Series	Feature Films	Total
A. Larger syndicators			
MCA			
MGM			
Screen Gems	45.0	79.6	67.6
Seven Arts			
United Artists			
Warner Bros.			
B. Smaller syndicators			
Four Star			
ITC	21.8	3.9	10.1
20th Century Fox			
C. Networks			
Network A[a]	7.0	−	2.4
Network B[a]	6.8	−	2.3
Network C[a]	5.5	−	1.9
D. Others	14.0	16.4	15.7
Total percentage shares	100.1	99.9	100.0
Total sales (million $)	40.0	76.0	116.0

[a]Network names not given.
Source: Little [336], p. 113.

Table 2-18
Shares of Domestic Syndication Market, 1967

| Distributor | Percentage Share | | |
	TV Series	Feature Films	Total
A. Larger syndicators			
MCA			
MGM			
Paramount			
Screen Gems	46.4	90.1	69.7
20th Century Fox			
United Artists			
Warner Bros.			
B. Smaller syndicators			
Four Star			
ITC	21.4	1.6	10.8
Metromedia			
Westinghouse			
C. Networks			
Network A[a]	8.3	–	3.9
Network B[a]	7.2	–	3.4
Network C[a]	2.6	–	1.2
D. Others	14.1	8.2	11.0
Total percentage shares	100.0	99.9	100.0
Total sales (million $)	65.1	74.1	139.2

[a]Network names not given.
Source: Little [336], p. 114.

3 Theories of Program Choice

Introduction

Chapter 2 investigated the economics of program production and syndication. It dealt with problems of supplying programs to broadcasters and networks, and reached the conclusion that program creation and distribution is a competitive business. It is not somehow "controlled" by a few program producers. If this conclusion is correct, then who does control the decision regarding what programs to produce? What factors influence this choice? Chapters 3 and 4 will examine this question in some detail. The basic difference between these two chapters is that Chapter 3 approaches broadcast markets from an abstract and theoretical point of view, with the intention of maintaining a broad perspective. In contrast, Chapter 4 delves more deeply into the realities and complexities of present broadcast markets by concentrating specifically on the behavior of the three existing commercial television networks.

Critics of broadcasting have charged repeatedly that television broadcasters provide excessive mass-appeal programming while simultaneously failing to offer programming for minority tastes.[a] Why should the television industry attract such criticism while magazine, book, and motion-picture industries do not? Are there properties peculiar to our broadcast institutions that dictate this outcome? If broadcasters do appeal only to mass tastes, what are the implications of this fact? If our television institutions were structured differently, would programming for minority audiences be more likely to appear?

To probe these questions, economists have constructed "theories of program choice." Under various assumptions regarding viewer preferences, program costs, and broadcast institutions, such models predict program patterns and compare the extent to which viewers receive preferred programs. Models of product competition by Steiner [523], Rothenberg [478], Wiles [617], and McGowan [343] will be reviewed and extended in this chapter. We extend these models in order to provide a more general theoretical framework upon which to formulate public policy as it relates to (1) "improving" present advertiser-supported television, with its limited channels, (2) evaluating the prospects of cable television, with essentially unlimited channels, and (3) evaluating the prospects

[a]For example see Minow, "The Vast Wasteland," speech delivered to the National Association of Broadcasters, May 9, 1961, reprinted in Minow [365], and N. Johnson [280].

49

for pay TV. Throughout the analysis, "performance" is measured in terms of the extent to which viewers receive their preferred programs.

Using a simulation methodology,[b] this chapter constructs a model that predicts program patterns and viewers' attainment of choices in a market of advertiser-supported television. The model considers alternative assumptions of channel-ownership structure, channel capacity, program costs, and viewer preferences. On pp. 78-88, the model is extended to cover subscriber-supported (pay) TV, and the resulting program patterns are compared with those under advertiser support. Finally, the direct policy implications are discussed. However, we save broader policy implications for later chapters.

We compare program patterns under two different ownership structures: a monopolistic structure, in which all channels are operated under unified management; and a "competitive" structure, in which each channel is operated under separate management, with each competitor engaged in noncollusive rivalry with other competitors.[c] These two structures are chosen for three reasons. First, Steiner and Wiles predicted that monopoly will provide superior viewer satisfaction under limited channels. Second, on the basis of Steiner's conclusions, monopoly at times has been proposed as an alternative to our present structure of rivalrous competition. Finally, a cable-TV operator possesses a potential monopoly control of programming in his market, although regulators may prevent him from exerting this power. What effect might this monopoly control have upon program patterns? Is it desirable to allow such control?

A major result of the model is that program patterns are particularly sensitive to the nature of viewer preferences. This result makes it imperative that one consider generalized preference structures and test how the model's predictions depend on alternative preferences. The model uses a wide range of preferences. Assumed viewer preferences of previous models are included as special cases, and in many cases the results of previous authors are found to be fragile.

Earlier Models

Theories of program choice can be considered extensions of Hotelling's classic article on product competition [257]. They pursue a question regarding

---

[b]A simulation methodology in this context is one that postulates a variety of alternative assumptions and uses a consistent set of rules to generate outcomes under each of the assumptions. The outcomes can then be analyzed to see how sensitive they are to the assumptions. With the exception of McGowan, previous papers have used simulation methodologies. For an enlightening discussion regarding simulation models of imperfect competition, see Shubik [502].

[c]In this chapter, the term "competitor" is synonymous with "rival." The competitive structure is really an oligopolistic structure of noncollusive rivalry. The game-theory formulation discussed later will formalize this structure. The important distinction to be made in competition of this nature is that stations view themselves as competitive with other stations and they know that their actions will bring forth reactions from other stations. Thus, the competition is "rivalrous."

broadcast programming similar to that which Hotelling analyzed in the competitive location of producers along a line: Can one explain the apparent result that rivalrous competitors market products of striking similarity, even though consumer desires would seem to dictate a more diverse product mix? Hotelling's model shows that under specific demand assumptions two firms will market products of "excessive sameness."[d] The result is analogous to what occurs under the two-party political system. If either candidate moves very far from center, the other candidate will move between him and the mass of voters. As a result, both candidates take a middle-of-the-road position.

Two extensions of Hotelling's model have important implications for the theory in this chapter. First, he compares the result of two rivalrous sellers with that of a single producer who attempts to maximize consumer satisfaction, but neglects to compare it to that of a single producer (monopolist) who attempts to maximize his own profit. Under the assumptions of Hotelling's model, the monopolist would offer *no* product variation. This extension will be explored below.

Second, Hotelling mentions the consequences of a third producer's entering the market, but fails to point out that his model is unstable for more than two competitors. Chamberlin [114] extends the model in a loosely formulated argument. He concludes that a static equilibrium will likely not obtain, but rather that "there might be continual shifting amongst the sellers" ([114], p. 261). Chamberlin does not pursue this point. It becomes an important prediction of the model formulated below.

Models of product competition in broadcast markets posit institutional assumptions that are far more specific than those pursued in the Hotelling vein. Steiner [523] has contributed the most comprehensive model, one rich in institutional detail and reaching conclusions that are consistent with the apparent failure of competitive broadcasting to satisfy a diversity of consumer tastes.

Steiner constructs viewer preferences by first dividing the potential audience into a number of subgroups. Consider a simple example in which a potential audience of 8750 individuals can be classified into three groups, each with internally homogeneous tastes.

Viewer group:	1	2	3
Group size:	5000	2500	1250

---

[d]Hotelling's results have been extended and shown to depend on rather strict assumptions (see Abbott [1], Archibald [18], Devletoglou [161], Lerner and Singer [324], Samuelson [481], Smithies [511], Telser [542], and Zeuthen [619]). All of these papers, including theories of program choice, define the product in terms which are quite narrow. The *general* economic problem that explains how firms in a market decide *which* products to produce and under what circumstances are these products the "right" ones from the viewpoint of economic efficiency remains unsolved.

Steiner also assumes that potential programs can be depicted as "program types." (This scheme of product representation is similar to Hotelling's, except that Hotelling's continuous line of finite length is in effect broken into a finite number of internally homogeneous segments.) To continue the above illustration, assume that the spectrum of potential programs is defined as three distinct program types. Each viewer group ranks the three program types and a fourth option, nonviewing. (The ranking of programs beyond the choice of nonviewing need not be specified, since if a group is offered only these lesser preferred choices, it turns off its sets.) Steiner's preferences for any given program type are exclusive—that is, in each case nonviewing is the second choice of an individual ([523], p. 199). A viewer is said to be "satisfied" if he is offered a program that he will view, and the measure for comparing alternatives becomes the number of "satisfied" viewers.

Viewer group:	1	2	3
Viewer program preferences:			
First choice	1	2	3
Second choice	nonviewing	nonviewing	nonviewing

Given these preferences, what programs will audience maximizing broadcasters offer? (Broadcasters attempt to maximize audiences in Steiner's model because advertising revenue is assumed to depend directly on audience size and the costs of programs are ignored.) Consider two ownership structures: all three channels controlled by a monopolist who operates the channels under unified management; and each of three channels operated by a separate competitor engaged in noncollusive rivalrous competition. Assume, furthermore, that where two programs of the same type are offered simultaneously, they share equally the total audience for that program type. What programs result under the two structures?

Monopoly

Program pattern:	1 channel of program 1—5000 viewers
	1 channel of program 2—2500 viewers
	1 channel of program 3—1250 viewers
Viewer satisfaction:	8750 receive first choice

Competition

Program pattern:	2 channels of program 1—2500 viewers each
	1 channel of program 2—2500 viewers

Viewer satisfaction: 7500 receive first choice

1250 do not view

How did these program patterns come about? The monopolist is interested in maximizing the total audience of the three channels. He does this simply by offering one program of each type. In contrast, each competitor is interested in maximizing the audience of his own channel. The first broadcaster to enter the market will show program 1, getting an audience of 5000 viewers. The second broadcaster then has a choice of (a) showing program 1, getting an audience of 2500 (sharing group 1 equally); or (b) showing program 2, getting an audience of 2500; or (c) showing program 3, getting an audience of 1250. Obviously, he will choose either (a) or (b). Suppose he chooses (b) and shows program 2. Now the third broadcaster enters. He has a choice of showing program 1, splitting group 1 with the first broadcaster; or showing program 2, splitting group 2 with the second broadcaster; or showing program 3, getting all of group 3. He will get the greatest audience if he duplicates program 1. Thus, under competition two broadcasters show program 1 and one broadcaster shows program 2, and this arrangement is "stable" (in this example) since none of the broadcasters can hope to gain by changing his program.

In this case, monopoly yields greater viewer "satisfaction." Groups 1 and 2 are indifferent as to the program patterns, and group 3 clearly prefers that of monopoly. Competitors fail to offer the "minority program," program 3. In this regard, monopoly yields greater "program diversity," for monopoly offers a wider range of programs. Furthermore, in competing for the mass of viewers, competitors engage in "program duplication," since two broadcasters simultaneously offer program one. Steiner's model predicts that, under competition, product imitation will occur, in the form of program duplication. This tendency toward excessive sameness is similar to that predicted by Hotelling, and reaffirms what critics of our broadcasting structure claim to observe.

The result of program duplication in this case is not only foregone minority programming, but a duplication of costs. Program duplication therefore results in a waste of resources, as well as a potential displacement of minority programming. (The existence of copyrights ensures that a broadcaster must offer a physically different program of the same program type. Hence, he must duplicate the production or purchase cost in order to engage in program duplication. In the real world, of course, "pure" duplication cannot occur, and one should think instead of programs that are more or less close substitutes.)

From his model, Steiner draws the following conclusion: "This suggests that a discriminating monopoly controlling all stations would produce a socially more beneficial program pattern" ([523], p. 206). But note the strong assumptions that are required to produce this result: (1) viewer groups are skewed (highly unequal) in size; (2) viewers watch only their first choices; (3) channel capacity is limited; (4) competitors duplicating a program share audiences equally; (5) all viewers are of equal value to broadcasters. These will be relaxed in the model to follow. Steiner's results also depend on his measure of satisfaction. This will be true of any measure, but Steiner's is quite narrow. Steiner discusses the effect of relaxing several of his assumptions. Steiner's paper still stands as the most comprehensive treatment of program patterns in broadcast markets, and in a later paper he applied the model to British television [522].

A brief treatment by Rothenberg [478] is complementary to Steiner's study, and offers valuable insights. He provides only two sketchy examples, but correctly focuses on two important variables: viewers' willingness to view programs other than their first choices, and the channel constraint. Rothenberg shows that if viewer groups each have a unique first choice, but as an alternative to nonviewing will watch some "common denominator,"[e] then competitors will likely engage in considerable duplication of this program before providing preferred programs. One can demonstrate this result by altering preferences slightly from those in the earlier example. Let the first program type be the common denominator.

Viewer group:	1	2	3
Viewer program preferences:			
First choice	1	2	3
Second choice	nonviewing	1	1
Third choice	nonviewing	nonviewing	nonviewing

Now note the result in the competitive market.

Competition

Program pattern:	3 channels of program 1—2917 viewers each
Viewer satisfaction:	5000 viewers receive first choice
	3750 viewers receive second choice

Under these conditions program duplication becomes even more attractive to competitors than Steiner had anticipated. Rothenberg concludes correctly,

[e]The term "common denominator" program is used throughout the book to mean any program that will be watched by a number of *different viewer groups*, i.e., the program is common to more than one group of viewers. In the viewer preferences that follow, the common-denominator program is never assumed to be the first choice of all viewer groups. In general, it will be a less-preferred choice. This use of the common-denominator-program concept is consistent with the (plausible) assumption that viewers would prefer to have programs somehow tailor made to their own tastes, but if this is impossible, will make do with some other program. It is in this context that the common-denominator program is interesting.

however, that competitive duplication is not a serious threat to viewer satisfaction if channel capacity is unlimited, because it does not displace minority programs (although duplication may result in a waste of resources). Rothenberg does not consider the effects of monopoly ownership.

Wiles [617] uses nine examples in an analysis of program patterns. He predicts differing program patterns under alternative ownership structures, channel capacities, and means of support, showing program patterns to be highly sensitive to alternate properties of these dimensions. A problem with his analysis is that his predictions are sensitive to specific assumptions. He concludes at one point, "Under the relationships between cost and revenue obtaining for TV, minimum differentiation is most profitable to an oligopoly or monopoly, maximum differentiation to a polypoly" ([617], p. 186). (The term polypoly is used to mean a large number of channels in rivalrous competition.) This statement needs to be examined carefully. Do oligopoly and monopoly necessarily produce minimum differentiation? Wiles's contention certainly disagrees with Steiner's result. For two of Wiles's examples, furthermore, monopoly produces maximum differentiation. At a later point in his analysis, Wiles appears to agree with Steiner, when he concludes that television should be monopolized because the spectrum is limited ([617], p. 188).

McGowan's model [343] of program patterns differs from the others'. Each producer determines an optimal program mix for the entire multiperiod "decision period" independently of other producers. His model fails to take into account the effect of one channel's program decision on another channel's audience, thereby ignoring the crux of small-group competition. McGowan also assumes away program duplication. As a result, his model generates unrealistic predictions. He draws the conclusion, "Industry performance given the number of broadcast stations will, on the average, be the same when the several broadcast facilities are independently operated as it would be if they were operated under unified management" ([343], p. 512). The present model takes channel interdependencies into account, thereby contradicting this conclusion for nearly all cases.

Measuring Viewer Satisfaction

Steiner's model, in which the second choice of all viewers is nonviewing, allows an appealing satisfaction criterion—maximization of viewers for a given number of channels. However, for generalized preferences in which viewers rank several choices above nonviewing, this criterion is too narrow. It measures only the extent to which viewers are persuaded to view. One clearly needs a satisfaction measure that registers not only total audience but also the extent to which viewers receive their preferred choices.

Our model constructs the following measures of viewer satisfaction. For each program pattern, the number of viewers receiving their first choices, second choices, etc., no program is tallied. Then the results under monopoly are compared to those under competition in terms of (1) which structure satisfies more first choices, (2) which structure attracts the larger audience, and (3) which structure wins a vote in which each viewer chooses the structure that gives him the higher choice.

For the voting scheme, viewers who receive the same choice under the two structures are assumed to cast a vote of indifference. The voting scheme is a populist notion and not one necessarily favored by economists. However, it provides a useful comparison of monopoly and competition, given that each member of the audience receives equal weight in the vote regardless of how intense his feelings are. We elect public officials the same way. Note that the results of the vote give no information as to which choices a program pattern is satisfying. The first two measures convey this information. (A full enumeration of viewers receiving each choice is omitted for expositional clarity.)

In the above example of Steiner's model, the monopolist's program pattern compares favorably to that of competitors, since (1) 8750 receive their first-choice program under monopoly, compared with only 7500 under competition; (2) monopoly attains a total audience of 8750, while competition attracts only 7500 (measures [1] and [2] are identical under the example's preferences); and (3) monopoly wins the populist vote, since groups 1 and 2 are indifferent while group 3 prefers monopoly.

A comparison of outcomes in terms of any of these measures does not avoid the problem of making "interpersonal welfare comparisons." For example, competition may give fifty viewers their first choices, while monopoly gives first choices to only thirty. We say, "Competition is better than monopoly in terms of first choices." But there is no guarantee that all thirty viewers who receive their first choices under monopoly *also* receive first choices under competition. The fifty to receive first choices under competition might be a totally different subset of the population. The measures count heads only. In this example, competition gives more first choices than monopoly, but *some* viewer might still get a higher choice with monopoly.

To measure viewer satisfaction, one could assign dollar values to choices. For a given program pattern, viewer satisfaction would then be expressed in terms of a single index number, which would represent the value of the program pattern to viewers. Because viewers receive programs free under advertiser-supported TV (ignoring the advertising costs a consumer pays when purchasing products), the value of this index number would then become a measure of consumer surplus.[f]

---

[f]Consumer surplus is a common measure used in welfare economics. It refers to the difference between the amount a consumer pays for an item and the amount it is worth to him. For total consumer surplus, the assumption is made that individual consumer surpluses can be added.

A more general framework should find the outcome that maximizes total (producer plus consumer) surplus. Total surplus for a given set of programs would be the total satisfaction (utility) derived from the set of programs minus the cost of the programs. Maximization of total surplus is consistent with the economists' concept of economic efficiency.

Although this measure of viewer welfare could easily be added to the model, it is not computed, for two reasons.

First, all that is needed to predict program patterns under advertiser support is a much weaker assumption regarding the order in which viewers rank programs. (A ranking of this nature is called an ordinal preference ranking.) In the absence of reliable empirical measures of the dollar satisfaction that viewers derive from programs, the assignment of dollar values must be arbitrary. (It is preferable at this point not to incorporate subjective weights in the measure of broadcaster performance. These weights will be added later in the analysis of pay TV. The pay-TV analysis requires that viewer preferences be stated in dollar terms.

The second reason for not expressing dollar satisfaction as a single index number is that the number would conceal information regarding which choices are being satisfied. For example, if a first choice is valued at 20¢, and a second choice at 10¢, does an index number representing 40¢ of total satisfaction mean that two persons received their first choices, or that four persons received their second choices? This detailed information will be valuable in analyzing the model's predictions.

To the extent that competitors duplicate programs and accordingly fail to offer unique programs, the effect on viewer satisfaction is recorded in the measures of choices. Since program duplication also implies duplicated resource costs, however, the total cost of duplication is not registered in the satisfaction measures. For this reason, the conditions under which program duplication occurs are discussed.

The Model Under Advertiser Support

The following assumptions hold throughout the analysis of advertiser-supported television:

1. There exists a television market that consists of a fixed number of potential viewers.

2. There exists a programming period of standard length during which each channel presents a single program type. The model deals with only a single program period. (The model will be extended to more than one period on pp. 132-137.)

3. The program is a free good to the viewer. The cost of advertising paid through product prices is ignored, as is the opportunity cost of viewer time. (The case of pay TV will be taken up on pp. 78-88.)

4. There are a finite number of identifiable and distinct "program types," defined in terms of viewer preferences.[g]

---

[g]Empirical testing of the model's welfare implications requires that program types be both empirically measurable and identifiable with viewer preferences. The present model does not attempt to make program types empirically measurable. See Levin's [330] use of industry categories and the accompanying comments, and other empirical studies by Lang [316], Land [317], and Bowman and Farley [82]. The model's predictions are testable in principle, but empirical work is left for the future.

5. Viewers in the market can be classified into a finite number of internally homogeneous "viewer groups."

6. Preferences are independent of the actual program types presented.

7. All channels simultaneously producing the same program type share equally in the total audience for that type. (The implications of relaxing this assumption are discussed on pp. 73-75.)

8. The cost of a program is not affected by the actual number of viewers; i.e., the marginal cost of an additional viewer is zero. (This assumption is reasonable for the single-period model here, but Chapter 4 will show that it is not valid for a given program over a period of time.)

9. Each program type has a given purchase cost associated with it. For a given program type, popularity is not a direct function of program cost. The relation between program cost and popularity is handled by defining different program types, and varying the popularity across program types. (The relation between program cost and popularity for network programming will be discussed in detail in Chapter 4.)

10. Advertising rates *per viewer* are fixed for the relevant decision period, and all viewers are worth the same amount to advertisers. Advertising revenues for a program depend upon the prevailing rate and the program's actual audience. (The assumption that all viewers are worth the same amount to advertisers is relaxed on pp. 75-78.)

11. (a) For the monopolistic system, the operator seeks to maximize the *joint* profits of all channels. If any channel's operation results in a net loss to the operator, he has the option of discontinuing use of that channel with the resulting zero net profit from that channel.

(b) For the competitive system, the operator of a single channel seeks to maximize his own profits in *noncollusive* rivalrous competition with other channels. The operator has the option of going off the air with a resulting zero net profit.

The calculations in the model can be simplified by using the fact that advertising rates per viewer are constant (assumption 10) to state the fixed program costs (assumption 9) in terms of minimum break-even audiences. The profit-maximizing broadcaster will then attempt to maximize the difference between total audience and break-even audience, this amount being a measure of profit. The model will be simplified with one further assumption—that break-even audiences are equal for all program types, i.e., program costs are the same for all program types. (Because popularities of programs will be varied, this assumption is not too restrictive. It will be discussed later.) Under these conditions, the monopolist will maximize profits by maximizing the *total audience* of all channels, provided that the *net* addition to audience from each channel is at least the break-even quantity. For the competitive system, the channel operator will maximize his own audience, provided that this audience is at least the break-even quantity.

The break-even audience is held constant across program types, so that formally there is no correlation between program cost and popularity. However, there is a symmetry between holding program popularity constant and varying costs, and holding program costs constant and varying popularity. The model does the latter by varying the distribution of viewers. The effects of program costs being correlated with popularity can be discussed, therefore, without introducing this relationship explicitly. (A detailed discussion of this relationship is left to Chapter 4.)

Viewer Preferences and Program Supply

Within the framework of the above assumptions, the model of advertiser-supported TV uses a range of viewer-preference structures and program-supply characteristics. Within the range of these dimensions, the performance of a competitive broadcasting structure will be compared to that of a monopolistic structure. The dimensions of viewer preferences and program supply are discussed below.

Viewer Preferences

The model uses three patterns depicting viewer choices. In the first pattern (no. 1 in Table 3-1), each viewer group has a unique first choice and will watch only that program (Steiner's assumption). If offered any other program, the group will not view.

The second pattern is more general. Each group still has the same unique first choice, but will view an alternate program (closely related on the program spectrum) if its first choice is not available (pattern 2 in Table 3-1). If neither of these two programs is available, the group will not view.

Similarly, additional lesser choices (third, fourth, etc.) can be added. However, a third case captures the effects of this expansion. Each group has a unique first choice and a closely related second choice, but in addition will always view some common denominator rather than turn its sets off (pattern 3 in Table 3-1). Under this assumption, there exists a program that all viewers will watch if offered nothing else, although a large fraction of the audience would actually prefer a different program. This case is suggested by Rothenberg and also is approximated by Hotelling's preference assumption.

These three patterns cover a wide range of possible preferences. However, the preference structure is not complete until the number of viewers in each group is specified. Again a range of values is assumed. The hypothetical audience of 10,000 viewers is divided into a maximum of twenty-five groups according to three geometric distributions: (1) a "highly skewed" distribution, in which each

Table 3-1
Assumptions of Viewer Preferences and Program Supply

The Nature of Viewer Choices

Ordinal Ranking of Program Types by Viewer Groups (Choices of Only the First Five Groups Are Shown)

1. Viewers will watch only their first choices.

2. Viewers have unique second or lesser choices.

3. Viewers have a common lesser choice (the common denominator.)

#1	Viewers				
Programs		1	2	3	4	5
1	1				
2		1			
3			1		
4				1	
5					1

#2	Viewers				
Programs		1	2	3	4	5
1	1	2			
2		1	2		
3			1	2	
4				1	2
5					1

#3	Viewers				
Programs		1	2	3	4	5
1	1	2	3	3	3
2		1	2		
3			1	2	
4				1	2
5					1

The Distribution of Viewers into Groups

(Only the First Five Groups Are Shown)

A. Highly skewed distribution

Group Size
1. 8,000
2. 1,600
3.   320
4.   64
5.   12

B. Skewed distribution

Group Size
1. 5,000
2. 2,500
3. 1,250
4.   625
5.   313

C. Nearly rectangular distribution

Group Size
1. 1,077
2.   970
3.   872
4.   785
5.   707

Program Costs

a. Higher program costs (the break-even audience is 1200 viewers)

b. Lower program costs (the break-even audience is 800 viewers)

The Channel Limitation

a. Channel capacity limited (three channels)

b. Channel capacity unlimited

successive group is only one-fifth as large as the previous group; (2) a "skewed" distribution, in which each group is one-half as large as the previous group; and (3) a "nearly rectangular" distribution in which each group is nine-tenths as large as the previous group (see Table 3-1). A rectangular distribution in which all groups are of equal size could also be used. However, many of the program patterns that result are indeterminate, without arbitrary rules for broadcaster decisions when a number of programs offer equal profitability. The nearly rectangular distribution captures the flavor of the rectangular distribution, but avoids indeterminacies. For the highly skewed distribution, "mass" audiences are very large relative to "minority" audiences. For the nearly rectangular distribution, all groups are of nearly comparable size.

Combining the three degrees of skewness in the viewer distribution with the three preference patterns yields viewer preferences that are very general. Since no one knows how preferences appear in reality, it becomes imperative to find predictions which hold under general preference assumptions.

Program Supply

The model includes two critical dimensions of program supply: the cost of purchasing programs and the number of channels available in the market. The explicit inclusion of program costs is important for two reasons. First, in a model that postulates profit maximization, programs must be economically viable. It is irrelevant to argue for "minority programming" in a purely profit-maximizing context without specifying the cost of such programs; and yet earlier models have omitted costs. Second, by altering assumptions regarding program costs, one can judge the effects of program costs on program patterns and viewer satisfaction.

Two levels of break-even audience size are used as proxies for program costs: "higher" program costs (break-even audiences of 1200 viewers for all programs) and "lower" program costs (break-even audiences of 800 viewers for all programs).

Finally, the number of channels is assumed either to be limited (arbitrarily to three channels) or unlimited. Numbers of channels other than three can be used, but these two options are sufficient to demonstrate the importance of the channel constraint.

Given the earlier assumptions about broadcaster and viewer behavior, and the alternative assumptions about channels and costs, it is possible to calculate numerically the program patterns that result from any particular combination of assumptions. This was done with the aid of a computer, and the results appear in the next section.

Program Patterns and Viewer Satisfaction

This section takes the reader through five important cases that are generated by the simulation model. These examples have been chosen to suggest some of the more interesting results that came out of the greater number of cases (thirty-six in all) included in the tables at the end of this section. The predictions from the five examples are representative, but not inclusive, of the more general predictions resulting from the full spectrum of cases. A discussion of the general predictions appears in the next section.

The first four cases presented here are chosen to examine Steiner's conclusions. Case 1 shows that under Steiner's assumptions, monopoly provides greater viewer satisfaction than competition—Steiner's result. Cases 2 and 3 show that if additional channels are allowed, or if viewer groups are nearly equal in size, both structures provide the same viewer satisfaction. Case 4 shows that if viewers will watch other than first choices, then viewers may well prefer competition to monopoly—the opposite of Steiner's result. Case 5 then demonstrates that program patterns may be unstable under competition, a complication not dealt with in earlier papers. These five cases only begin to demonstrate the wider range of cases tabulated at the end of the section.

Steiner concludes that under limited channels "a monopoly controlling all stations would produce a socially more beneficial program pattern" ([523], p. 206). Let us use the simulation model and the dimensions of preferences and program supply in Table 3-1 to examine this conclusion. First, consider a case analogous to Steiner's.

Case 1—Steiner's case

    a. Preference assumption 1A (viewers will watch only their first choices and the viewer distribution is highly skewed)
    b. Break-even audience is 800
    c. Number of channels limited to three

Monopoly

Program pattern: 1 channel of program 1—8000 viewers

                         1 channel of program 2—1600 viewers

                         1 channel dark

Viewer satisfaction: 9600 receive first choice

                         400 do not view

Competition

Program pattern: 3 channels of program 1—2667 viewers each

Viewer satisfaction: 8000 receive first choice

2000 do not view

Under competition, broadcasters find it more profitable to engage in program duplication than to offer a diversity of programs. The monopolist, however, offers all programs that are economically viable. Monopoly clearly produces superior viewer satisfaction (without incurring the cost of program duplication). Can one conclude from this, as did Steiner, that viewers would prefer all stations to be operated under unified management? This conclusion is sensitive to at least three of the example's assumptions: the number of channels is limited; the viewer distribution is highly skewed; and viewers will watch only their first choices. The next three examples will relax each of these assumptions in turn.

Case 2—Additional channels

    a. Preference assumption 1A (same as before)

    b. Break-even audience is 800 (same as before)

    c. Six channels in the market

Monopoly

Program pattern: 1 channel of program 1—8000 viewers

1 channel of program 2—1600 viewers

4 channels dark

Viewer satisfaction: 9600 receive first choice

400 do not view

Competition

Program pattern: 5 channels of program 1—1600 viewers each

1 channel of program 2—1600 viewers

Viewer satisfaction: 9600 receive first choice

400 do not view

When the number of channels is expanded to six, the monopolist leaves the additional channels dark. In contrast, competitors fill the additional channels by continuing to duplicate program 1, further splitting the mass of viewers. However, given enough channels, it finally becomes profitable for competitors to offer program 2. Given ample channels, minority programs (if economically viable) eventually appear under competition in spite of program duplication. *Under unlimited channels, competitive duplication of programs causes no loss in viewer satisfaction* (although it wastes resources). Even under Steiner's strict preference assumption, if there are unlimited channels, monopoly no longer provides superior choices. Now consider what happens if the preference assumption is relaxed.

Case 3–Viewer distribution no longer skewed

    a. Preference assumption 1C (viewers will watch only their first choices and the viewer distribution is nearly rectangular)

    b. Break-even audience is 800 (same as before)

    c. Number of channels limited to three

Monopoly

Program pattern: 1 channel of program 1–1077 viewers

                        1 channel of program 2– 970 viewers

                        1 channel of program 3– 872 viewers

Viewer satisfaction: 2919 receive first choice

                        7081 do not view

Competition

Program pattern: 1 channel of program 1–1077 viewers

                        1 channel of program 2– 970 viewers

                        1 channel of program 3– 872 viewers

Viewer satisfaction: 2919 receive first choice

                        7081 do not view

Competitors no longer engage in program duplication! Program duplication under competition results when a mass of viewers who prefer one program is considerably larger than another mass who prefer a different program. But this occurs only if viewer groups are skewed in size (or, as will be seen later, if a common denominator exists). If duplication does not occur and if viewers will watch only their first choices, then the two ownership structures provide identical program patterns. Again, monopoly does not necessarily provide superior viewer satisfaction.

So long as viewers refuse to watch any programs except their first choices, then the model predicts that monopoly always provides viewer satisfaction at least as great as that provided under competition. However, it seems reasonable that in actuality viewers will watch less-preferred choices if their first choices are not available. In this case, it no longer holds that monopoly necessarily provides satisfaction as least as great as competition. Two more examples will demonstrate this result.

Case 4—Viewers will watch lesser choices

    a. Preference assumption 2B (viewers have both a first and a second choice and the viewer distribution is skewed)
    b. Break-even audience is 800 (same as before)
    c. Number of channels limited to three (same as before)

Monopoly

Program pattern:	1 channel of program 1—7500 viewers
	1 channel of program 3—1875 viewers
	1 channel dark
Viewer satisfaction:	6250 receive first choice
	3125 receive second choice
	625 do not view

Competition

Program pattern:	2 channels of program 1—2500 viewers each
	1 channel of program 2—3750 viewers
Viewer satisfaction:	7500 receive first choice
	1250 receive second choice
	1250 do not view

Where viewers will watch lesser choices, the monopolist capitalizes on this fact by offering only audience-maximizing common denominators! Why should the monopolist produce program 2 (the second group's first choice) when he captures group 2 by offering only program 1? His only concern is that viewers choose television over other activities, not that they receive their favorite programs.

On the other hand, competitive broadcasters must gain audiences by attracting viewers away from other channels as well as from preoccupations other than television viewing. Therefore, competitors find it profitable to offer preferred choices. In the example, a competitor offers program 2, thereby attracting group 2 away from the other channels that offer program 1. (If there were more channels, program 3 would appear under competition in addition to programs 1 and 2. The monopolist, however, would never produce program 2.) The comparison of monopoly and competition looks very different when lesser choices are allowed. No longer do the monopolist's program patterns provide viewer satisfaction at least as great as competitors' program patterns. (Under preference pattern 3, the monopolist always offers only the common denominator, regardless of other variables.)

For the above example, competition satisfies more first choices while monopoly attains a larger audience. Therefore, neither structure is strictly preferred by viewers. (However, competition wins the populist vote. Group 2 votes for competition, groups 3 and 4 vote for monopoly, and all other groups are indifferent.)

One further example will demonstrate that where lesser choices exist, an equilibrium in pure strategies may not always occur under competition. Instead, a mixed strategy or probabilistic outcome occurs.[h]

Case 5—Competitive mixed-strategy equilibrium

    a. Preference assumption 2C (viewers have both a first and a second choice and the viewer distribution is nearly rectangular)
    b. Break-even audience is 800 (same as before)
    c. Number of channels is limited to three (same as before)

<u>Monopoly</u>

Program pattern:	1 channel of program 1—2047 viewers
	1 channel of program 3—1657 viewers
	1 channel of program 5—1343 viewers
Viewer satisfaction:	2656 receive first choice
	2391 receive second choice
	4953 do not view

<u>Competition</u>

Program pattern:	Three channels in a mixed strategy such that programs 1-4 are each shown with 75 percent probability. Each producer attains a probable audience of 1322 viewers.
Viewer satisfaction: (mixed strategy averages)	2778 receive first choice
	1187 receive second choice
	6035 do not view

The example illustrates an important facet of competition in product space. There is no reason to suppose that a fixed set of program patterns should always

[h]For the reader not familiar with game theory, a pure strategy equilibrium means that every player finds it most profitable to continue showing his profit-maximizing program so long as the other broadcasters continue to show their profit-maximizing programs. The mixed strategy means that each broadcaster finds it optimal not to reveal his program decision until absolutely necessary, and to calculate probabilities as to which program he will offer viewers. This way he keeps his competitors guessing, so that they cannot play on the fact that they know what he will do.

occur under competition. As noted earlier, Chamberlin [114] suggests this result in his discussion of Hotelling's model. Perhaps we see it demonstrated in the present three-network rivalry situation where program strategies are always changing, and in the magazine industry where new products are continually emerging, and existing products changing or disappearing.

The game used in the simulation model to produce the competitive program patterns is an n-person non-zero-sum noncooperative game, where n is sufficiently small that one channel's program decision directly affects profits on other channels. This formulation is common in game theory, and is discussed in detail in Beebe [57]. Each producer is treated symmetrically; that is, each competitor is allowed the same payoff from a given strategy. A solution in pure or mixed strategies is approached or found using a method of fictitious play. Consider how the mixed strategy comes about. First suppose the three competitive broadcasters offer programs 1, 2, and 3 respectively. In this situation it obviously pays either of the producers of programs 1 or 2 to shift to program 4, thereby attaining a net gain in audience. If this occurs, then it pays the producer of program 3 to shift to program 1 or 2. But given this move, it pays the producer of program 4 to shift to program 3, and so forth. The three producers will continue to shift among the four programs. No stable pattern of pure strategies exists, and the result is a mixed strategy for each producer. (For the mixed strategy, the resulting program patterns and viewer satisfaction are calculated in probabilistic terms for the cycle over which the mixed strategy occurs.)

As in Case 4 above, one cannot say unambiguously that one structure provides preferred choices. Competition satisfies more first choices, but monopoly gains a greater total audience. (For this case, monopoly wins the populist vote.)

The examples above are representative of those generated under the simulation model. The broader results are summarized in Tables 3-2 and 3-3. The thirty-six cases included in the tables are generated across the spectrum of three preference patterns, three viewer distributions, two break-even audiences, and two channel options.

Table 3-2 provides predictions of the highest numbered program type offered by monopoly and competition. This is a measure of programming for minority-taste audiences, since higher numbered programs (by convention) are always those aimed at smaller audiences. The table also gives the number of channels used, since this is a measure of the spectrum crowding that is necessary to obtain this extent of minority programming. These results are given for a system with three channels and for one with unlimited channels, for each of the viewer preference and program cost assumptions in Table 3-1. (The reader should refer to Table 3-1, p. 60, to remind himself of the preference assumptions that appear in the first two columns of Tables 3-2 and 3-3.)

Table 3-3 compares monopoly and competition in terms of first choices, total

Table 3-2
Highest Numbered Program Type Offered and Number of Channels Used Under Monopoly and Competition

Pref. Pattern	Viewer Distr.	Min. Aud.	Three Channels				Unlimited Channels			
			Highest Numbered Program Type Offered		Number of Channels Used		Highest Numbered Program Type Offered		Number of Channels Used	
			Monopoly	Comp.	Monopoly	Comp.	Monopoly	Comp.	Monopoly	Comp.
1	A	1200	2	1	2	3	2	2	2	7
2		800	2	1	2	3	2	2	2	12
3	B	1200	3	2	3	3	3	3	3	7
4		800	3	2	3	3	3	3	3	10
5	C	1200	0	0	0	0	0	0	0	0
6		800	3	3	3	3	3	3	3	3
7	A	1200	1	1	1	3	1	2	1	7
8		800	1	1	1	3	1	2	1	12
9	B	1200	3	2	2	3	3	3	2	7
10		800	3	2	2	3	3	3	2	11
11	C	1200	5	4(75%)[a]	3	3	5	6(96%)[a]	3	5-6[b]
12		800	5	4(75%)	3	3	9	9(96%)	5	9-10
13	A	1200	1	1	1	3	1	2	1	7
14		800	1	1	1	3	1	2	1	12
15	B	1200	1	2	1	3	1	3	1	7
16		800	1	2	1	3	1	4	1	11
17	C	1200	1	1	1	3	1	6(96%)	1	9-10[c]
18		800	1	1	1	3	1	9(92%)	1	13-15[c]

[a]The percentage represents the probability that this program appears in the mixed strategy.
[b]The range is taken over the mixed strategy.
[c]For these cases the occurrence of a mixed strategy under the Cournot assumption leads to losses for some broadcasters.
Source: See text.

Table 3-3
Viewer Satisfaction Under Monopoly and Competition (Ownership Structure Satisfying More Viewers[a])

	Pref. Pattern	Viewer Distr.	Min. Aud.	Three Channels			Unlimited Channels		
				First Choices	Total Viewers	Populist Vote	First Choices	Total Viewers	Populist Vote
1	1	A	1200	M	M[b]	M	E	E[b]	E
2			800	M	M	M	E	E	E
3		B	1200	M	M	M	E	E	E
4			800	M	M	M	E	E	E
5		C	1200	E	E	E	E	E	E
6			800	E	E	E	E	E	E
7	2	A	1200	E	E	E	C	C	C
8			800	E	E	E	C	C	C
9		B	1200	C	M	C	C	E	C
10			800	C	M	C	C	C	C
11		C	1200	C	M	M	C	C	C
12			800	C	M	M	C	M[c]	C
13	3	A	1200	E	E[d]	E	C	E[d]	C
14			800	E	E	E	C	E	C
15		B	1200	C	E	C	C	E	C
16			800	C	E	C	C	E	C
17		C	1200	E	E	E	C	E	C
18			800	E	E	E	C	E	C

[a]M = Monopoly satisfies more viewers. C = Competition satisfies more viewers. E = The two structures satisfy equal numbers of viewers.

[b]For preference pattern 1, viewers receiving first choices are identical to total viewers.

[c]Monopoly attains a slightly larger audience because the monopolist always shows program 9, but it is shown with 96 percent probability under competition (see Table 3-2). This is a peculiarity of the simulation model that can occur under a mixed strategy because audience groups are lumpy in size.

[d]For preference pattern 3, so long as program 1 is shown the entire audience will view.

Source: See text.

audience, and a populist vote between the two structures. Tables 3-2 and 3-3 together provide data that have been assimilated by examining the full program patterns of the thirty-six cases. The tables provide a means for the reader to examine the general predictions of the next section in terms of the particular results of the simulation model.

Predictions from the Model

Result 1

Two important aspects of profit-maximizing product variation stand out for their impacts on program patterns and viewer satisfaction: competitors' tendencies toward program duplication and imitation, and the monopolist's search for audience-maximizing common-denominator programs.

Competitive duplication results under the skewed viewer distribution (viewer distributions A or B in Table 3-1) and/or the existence of common denominators (preference pattern 3). Duplication exemplifies the Hotelling-Steiner criticism of competition.

The monopolist's behavior is the result of protection from product competition. The monopolist never engages in duplication, and under advertiser-supported TV avoids producing substitutes. Hence, if viewers accept other than their first choices (preference patterns 2 or 3), then the monopolist specifically seeks out common denominators.

Where viewers prefer some common denominator to nonviewing (preference pattern 3), then this is the only program the monopolist will offer (see Table 3-2). Competitors are likely to duplicate this program, but given ample channels (and sufficient demand for preferred types to cover costs) competitors eventually cater to higher choices. Under monopoly, if viewers expect preferred choices, they must exercise their power of nonviewing when offered lesser choices. But under competition with unlimited channels, viewers' likelihood of receiving preferred choices is independent of whether they rank lesser choices.

Result 2

Steiner's model ignores program costs, and hence assumes implicitly that channel capacity is the only binding constraint. The implication is profound: Whenever program duplication exists, it displaces minority programs. But when program costs are introduced, there exists the possibility of excess channel capacity. Under excess channel capacity, duplication does not displace minority programming, but appears in addition to it, and hence causes no loss in viewer satisfaction. Although duplication results in a waste of resources, viewers are not denied alternative programs.

We feel that the displacement of minority-taste programs (which occurs only under limited channels) is probably a more serious cost of duplication than is the cost of duplicated inputs. Does duplicated editorial effort in magazines comprise a competitive waste of resources? In reality, are programs or magazines ever perfect substitutes? Might the threat of duplication have a beneficial effect upon quality? The point is that duplicated editorial effort in magazines might pose a serious problem if only three magazines were allowed in the market.

Result 3

If one wishes programs for minority-taste audiences, then adequate channel capacity is a necessary but not a sufficient condition under profit-maximizing ownership and advertiser support (see Table 3-2). Sufficient conditions under competition are (1) adequate channel capacity, and (2) some audience subset greater than the break-even audience size that ranks the program as a first choice. Sufficient conditions under monopoly are the above plus (3) the group's refusal to view lesser preferred programs (preference pattern 1).

The addition of channels, *ceteris paribus*, never leads to a decrease in program offerings or viewer satisfaction. The model provides the opportunity to measure the value to viewers of additional channels in terms of foregone viewer satisfaction, although this is not done.

Under unlimited channel capacity, the number of channels used varies considerably depending upon assumptions about preferences, costs, and ownership structure (see the last two columns of Table 3-2). The model suggests, therefore, that there is no way to know a priori what will be an "adequate" number of channels for a cable television system, for instance, without specifying preferences, program costs, and institutional structure, as well as the cost of additional channels. Many of these variables, particularly viewer preferences, will be very difficult to predict ahead of time. Thus, it will be almost impossible to determine a priori the "correct" number of channels to build into a cable television system. A strong case exists, therefore, for building flexibility into capacities of future cable television systems, if technically feasible and not excessively costly. If flexibility is impossible or uneconomic, then systems might be built with an anticipated risk of excess capacity to encourage programs for minority tastes, for under advertiser-supported TV it is necessary that there be ample channels if minority programs are to appear. To ensure excess capacity, one should provide more channels for a competitively owned system than for a monopolistically owned system. Under advertiser support monopoly never uses more channels than does competition, *ceteris paribus* (see the last two columns of Table 3-2).

Result 4

The effect of program costs being correlated with popularity is analyzed by varying the distribution of viewers among groups. If break-even audiences are lower for less popular programs, then *ceteris paribus*, more programming is likely to appear for minority audiences. If channel capacity is binding, or if enough viewers switch to these programs from previously produced more popular programs, then these programs are likely to replace more popular (and more costly) programs. Otherwise they are likely to appear in addition to them. If costs appear greater for the less popular programs, then the opposite result will hold.

Result 5

Under limited channels, the model yields the following predictions: (1) If viewers watch only their first choices (preference pattern 1), then monopoly provides at least as many program types and viewer satisfaction at least as great as competition; (2) If viewers watch only their first choices and the viewer distribution is skewed (viewer distributions A or B), resulting in program duplication under competition, then monopoly provides more program types and greater viewer satisfaction than competition; (3) If there exists a common denominator (preference pattern 3), then competition provides at least as many program types and viewer satisfaction at least as great as monopoly (which provides only the single program).

Steiner and Wiles reach the following conclusion: If channel capacity is limited, then monopoly will likely produce more program types and yield higher viewer satisfaction than will competition. This prediction is necessarily true only under the strong assumptions of prediction (2) in the preceding paragraph. Under more general (and realistic) preferences, the conclusion of Steiner and Wiles is not necessarily true. *Under general preferences and limited channels, one cannot say (without stating specific preference assumptions) which ownership structure offers more program types and yields higher viewer satisfaction.* (See Tables 3-2 and 3-3, columns under "Three Channels.") If viewers will watch only their first choices, then monopoly is likely to be the preferred structure. If viewers will watch lesser choices and viewer groups are not highly skewed in size, then competition is likely to provide more first choices, but monopoly is still likely to attract a larger audience.

Result 6

Under unlimited channels, competitive program duplication does not displace minority programs. The minority programs (if preferred by viewers and if economically viable) appear in addition to the duplicated programs. (See Table 3-2, columns under "Unlimited Channels.") Under unlimited channels, therefore, competitive program duplication causes no loss in viewer satisfaction. In their attempts to attract audiences from other channels, competitors offer all economically viable programs, so that viewers are guaranteed of receiving preferred choices.

Under unlimited channels, the monopolist still seeks out common denominators. (See Table 3-2, columns under "Unlimited Channels.") If he captures an audience with a lesser choice, he has no incentive to provide a preferred choice, even though channel capacity is available.

Because of these results for competition and monopoly, the model predicts the following: *Under unlimited channels, competitive ownership of channels always results in at least as many program types, and where lesser choices are specified, more program types than does monopolistic ownership.* This does not necessarily mean that competition always offers the same program types as monopoly plus additional types. Rather, it implies that the total number of different program types being offered under competition will exceed that under monopoly. The reason that competition does not always offer the same program types as monopoly plus additional types is that in the mixed strategy, programs offered by the monopolist will not always be offered with certainty by competitors. Case 5 provides an example.

Competition never satisfies fewer first choices than does monopoly. (See Table 3-3, columns under "Unlimited Channels.") Where viewers will watch lesser choices, competition always satisfies more first choices. Where viewers will watch only their first choices, the two structures satisfy exactly the same number of viewers.

Competitors under unlimited channels will always satisfy (economically viable) preferred choices (although they may not offer these programs with certainty). This is not true of the monopolist under unlimited channels, however. Furthermore, under unlimited channels, competitors will almost always attain a total audience as great as the monopolist (who specifically seeks to maximize total audience). (See the last column in Table 3-3.)

The model's predictions point to the conclusion that under advertiser-supported TV, if channel capacity is constrained (the present situation for VHF), then one cannot say which ownership structure will yield greater viewer satisfaction for general preferences. However, if channel capacity is effectively unconstrained (as with cable TV), then the competitive structure will yield greater viewer satisfaction than the monopolistic structure for general preferences (although costs attributable to program duplication will occur under the competitive structure).

Relaxing Two Assumptions

Two assumptions in the model can now be relaxed: First, channels that duplicate a program share equally in the audience for that program (assumption

7); and second, all viewers are equally valuable to advertisers (assumption 10). The former assumption will be relaxed because program duplication is an important result in the model, and the degree of program duplication under competition obviously depends on the way broadcasters duplicating a program actually divide the audience (or think they will divide the audience). It is important to examine the second assumption, because advertisers may be willing to pay more (or less) for various minority-taste audiences. If this is the case, then it has important implications for the quantity of minority programming that will result.

To relax the first assumption, consider what happens to program duplication if broadcasters do not split the audience equally. Suppose that each successive broadcaster duplicating a previously offered program receives one-half of the audience of the preceding broadcaster. For example, two broadcasters split the audience 2/3 and 1/3; three broadcasters split it 4/7, 2/7, 1/7. (In deciding to duplicate a program, the entering broadcaster assumes that he will obtain a fraction of the total audience for that program equal to $1/(2^n-1)$, where n is the number of broadcasters duplicating the program, including himself.) Consider again Case 1, which was used to exemplify program duplication under competition (p. 62). The preference assumptions for Case 1 were:

Viewer group:	1	2
Group size:	8000	1600
Program preferences:		
First choice	1	2
Second choice	nonviewing	nonviewing

Now, what program patterns emerge under the competitive broadcast structure with three channels, given the alternative assumptions regarding how broadcasters split audiences?

Assumption (a): Broadcasters duplicating a program share audiences equally.

Program Pattern

3 channels of program 1—2667 viewers each

Assumption (b): Each successive duplicating broadcaster receives one-half the audience of the preceding broadcaster.

Program Pattern

2 channels of program 1—5333 and 2667 viewers respectively

1 channel of program 2—1600 viewers

Where broadcasters duplicating a program do not share the audience equally, less duplication results. The degree of duplication under the competitive structure is sensitive to the way in which broadcasters split audiences. At one extreme, a broadcaster who considers duplicating a program might think that he can take the entire audience from the other broadcaster(s). This assumption leads to maximum duplication (and an obvious instability in program patterns). At the other extreme, a broadcaster who considers duplicating a program might think that the entire audience will remain loyal to the previous broadcaster. This assumption leads to no duplication. The model's assumption that broadcasters duplicating a program split the audience equally is admittedly arbitrary. However, so long as it is possible for a successive broadcaster to obtain *some* fraction of the program's audience, then program duplication may occur under competition. (*Playboy* and its imitators may provide an example.) In this case, the qualitative results of the model are independent of the actual shares assumed, even though the quantitative degree of program duplication is sensitive to this parameter.

Now let us relax the assumption that all viewers are equally valuable to advertisers. Suppose that incomes, tastes, and expenditure patterns differ across viewer groups. As a result, advertisers value some groups more highly than others. (Each individual advertiser will have his own valuation of viewer groups. But here we are concerned with the net effect of individual advertiser demands, that is, how the advertising market as a whole values each viewer group.) To be consistent with the methodology of the model, we shall assume that either (1) the smaller audience groups (the minority audiences) are worth more per viewer in the advertising market than are the larger (mass) audiences, or (2) the opposite is true. Which of these assumptions is more realistic is not obvious. Some discussion will be devoted to this issue at the end of the section.

In generalizing the model of advertiser-supported TV, assume first that all viewers will watch only their first choices (preference pattern 1). Assume also that advertising rates (per viewer) accurately reflect the values of viewer groups in the advertising market. Then the potential revenue to a broadcaster of attracting any particular group is the number of viewers in the group weighted by the group's value per viewer to advertisers.

Return again to Case 1. The viewer preference structure is:

Viewer group:	1	2
Group size:	8000	1600
Program preference:		
First choice	1	2
Second choice	nonviewing	nonviewing

But now assume that different viewer groups generate different revenues *per viewer* to the broadcaster. One can no longer use the concept of audience maximization; instead, one must revert to the more fundamental assumption of profit maximization. (See assumption 11, p. 58, for the initial postulate of profit maximization.) Assume exposure to viewers in group 1 is worth 1¢ per viewer and exposure to group 2 is worth 2.5¢ per viewer. (For completeness, the minimum audience sizes used earlier must also be converted to costs. For the minimum audiences of 1200 and 800 used earlier, substitute $12 and $8 as break-even costs. For the simple examples in this section, however, these costs are not needed.) Then the revenues generated from programs 1 and 2 are:

Program 1:   8000 × $.01   = $80.00

Program 2:   1600 × $.025 = $40.00

Based on this revenue structure across program types (and taking into account the break-even costs) profit-maximizing program patterns can be calculated for the model just as they were earlier. Note for this example that the audience for program 2 generates exactly one-half the revenue which the audience for program 1 generates. (Program 3 would generate half the revenue of program 2, and so forth.) For this example, the *relative* revenues across program types are identical to those of the original model assuming the second viewer distribution—that is assuming a viewer distribution of 5000, 2500, 1250, etc. The predictions that result from the model are also identical. Therefore, one can interpret the effect of viewer groups' being worth differing amounts within the context of the original model by merely altering the viewer distribution. (This is strictly true where viewers watch only their first choices.) The result is that if minority audiences are worth more per viewer to advertisers, then this is equivalent to assuming a less skewed viewer distribution in the original model, with the same effect on program patterns. Minority programs are more likely to appear under both competition and monopoly, and program duplication is less likely to occur under competition. If mass audiences are worth more per viewer to advertisers, then the opposite will hold true.

For preference patterns in which viewers rank more than a single choice, calculating revenues received by broadcasters and resulting program patterns is a bit more complicated. However, the predictions are basically the same as those which hold for the simpler case where viewers watch only their first choices. Where advertisers are willing to pay more for exposure to certain viewers, then the viewers who are worth more to advertisers will receive heavier weighting in the calculation of potential advertising revenues.

Does this mean that the groups that are worth more to advertisers are more likely to receive their preferred programs? The answer is Yes. But does it also mean that viewers in general are more likely to receive their preferred programs? The answer is No, at least not necessarily. The signals that enter broadcasters' profit calculations and hence determine program patterns are the advertisers' values of exposure to viewers, *not* the viewers' values of programs. Therefore, one cannot expect that, because prices in advertising markets reflect the amounts that advertisers are willing to pay for different viewers, program patterns will more nearly reflect those desired by viewers.

In reality, are advertisers more likely to consider mass audiences or minority audiences more valuable per viewer? Obviously, viewers with some common interest are valuable to advertisers who sell products aimed at that market. But this does not answer the question. After all, beer drinkers have a common interest and are of considerable value to firms selling beer. But can we classify beer drinkers as a minority audience? What we can say, however, is that under our present television structure—limited channels and large audiences per channel—the cost of advertising time is sufficiently high and the program content sufficiently broad that little advertising for minority audiences appears in prime time. (This does not say whether minority audiences are necessarily more or less valuable per viewer than are mass audiences.) Advertisers interested in minority audiences cannot afford to pay the opportunity cost of the spectrum in order to reach their particular audiences. Such advertisers must turn to other media—special-interest magazines, newspapers, radio programs, or throwaways, where the cost of advertising space is not held artificially high and content for minority groups held artificially low by limited capacity.

Because of limited spectrum and large audiences, many viewers who may be worth a considerable amount to specific advertisers cannot be reached economically through the present television medium. In fact, the broad demographic variables that are used to characterize audiences in Neilsen and American Research Bureau ratings lead one to surmise that mass audiences are the only audiences of significance to the present television medium. (For information on the Neilsen and ARB polls, see U.S. Congress [565] and [586].) Demographic characteristics reported by these companies include data such as age and sex characteristics and incomes by market area. Given the cost of collecting data *and the fact that mass-appeal large-audience programming is more profitable under television with limited channels*, collecting more detailed data is probably not justified. Under unlimited channels, however, the value of detailed data might be much greater.

If mass audiences are worth more per viewer than minority audiences in the advertising market, then this will cause less diversity and more duplication of programs than the model of advertiser-supported television, with all viewers worth equal amounts, predicts. It seems plausible, however, that if television had unlimited channels, advertisers who seek out minority groups would find the television medium more attractive as an advertising vehicle whether or not these viewers are worth inherently more than mass-audience viewers. The reason is simply that the opportunity cost of a channel would be much lower (or zero), and an advertiser could afford to purchase time on a program that attracted only a small subset of the total viewing audience. With unlimited channels, more advertising for minority audiences would appear than is now the case. In the limit, one might expect programs in which both advertisers and viewers have common interests, such as literary programs, sewing programs, or outdoor and nature programs. (The extent to which this would actually occur depends on the costs of producing programs and the efficiency of television as an advertising vehicle relative to other media.) But note two important points: additional channels are a necessary condition for specialized programs to appear; and program patterns would still reflect the advertisers' values of exposure to viewers, not the viewers' values of the programs. With this final comment, we turn to an analysis of pay TV.

Program Patterns Under Pay TV

Up to this point in the chapter, programs have been supported wholly through advertising. Now consider the case of "pure" subscriber-supported, or pay, TV—that is, pay TV in which the only revenues broadcasters receive are those which viewers pay on a per-program basis. Broadcasters purchase programs in the programming market; they then sell these programs directly to viewers.

In actuality, pay TV will probably not be "pure." It is likely that, unless regulation prohibits it, programs under pay TV will be partially supported by advertising revenues, just as magazines and newspapers are supported by both advertisers and subscribers. (It may be that viewers prefer programs interspersed with advertising, particularly if advertising revenues result in lower direct viewer charges.) It is also probable that programs will be "packaged" (especially if exclusion and billing costs are substantial), so that viewers will purchase pay TV by the channel. Under this scheme, viewers would pay, say, a monthly charge to receive a sports, news, or movie channel. Discussions of public policy must consider these alternatives as realistic structures for pay TV. This chapter is confined, however, to predicting program patterns under the case of "pure" pay TV. Problems of public policy will be dealt with in later chapters.

The measure of viewer satisfaction used will be the same as that used for the model under advertiser support: the extent to which viewers receive their preferred choices (specifically, first choices). In Chapter 5 we shall discuss viewer satisfaction in terms of consumer surplus, and consider the implications for public policy.

Public Goods, Pay TV, and
Economic Efficiency

Let us reintroduce the notion of the program as a public good, as first discussed in Chapter 1. A public good is a good whose cost of production is independent of the number of persons who consume it (i.e., there are economies of scale in *consumption*). Alternatively, one person's consumption of the good does not reduce the availability of the good for another person's consumption. Clearly, television programs have the characteristics of a public good. (For over-the-air TV, the broadcast is also a public good. But in this section we are concerned more with the program.) Up to this point in the analysis, broadcasters have not been selling programs. Under advertiser-supported TV, programs are used to attract audiences, and then the audiences are sold to advertisers. Under pay TV, however, the programs are sold directly to viewers. But whether audiences or programs are sold, programs still are public goods.

Note from the definition of a public good that the program is still a public good regardless of whether viewers receive it free or must pay for it. Being able to exclude viewers by enforcing payment does not convert the public good to a private good. Furthermore, the program is a public good whether or not the broadcasting medium is also a public good—that is, whether the medium is over-the-air broadcasting (a public good) or cablecasting (closer to a private good).

There is every reason to suspect that advertiser-supported TV leads to an allocation of resources in television that is inefficient. In fact, one can prove that the allocation is inefficient so long as advertisers' values of viewers differ from viewers' values of programs. But economic theories of public goods raise serious doubt whether even pay TV would necessarily lead to an efficient allocation of programs. The purpose of this section is to use the theory of public goods to show why pay TV will probably *not* lead to an efficient resource allocation in television, and to assess where this leaves us in comparing advertiser-supported and pay TV. In particular, which system is likely to be more efficient? Since neither is efficient, it becomes very difficult to prove for certain which will be *more* efficient. The arguments of this chapter attempt to show that *under certain assumptions* pay TV with unrestricted channels will be "more efficient."

Consider the dilemma that is posed by private (free-enterprise) production of a public good. Once a program is created, the marginal cost of having an additional person receive it is limited to the transmission expense of reaching that extra person. If the price charged exceeds this incremental transmission cost and thereby excludes the person, then society has lost some costless benefit. On the other hand, at a zero price above the incremental transmission cost, there will be no incentive for the private production of programs, because the fixed cost of producing the program will not be covered. This is a dilemma of some importance. *The existence of a market for the public good depends on the presence of potentially inefficient exclusion in the market.*[1]

The problem has been put within a rigorous framework by Samuelson, in

[1]This is a general problem in monopolistically competitive markets. Professor A. Michael Spence of Stanford University is working on a model of product competition that shows it to be true for monopolistically competitive markets in general and for public goods—pay TV—in particular.

which he derives the conditions for the efficient allocation of a public good. (The theoretical exposition appears in Samuelson [486] and [484]. The relevance of public goods to television is first discussed by Samuelson [482].) Since public goods can be *jointly consumed*, there is a fundamental difference between the efficient allocation of a public good and that of a private good (which cannot be jointly consumed).

Can we expect the private-enterprise system (in this case, pay-TV broadcasters) to provide an efficient allocation of a public good? We are skeptical (although we shall describe a pay-TV institution that might at least come close). Under conditions of decreasing costs per consumer, one cannot expect the entrepreneur to price at the marginal cost of serving the consumer. The (fixed) cost of production simply would not be covered, and at this price the producer would have no incentive to produce the public good. So long as consumers do not all value the public good identically, there may not exist a (uniform) charge for the good's consumption that brings forth the efficient level of the public good.

One way out of this dilemma is to allow the firm to practice price discrimination among consumers, charging each the highest price he will pay for the public good. The perfectly price-discriminating producer could theoretically produce an efficient allocation of the public good. Each consumer would pay a price equal to his true value of the good, and no consumer would be excluded. Such a scheme *could* satisfy Samuelson's conditions for the efficient provision of public goods.

The price discrimination analogy *suggests* an industry structure which *in the extreme* might provide a product allocation close to that deemed efficient. Magazine, book, and movie production (creation, not transmission) suggests that the efficient firm size in *creating* these messages is quite small, that entry costs are low, and that numbers will be large. The analysis of Chapter 2 suggests that this might be the case with pay TV also. The very structure of pay TV with unrestricted entry and many competing channels (large numbers of differentiated products produced under monopolistic competition) may at least begin to approach efficiency. Consider the extreme case in which there are so many competing sources that each one finds it necessary to deal with only a single customer. This case is of course very extreme. But if the industry can be encouraged to develop in such a way that there is great diversity and specialization, then the potential demand for any one message will be from a relatively small and homogeneous group of consumers, as it is today with many periodicals. The prices charged for such a product spectrum, taken together, will be in effect a close approximation to perfect price discrimination. By ensuring sufficiently large numbers of competitors, each specializing extensively, one can perhaps come close to efficient allocation of public goods. (For a detailed treatment of the economic rationale supporting this conclusion, see Demsetz [157] and [156] and Owen [415].)

The above analogy to the print and cinema media suggests an institution for pay TV in which resources might be allocated reasonably efficiently in the production of television programs. There would be many program producers with unrestricted access to many channels in each market, and each producer would be able to charge viewers directly for his program (i.e., cable television with unrestricted access and pay TV). Although such an institution is logically plausible, the conditions for efficiency will in reality only be approximated. (Whether the result would come close to efficiency depends very much on the costs of producing programs, among other things.) We shall have more to say about pay TV in this context in Chapter 6.

Where does this leave us in the dilemma of finding a television institution that provides an efficient allocation of resources? Just because advertiser-supported TV offers programs to viewers at a zero direct charge (which is close to the marginal cost of the viewers' tuning to the program), we cannot assume that the institution provides programs closer to an efficient allocation than would TV with imperfect exclusion and imperfectly discriminating prices. (Minasian mistook Samuelson to imply that this was in fact the case. For the ensuing debate, see Minasian [364], Samuelson [485], and Buchanan [96].) There is simply no reason advertisers should value programs as vehicles for reaching audiences such that the conditions for an efficient provision of programs are satisfied.

Minasian makes a rational and intuitive plea that what is needed is an "analysis of the effects of different institutional arrangements," which would attempt to compare the use of scarce resources both within broadcasting and between broadcasting and competing uses. "The real problem, therefore, is the choice between the results of the two systems and not the rules of rationing they contain" (Minasian [364], p. 77). We can go farther than this. It is possible that where entry is unrestricted (channel capacity is unlimited and access to channels is organized on a competitive basis), the monopolistically competitive provision of public goods with price and product competition might result in an allocation of resources in television that is reasonably efficient. The attraction of pay TV with many channels is precisely that it will provide an economic incentive for program producers to create programs for small groups of viewers who have strong interests in specialized programs.

Keeping in mind that we cannot prove that pay TV will in fact provide an efficient allocation of programs (although we suspect that without channel restrictions and monopoly control it might begin to come close), let us now turn to how program patterns might differ under pay TV from those we have already predicted under advertiser-supported TV.

The Behavior of Competitive
Pay-TV Broadcasters

In the model of advertiser-supported TV, the price per viewer that accrued to broadcasters was determined in the advertising market. Competitive broadcasters attracted viewers through product competition, not price competition, and a result was duplication of programs. Under pay TV, however, broadcasters will compete for viewers through both *product and price* competition. Does the addition of price competition significantly alter the extent of competitive program duplication? The theory of public goods provides a basis for expecting competitive program duplication to be less serious under pay TV than under advertiser-supported TV. Let us demonstrate this possibility with a few examples.

Suppose broadcaster A purchases program A at a cost of $400 and sells it to 10,000 viewers at 10¢ each. His profit is $600. Broadcaster B now considers duplicating program A at a cost of $400, splitting the audience at 10¢ each, thereby earning a profit of $100 while reducing A's profit to $100.[j] As B contemplates duplicating program A, what reaction might he expect from broadcaster A? Since A has already incurred the $400 fixed cost, he will threaten (or carry out) price cuts in order to deter B from entering his market. If one ignores costs of transmission and billing, then broadcaster A will threaten price cuts to the point where price equals marginal cost which equals zero. The expected price competition from broadcaster A will render B much less enthusiastic about the prospect of duplicating program A than would be the case if there were no price competition.

The example assumes that broadcaster A has already incurred the $400 program purchase cost, and is serving the market prior to B's appearance. Alternatively, we can assume that both A and B are simultaneously contracting with viewers to determine which broadcaster viewers will buy from, and neither broadcaster has yet incurred the $400 program cost. (This is similar to the mechanism considered by Demsetz [157].) In competing *for the market*, only *one* broadcaster will end up offering the program. (It is entirely possible that *no* broadcaster will produce the program due to the uncertainty of an additional entrant, and the almost certain price war that would ensue if the second broadcaster did enter. The point here, however, is that only one broadcaster will enter at most.) Furthermore, the price charged will in a sense be "competitive" (in this case close to 4¢ per viewer), because the broadcaster who "wins the contract" does so by offering the program at the lowest possible price. Here the price is determined in a competitive framework, whereas in the example above it was simply assumed to be 10¢.[k] The result regarding program duplication is the

[j]An important consideration here is that B must also pay the $400 fixed cost. This is ensured by copyright laws, so that B faces two alternatives. If A does not have exclusive rights to the program, then B can purchase the program at the same price paid by A. Or, if A has exclusive rights, then B must purchase a different program for which viewers have identical preferences—hence, the different program is still of the same "program type," or a perfect substitute.

[k]It is possible to specify assumptions about pricing and entry such that entry is avoided at some price between 4¢ and 10¢. A "limit price" of 8¢ is a possibility because at this price, the second broadcaster would be indifferent about entering and splitting the audience.

same, however. *Where price competition is a real possibility, program duplication* (i.e., the duplication of perfect substitute public goods) *does not occur.* Again, why does duplication of programs occur for the competitive channel structure under advertiser support? Under advertiser-supported TV, broadcasters do not sell the public good; they *use* the public good to attract audiences, and then sell the audiences. For this reason, and because prices are set in advertising markets, competitive program duplication is prevalent.

Price competition in the production of public goods will certainly lessen program duplication, and will therefore have an important effect on program patterns under pay TV with a competitive channel structure. The only two existing economic models of pay TV, models by Wiles [617] and Rothenberg [478], both assume that prices are somehow fixed in pay-TV markets. As a result, both authors conclude that program duplication will be prevalent under pay TV, just as it is under advertiser-supported TV. Curiously, if prices are set by regulators in competitive pay-TV markets, then these models may indeed predict the program patterns that result. Regulated (minimum or fixed) prices in a competitive pay-TV market may well generate program duplication. The result has a striking similarity to the case of competitive airlines, where minimum air fares are regulated but flight schedules are left to the discretion of the firms. One finds that competing firms cluster their flights unduly about the peak periods in an attempt to split the mass of customers. Price competition would undoubtedly alleviate (but perhaps not solve) this problem.

We have argued that price competition in the production of public goods renders product duplication and imitation potentially unprofitable. Is this result empirically plausible when one considers movies, magazines, and newspapers? This question is difficult to answer, and a study should probably best be confined to movies, because of the obvious analogy to pay TV.

We suspect that price competition, or at least the omnipresent *possibility* of price competition, among movie theaters does reduce the tendency toward product imitation and audience splitting.[1] But this hypothesis needs to be tested before it can be asserted as fact. The most difficult analytical problem faced in such a study would be in constructing empirical measures of product differentiation. (This is the same problem that makes testing our television model difficult.)

The Behavior of a Monopolist
Pay-TV Broadcaster

Suppose that all channels in a pay-TV market are operated under unified management by a pay-TV monopolist. (Perhaps he is the owner of the local cable television system.) A conclusion of the model under advertiser support was

---

[1]The competitive game among movie theaters leads also to a promise for more profits if theaters collude, determining jointly both product and price. Such tactics of monopoly or joint maximizing behavior have indeed been attempted by theaters. The result would probably occur in television also if competition were not somehow enforced.

that where viewers were worth equal amounts in the advertising market, the monopolist sought out common denominator programs. So long as he could capture a viewer, he had no incentive to provide the viewer with a preferred choice. Does this still hold for the monopolist in a pay-TV market?

Viewers are presumably willing to pay higher prices to view their preferred choices. Under pay TV, unlike advertiser-supported TV, the potential revenue per viewer is higher for preferred choices. The pay-TV monopolist will take account of this fact, and will no longer produce only common-denominator programs. To see this, consider a simple example with only two viewer groups and program types. Viewers in group 2 will pay 10¢ to view program 1, but will pay 20¢ to view their preferred program, program 2.

Viewer Groups

	Group Size
1	5000
2	2500

Viewer Preferences

(Amounts viewers will pay for programs)

		Viewers	
		1	2
Programs	1	10¢	10¢
	2		20¢

If programs cost $200 to purchase (or produce), then the monopolist offers both program 1 (at a price of 10¢) and program 2 (at a price of 20¢), thereby maximizing his profit of $600. (The marginal profitability of adding program 2 is 20¢ x 2500 − 10¢ x 2500 − $200 = $50. His profit would be $550 if he offered only program 1.) Because viewers will pay more for preferred choices, the monopolist in this example caters to preferred choices. This never occurs in the model under advertiser support, where viewers are worth identical amounts in advertising markets.

Suppose for the above example that viewers in group 2 are willing to pay only 14¢ for their preferred choice. Viewer preferences appear as follows:

Viewer Preferences

		Viewers	
		1	2
Programs	1	10¢	10¢
	2		14¢

What is the monopolist's profit-maximizing-program pattern? He offers program 1 only, receiving a profit of $550. (He would earn only $450 if he produced both programs 1 and 2.) Although the monopolist responds to viewers' demands for preferred programs, the additional revenue generated by an additional program must cover the cost of the program *and the revenues lost from other programs due to viewers' switching from these other programs.* In other words, the monopolist takes direct account of the lost profits on his other channels in his decision to add an additional program.

Suppose that group 2 is still willing to pay 14¢ for program 2. But instead of having the two channels operated by a monopolist, they are operated by competing broadcasters. What programs will be offered viewers? One broadcaster will offer program 1, receiving a profit of $300, and the other will offer program 2, receiving a profit of $150. Note that without price competition, the second broadcaster would duplicate program 1, also charging viewers 10¢. In this case his profits would be $175 and the first broadcaster's would also be $175. But we can rule out program duplication, because the first broadcaster has a strong incentive to avoid duplication and will threaten. or carry out price cuts. Competitors offer both programs, whereas the monopolist offers only program 1.

What do these two examples suggest? First, under pay TV, a monopolist of all channels will respond to preferred choices, because he can charge viewers according to their preference intensities. Second, in deciding to offer additional programs, the monopolist includes in his profit calculations the expected revenues lost on other channels. Third, competitive broadcasters are likely to provide more programs than the monopolist under pay TV (where channel capacity allows it), because each competitor does not take direct account of the diminished revenues on other channels due to his program decision on his own channel.

Another difference under monopoly and competition is important. Prices will probably be lower under competition. The argument of the previous sections shows how competitors are forced to charge "competitive" prices.

Resource Allocation in Pay TV

In the prior two sections we found that under pay TV, competitors will engage in price competition and hence will tend to avoid program duplication. We found also that the monopolist will produce preferred programs if viewers are willing to pay a "profitable" premium. These results are substantially different from those reached under the model of advertiser-supported TV. But program patterns under pay TV will differ from those under advertiser support in other fundamental respects. *Specifically, both the quantity of resources devoted to television and the allocation of resources among program types will differ under pay TV and advertiser-supported TV.*

Although we can only guess how viewer preferences might actually look, a few simple examples will illustrate this crucial point.[m] How might viewer preferences have to look in order for the potential revenue structure under pay TV to be similar to that under present advertiser-supported TV? We know that present advertising revenue per viewing household for a half-hour program in prime time is approximately 1¢ to 2¢. (For the determination of these rates, see the appendix to Chapter 2.) Assume for simplicity that viewers will watch only their first choices, and that they will pay 2¢ to view their preferred programs.

Viewer Preferences

		Viewers	
		1	2
Programs	1	2¢	
	2		2¢

For viewer preferences as depicted above, potential revenues under pay TV will be identical to potential revenues under present prime time over-the-air advertiser-supported TV.

Are viewers likely to value half-hour programs at approximately 2¢? The prospect does not seem very probable. Some viewers may be willing to pay only 1¢, while others will pay a good deal more. The point to be made here is that advertiser-supported TV registers no intensity response, and the chances are

[m]A few pay-TV experiments have been conducted, and empirical inferences regarding viewer preferences have been drawn using these data (see especially Blank [76] and Noll, Peck, and McGowan [394]). Also, consumer demand for television has been estimated using cable-television data (see Comanor and Mitchell [137], Park [427], and Noll, Peck, and McGowan [394]). Earlier, Lang attempted measuring radio preferences [316]. These studies provide insights, but their use for developing public policy is subject to limitations (see Besen and Mitchell [70]).

great that advertising revenues will be substantially below viewers' willingness to pay. The resources allocated to pay television, however, and the resulting program patterns under pay TV will respond to these preference intensities.

Suppose all viewers are willing to pay 10¢. Then potential revenues under pay TV are five times those under advertiser-supported TV. (In order to make a direct comparison of the amounts of resources that would flow into program production under pay TV compared to advertiser-supported TV, one needs estimates of the differences between transactions and billing costs under the two structures. It is almost certain that these costs will be higher for pay TV.) Under pay TV, program prices will respond in the market and additional resources will flow into television. *If there is adequate channel capacity*, programs will be added at the margin, since minority programs that are not profitable at 2¢ per viewer will now be profitable at 10¢. If channel capacity is limited, however, additional programs will not be possible. In this case, one might expect a monopolist of all channels in the market merely to raise prices and extract a greater profit. One might expect competitors to charge higher prices also, but in their competition for viewers to bid up program production (or purchase) costs and hence to raise program quality. (This will be discussed further in Chapter 4.)

Note that it is possible, but not probable, that half-hour programs are worth less than 2¢ to viewers. In this case, pay TV will allocate fewer resources to television than does present advertiser-supported television.

Not only will the total amounts of resources devoted to television be more responsive to viewer tastes under pay TV, but the mix allocated to specific programs will also be more responsive to tastes. In determining which programs to offer, broadcasters will weight the number of viewers who prefer a program by their preference intensities, as measured by the amounts they are willing to pay. To the extent that smaller groups are willing to pay a premium for their programs, then the profitability of these programs will reflect these viewers' desires.

A word of caution is needed at this point. Pay TV is often discussed in terms of the minority-taste programming that it would produce. The existence of pay TV does not necessarily imply that mass programs would disappear from the spectrum. Mass programs are still likely to be relatively profitable under pay TV, either because viewers of these programs will be willing to pay relatively high prices or because the sheer numbers of potential viewers will make these programs profitable at low prices. *The point here is not whether minority programs should displace mass programs, but rather that for economic efficiency, some measure of preference intensities should at least enter the broadcasters' program decisions.*

The discussion above suggests that pay TV (particularly with unconstrained channels and a competitive structure) is likely to approach more closely an efficient allocation of resources in television production than is advertiser-supported TV. The reason is quite simple: Revenues per viewer are more likely to reflect viewers' program preferences than are revenues per viewer under advertiser support (which reflect advertisers' values of viewers).

The analysis of pay TV asserts some important differences between program patterns under the alternative means of support. First, competitive program duplication is not nearly as likely to occur under pay TV as under advertiser-supported TV. Second, a monopolist controlling all channels in the market will have an incentive to produce preferred programs under pay TV. He will have little incentive to do this under advertiser support, where viewers are worth equal amounts in advertising markets. Third, in pay-TV markets with ample channels, the competitive channel structure, through competition for audiences, is likely to produce more programs (at lower prices) than is the monopolistic structure. The reason for this result is that in maximizing the joint profits of all channels, the monopolist takes direct account of how increasing his audience on one channel may decrease it on other channels. Finally, where the number of channels is ample, both the total amount of resources devoted to television and the amounts allocated to individual programs are more likely to approach an economically efficient allocation under pay TV than under advertiser-supported TV.

One caveat should be mentioned. This chapter has asserted that program patterns under pay TV will more nearly reflect viewer tastes than will program patterns under advertiser-supported TV. But note that under pay TV viewers must pay for a product, whereas they received a different product free under advertiser-supported TV. To say that some or all viewers will be "better off" under pay TV, one needs to consider empirical measures of consumer surplus under the two structures. But consumer surplus is very difficult to measure. To say that viewers will receive a greater consumer surplus under pay TV than under advertiser support, one needs empirical measures of (1) the consumer surplus currently being received under "free" TV; (2) demand curves for the kinds of programs likely to appear under pay TV; and (3) prices that would result under pay TV. To obtain such measures is indeed an ambitious task. Even this analysis would abstract from the effects of pay TV on advertising markets, consumer incomes, commodity prices, and on substitute forms of entertainment such as movie theaters, magazines, and so forth. We shall have more to say on the relative merits of pay TV in Chapters 5 and 6.

Conclusions and Policy Implications

Predictions derived from models of product competition are highly sensitive to the nature of consumer preferences. Steiner's model, although it offers a most significant contribution toward examining product competition in broadcasting, is limited by its strict preference assumption.

The model presented here retains the institutional detail of Steiner's model, but generalizes preferences by including less-preferred substitutes and by varying the distribution of viewers. The model also formulates and alters explicit assumptions for program costs and channel capacities, and includes a formal comparison of monopoly and competition. The analysis is then extended to pay TV.

Modeling a television market is especially difficult because the number of channels is usually small, and the program decision on one channel cannot be isolated from its effects on other channels. The monopolist is faced with the problem of maximizing the joint profits of the system. Competitors are faced with maximizing the profits of their own channels, knowing that doing so will bring forth reactions from other competitors. The model compares the monopolist's program patterns with the program patterns offered by competitors. Scrutiny of the program patterns allows general predictions regarding both the monopolist's and competitors' outputs.

Predictions under advertiser support have several important implications regarding public policy. First, Steiner concludes that under limited channels, monopoly will provide a more diverse program mix and satisfy a greater number of viewers than will competition. This is shown to be true only for very special cases. In general it is not true. The conclusion depends critically upon his strong (and perhaps unrealistic) assumption that viewers will watch only their first choices. Under limited channels and more general preferences, one cannot say which structure provides superior program diversity or viewer satisfaction.

Second, Steiner's model, by assuming exclusive preferences, does not pick up the most interesting result of the profit-maximizing monopolist's behavior. The monopolist under advertiser-supported TV specifically seeks common-denominator programs. If viewers are subjected to a monopolist broadcaster under advertiser-supported TV, then the *only* way that they can get programs that they prefer is to *refuse* to watch less-preferred programming. This result does not hold under competition.

Third, the model reveals ample channel capacity to be a necessary, but not a sufficient, condition for minority-taste programming under advertiser support. If minority programs are to be encouraged, then the model's predictions support promoting additional channel capacity. At present, cable TV appears to provide the most economic means for many areas. But the model also shows channel use to vary depending on assumptions of preferences, program costs, and ownership structure. "Adequate" channel capacity of future cable systems, therefore, will be nearly impossible to predict. If one wishes to structure a cable system such that minority programs can appear under advertiser support, then it is necessary that the system have either flexible channel capacity, or if this is uneconomic, an anticipated risk of excess channel capacity. A competitive structure, furthermore, will undoubtedly require more channels than a monopolized structure.

Fourth, the model under advertiser support shows that where channel capacity is unconstrained (a possibility under cable television), a competitive system always results in at least as many program types being offered as does a monopolized system. Under unlimited channels and advertiser support, one can say unambiguously that competition provides viewer satisfaction that for general preferences is greater than that provided by a monopolist controlling all channels. Under a competitive system, furthermore, whether viewers are offered first-choice programming does *not* depend upon whether they accept less-preferred choices. For cable television systems where channel capacity is "ample," the model argues strongly in favor of structuring program decisions under a competitive system.

The pay-TV analysis suggests that both the quantity of resources devoted to television and the specific programs that result will come closer to approaching the desires of viewers under pay TV than under advertiser-supported TV. Furthermore, extensions of the theory of public goods argue that it is even logically plausible (although perhaps not realistically probable) that with unlimited channels, free competitive entry, and pure pay TV the allocation of resources in television might approach an economically efficient level.

Other important implications arise from the pay-TV analysis. First, under competitive pay TV, price competition for viewers will lessen the degree of program duplication and imitation that is prevalent in competitive advertiser-supported TV. Second, the monopolist of a pay-TV market, unlike the monopolist of an advertiser-supported-TV market, will offer viewers other than audience-maximizing common denominators, because he can charge viewers higher prices for preferred choices. Finally, under pay TV competitors are likely to offer more programs (at lower prices) than a monopolist controlling the entire market would offer. Where channel capacity is not an effective constraint, the pay-TV analysis favors a competitive pay-TV structure over a monopolized structure.

In short, for commercial broadcasting the model's predictions support the expansion of channels as a necessary condition for viewers' attainment of preferred choices. If this is possible, then the predictions argue strongly in favor of a competitive channel structure. To attain this structure under cable TV, regulatory policy will have to ensure that the cable operator is denied monopoly control of program decisions. Furthermore, given that the channel constraint can be effectively relaxed, the analysis argues for encouraging a competitive pay-TV structure with free entry for firms wishing to sell programs directly to audiences—an issue that we shall deal with in some detail in Chapter 6.

Chapters 5 and 6 will continue discussion of the policy issues raised here. It will turn out that if channels are effectively limited, then it is not clear that viewers would be "better off" with pay TV. With effectively unlimited channels, however, pay TV should probably be encouraged, or at least be allowed to develop, in addition to existing advertiser-supported television.

The Behavior of Networks

Introduction

This chapter analyzes the behavior of the three commercial television networks, in order to shed light on their past performance and related policy issues. Although local stations nominally control their programming, the networks purchase and distribute to the stations the bulk of the programs that the average viewer sees. Thus, any attempt to alter television performance must be founded on an understanding of network behavior.

The principal point to be developed here is that the networks are engaged in a market rivalry where each chooses not only the type of program, but the "quality" or "audience appeal" of each program as well. As a result the networks tend to duplicate programming, as indicated in Chapter 3, *and* find themselves continually increasing the level of inputs to programming. The characteristics and implications of this rivalry will affect the policies that we examine in the following chapters.

The behavior of the three television networks is controlled indirectly by Federal Communications Commission rules, which forbid individual stations from entering into affiliation contracts with "any network" that fails to comply with FCC standards (*National Broadcasting Co. vs. U.S.* [319 U.S. 190 (1943)]). Since the networks supply most of the programs that are broadcast on affiliated stations, FCC regulation of program content and other station behavior potentially has both direct and indirect effects on the networks' behavior.

The principal problem facing the FCC in its regulation of the television networks has been the issue of network market power vis-à-vis stations and programmers. As we saw in Chapter 2, this network dominance is due in part to public good and networking economies.

This issue was of concern in the late 1950s, principally because economic reality flew in the face of the Commission's cherished doctrine of "localism" in the control and origination of programming; affiliates found it more profitable to use network programs than local or syndicated series. The Commission's "solution" to this problem was to restrict the terms and conditions of affiliation contracts, with the aim of reducing the ability of station licensees to relinquish blanket control of programming to the networks (*FCC Rules and Regulations*, Section 73.658, parts (a) through (h). The Commission can also reach the networks through their owned and operated (O & O) stations, e.g., by the threat of revoking O & O licenses). As we shall see in this chapter, the effect of these

91

rules has been minimal, since the bargaining power of the networks is based on their ability to affiliate with other stations in the same local market. This power is related to the number of stations relative to the number of networks, rather than to any specific clauses in affiliation contracts. The FCC's restrictions on contract clauses have not significantly altered this power structure, and hence have had little effect on network and station behavior. Localism remains an elusive goal, which we will discuss further in Chapters 5 and 8.

In the middle and late sixties, the FCC again faced the network power problem, this time in response to program producers in Hollywood and elsewhere who regarded themselves as victims of network control (Federal Communication Commission [192], [193]; U.S. House of Representatives [559]). The FCC's response was the prime time access rule, which prohibited the networks from acquiring equity and profit rights in programs produced by others, and limited to three the number of hours per evening in "prime time" which could be programmed by the networks (*FCC Rules and Regulations*, Section 73.658, parts (j) and (k). Prime time is 7 to 11 PM, Sunday through Saturday). The purpose of the rule was to give other program producers "access" to individual station broadcast time, through the program syndication market. (The syndication market had previously been limited, as a practical matter, to nonaffiliated stations and to periods other than prime time on affiliated stations.) As Crandall [152, 153] and others have argued, the rule shows little understanding of the economics of TV program production and distribution. We will return to the prime time access rule later in this chapter.

Why does the FCC make rules to regulate the networks that either fail to be effective or have economically perverse or probably unintended effects? What makes network economic behavior such an elusive object for FCC regulation? Answers to these questions will be especially important in view of the latest alleged symptom of network economic power—increased reruns (*Broadcasting*, September 18, 1972, pp. 12-13). The FCC has been invited to study this phenomenon and to make rules to stem the tide of rerun programming, supposedly to benefit viewers and unemployed actors. A better understanding of network economics may enable us to predict the consequences of alternative policies directed at the rerun issue, as well as the broader and historically more important problems of network power, diversity, localism, and freedom of expression.

The following section will describe very briefly the economic and regulatory environment in which the networks are imbedded. In the next section we review older theories of broadcast behavior, and propose a new one of our own, based on Stigler's [531] theory of oligopolistic rivalry. In the final section we explore the policy implications of this theory for the prime time access rule and limiting reruns.

Economic and Regulatory Environment

The networks are engaged as brokers on behalf of local affiliated TV stations in the business of selling access to audiences. The prices quoted for a 20-, 30-, or 60-second commercial vary with the size of the audience, and are often spoken of in the trade as "price per thousand viewers (or households)." The process by which the networks acquire the ability to sell audiences to advertisers is as follows: Television programs are purchased by the networks from the program production industry, or produced by the network themselves. These programs are delivered to individual TV stations across the country in partial return for access to local audiences. The network thus serves as a broker between local stations and both advertisers and program producers, and (to the extent that it performs the function of program "selection") between local stations and viewers.

A description of the environment in which this process takes place requires an examination of the character of each of the three groups with which the networks must deal: advertisers, viewers, and program producers. We must also describe the nature of the relationship between the networks and their affiliated stations.

The Advertising Market

Despite the prominence of TV commercials as a form of advertising, only about 8 percent of total U.S. advertising expenditure, or about 15 percent of all national advertising expenditure, goes to network television (see Table 1-3). There are relatively few products for which network television has a comparative advantage as an advertising vehicle, and there are a number of more or less good substitutes: spot television advertising,[a] network and spot radio, national magazines, direct mail, billboards, and newspapers. It is true that none of these substitutes reaches as large an audience as network television, but it is also true that many advertisers prefer a smaller audience to a larger one, if that audience contains a greater proportion of likely customers. (Firms whose sales are geographically concentrated provide the most obvious example.) The networks do make an attempt to supply audiences with characteristics which advertisers find desirable (principally women between the ages of eighteen and forty-nine) by careful program selection.

Advertisers can buy access to network audiences in a number of ways. First,

---

[a]"Spot" advertising is the purchase by national advertisers or their agencies of commercial time directly from local stations or their representatives, rather than from the network. It differs from network advertising and from local advertising. See Chapter 1.

they may sponsor an entire program or series of programs. This is now quite rare, except for special-event programs in the high culture or public-affairs categories. More common is the purchase of "participations," or partial sponsorship of programs selected by the network. A large network television advertising account will typically buy, long in advance, a package of commercial minutes spread over a number of programs throughout the year. It is not uncommon for some commercial minutes to remain unsold until days or even hours before they are broadcast, with the price of the perishable commodity, time, generally being observed to fall as the time of broadcast approaches. Commercial minutes that cannot be sold are filled with public service announcements or network promotional announcements.

The National Association of Broadcasters (NAB), through its industry "code,"[b] sets an upper limit of six minutes per hour in prime time for network commercial messages, and the FCC implicitly endorses this practice. The result is, presumably, to keep the number of commercial minutes per hour lower than competitive conditions would warrant. (At least this is the presumption if the industry association is attempting to maximize industry profits.)

There is reason to believe that, except for the effects of the NAB Code, the network advertising market is rather highly competitive. Buyers are well informed and are typically advised by expert advertising agencies; the commodity is perishable; more or less close substitutes exist and are typically already in use by major advertisers. The result is that it is unlikely that any one network possesses significant market power vis-à-vis most advertisers, although such power may exist with respect to advertisers of some products. The arguments above suggest that the networks' ability to capitalize on recognition of their interdependence is probably slight, because the advertising market is fairly competitive.

Program Markets and Syndication

A television station has two external sources of programming material—affiliation with one of the three national networks and the syndication market. The networks distribute programs that have been (1) obtained directly from program producers; (2) supplied by advertisers who buy network time; or (3) produced internally. Stations can acquire nonnetwork fare by going directly to syndicators for television series, specials, and feature-length films.

As indicated in Chapter 2, the supply of programming to the networks is best described as competitive. The factors that guarantee this are: (1) the fact that the networks distribute the programs, taking advantage of any economies of distribution; (2) the continued viability of a wide range of firm types and sizes; (3) the existence of a well-developed rental market, which spreads the cost of lumpy inputs (such as sound stages) over several producers; and (4) the ease of

---

[b]For the text of this code, see *Broadcasting Yearbook* (Annual).

entry by new competitors, which frustrates any attempt by packagers to earn monopoly profits through collusion.

The supply of syndicated programming is rather less competitive than the supply to the networks, but still not monopolistic. Any economies from distributing programs, with their public-good characteristics, appear to be quickly exploited. Several firms are viable, with only 3 to 5 percent of total syndication sales.

To what extent is syndicated material, especially first-run, competitive with network fare in the eyes of station program managers? Talent costs may be lower because talent is available at a lower wage for a first-run syndicated show than for a network program, since more work can be guaranteed (rather than guaranteeing just a pilot, or just a pilot and thirteen weeks). All other things being equal, this cost advantage would result in syndicated programming dominating network programming on affiliates; but exactly the opposite occurs. Networks can easily compete with syndicated programming for two reasons: station profits are higher with network fare, or the extensive use of syndicated material might cause the loss of affiliation.

Talent cost is only one component of the cost of a program. Although the syndicated program has lower talent costs, it may have other costs which are higher. Economies in simultaneous networking confer a competitive cost advantage on network fare, because of the effect of sharing program costs over a larger audience and the networks' lower distribution costs. (Note that syndication does not take advantage of simultaneous networking, and it must check films repeatedly for wear; both are costly.)

The affiliates may also use network fare because they fear loss of their affiliation agreement. If the threat of cancellation were credible the affiliate would maintain his affiliation only if it were more profitable than independent status. As an affiliate he could show network and some syndicated fare, while as an independent he could show only syndicated programs. The preceding arguments suggest that affiliates are affiliates because the network supply of programming *as a whole* is more profitable than syndicated material.

Viewer Behavior

The actual behavior of television viewers is perhaps less important than the perception of that behavior by network executives and advertisers. It is clear that the audience produced by any given network is related to the popularity of its programs relative to those offered on other networks. But the total audience for all three networks combined seems to be determined almost completely by exogeneous factors, such as seasonal patterns of family entertainment. As an example, the average total prime-time audience (expressed as the percent of TV-homes tuned in) in the month of April between 1953 and 1972 varied almost at random between a minimum of 57.3 (1963) and a maximum of 62.0

(1957). (See OTP Report [599], appendix table 29.) This stability occurred despite drastic changes in the kinds and qualities of programs offered, the advent of color, the fact that April is now (as it was not in earlier years) occupied almost entirely by rerun programming, and the total number of TV homes has increased, as has the average number of hours per day during which each TV home views. Similarly, the audience for any given program is believed by network executives to depend to a very significant extent on the popularity of adjacent programs, as well as the nature of the program itself (Epstein [178], pp. 93-97). The audience is believed to be passive, switching channels only as a result of rather extreme provocation.

This perception of viewer behavior implies that a network must pay attention not merely to the popularity of individual programs, but to its whole schedule, in relation to the schedules of its rivals. The ability of the network to produce audiences thus involves rather complicated "adjacency" problems, in which the audience for a given program may depend more on the type and nature of preceding and succeeding programs than on the program's "intrinsic" popularity. (This behavior is consistent with the assumptions of Chapter 3. Instead of viewing a single program as the choice variable, the viewer may regard a schedule of programs as the object of choice. This could result from lethargy, or because programs on different channels do not begin and end at the same times.)

Thus, a given network can increase its instantaneous audience only at the expense of its rivals, and then more by increasing the popularity of its whole program schedule than by variations in the popularity of individual programs.

A program's quality is measured in this chapter by its contribution to the audience of the network. Generally, popularity can be increased by a very uncertain process of feeling out public tastes in relation to the offerings of rival networks. There is a role here for the "novel idea," but most quality variation takes the form of providing more of those program "values" or types that appear to be popular on other networks. A network can do this by producing more elaborate versions of the same type of program, or by bidding away the talent inputs of existing programs. Either action is likely to increase the cost of the program. Hence, it is generally valid to speak of program "popularity," "quality," and cost as being highly correlated. There are exceptions to this, of course, whenever a popular new program is discovered. An unexpectedly popular program will, at first, cost less than programs of equal popularity that are older, and whose input factors have been evaluated properly by the market. If the returns to most popular network television talent inputs are higher than their opportunity costs in alternative activities, scarcity rents for the popular factors of production will arise.

The remaining question concerning viewers is the issue of fashion demand, its causes and effects. Some network behavior can be explained equally well by models of audience passivity in the face of oligopolistic gamesmanship by the networks, or by models of a fickle audience with rapidly changing tastes, to which the networks react more or less passively in their choice of program type and quality. There is very little evidence available to distinguish among these alternative views of audience behavior. The total audience for network television at a given moment is evidently not much affected by program content or type within the range of variation with which we have experience.

Affiliated Stations

Affiliated stations can have contracts of maximum length of two years with the networks, the terms of which are restricted by the FCC in the stations' favor. (See the summary of FCC restrictions on affiliation in *Broadcasting Yearbook*, 1973, C-31 to C-33.) The networks try to line up as many "clearances" with affiliated stations as they can. The stations have an incentive to "clear" network programs only if the compensation they receive from the network exceeds the profits they could earn by using other program sources. This opportunity cost is determined by the revenue for spot and local commercials less the cost of originating local programming or acquiring syndicated programming and the selling costs involved, taking account of the effects of this on audience size and on "audience flow" among adjacent programs. Network programs are sometimes carried at a net loss by local affiliates because the programs satisfy FCC requirements (Epstein [178], pp. 84-91).

The networks exist only to the extent that their brokerage function serves the interests of local stations. Their ability to serve this interest at a profit derives from economies of scale in simultaneous sharing of program costs over large audiences, possibly from economies of scale in selling commercial minutes to advertisers, and *perhaps* from a degree of domination of the program markets that individual stations would not attain. The fact that most stations do affiliate with a network suggests that economies of scale and other advantages of network brokerage outweigh the disadvantages to stations of having to carry a program that is not always the one that maximizes audiences in their particular market, due to differing local tastes. In general, it appears that network affiliation is the most profitable choice for a local station to make. "Most stations consider network affiliation their most important single asset, next to their Commission License" (U.S. House of Representatives [559], p. 207).

However, the power of the networks over local stations is limited by their ability to find other stations in the same market with whom to affiliate. Only about sixteen cities have more than three commercial VHF stations, and it is presumably only in these cities that the network's threat to cancel the affiliation contract can be effective. In three-station markets neither the stations nor the networks have any particular bargaining power in this respect, since neither side has a viable alternative. Of course the "strongest" network has bargaining power by virtue of its attractiveness to stations affiliated with "weaker" networks;

similarly, the station affiliated with the "weakest" network will be the bravest of the affiliates in a market. In one- and two-station markets, power lies on the side of the stations. The opposite holds in four- and more station markets. Since affiliates in markets with more than three stations are in larger, and hence more profitable markets, their profits will be larger than those in two station markets. This will occur despite their weaker position vis-à-vis the networks. Also many of the affiliates in the largest markets (more than three stations) are owned and operated (O & O) by the networks. In such cases there is no bargaining problem, only an accounting one. The networks may bury their profits in such stations by generous compensation in order to enhance their bargaining position with non-O & O stations in smaller, less profitable markets. If they can hide profits in O & O's, other affiliates will believe that the joint profits of the network are smaller than they actually are. With imperfect information, the other affiliates will settle for smaller compensation than they might have if they knew the real magnitude of network profits. Even in the three-station markets the FCC rules on affiliation give considerable latitude to local affiliates in dealing with the networks. Let us examine the reasons.

The nature of the station-network relationship can best be understood in terms of a bargaining problem. Consider the case of only one network and a single local station, where each can earn $1 million operating alone or in other markets, but together they can earn $3 million profit. If a bargain of affiliation is struck, each will settle for no less than $1 million. Any division of the remaining $1 million will maintain the contract; for example, $1,999,995 for the network and $1,000,005 for the station or vice versa, or somewhere in between. Both the station and the network are better off by affiliating, and neither has a viable alternative. Game theorists will recognize this as a problem of finding the core in a cooperative game with side payments; see Rapaport [457].

Now, consider a case of only one network and two local stations, where the local stations are effectively prohibited from colluding by FCC regulations and antitrust laws. Separately the network and the two stations can each earn profits of $1 million. An affiliation contract between the network and either station yields joint profits of $3 million. Clearly the network captures the extra $1 million generated by networking. If station A has the affiliation contract and asks for more than $1,000,005, the network will offer station B the contract for $1,000,004. Since this will increase station B's profits, it will take the contract. This process can be repeated until the network receives $1,999,999.99, the affiliated station gets $1,000,000.01, and the unaffiliated station earns $1,000,000.00. (In the real world, with imperfect information, affiliates will receive more than 1¢ from affiliating with the single network.) If there were two networks and one station the bargaining positions would be reversed, with the station capturing all the extra profits from the bargain.

The bargaining between networks and stations is more complex than these two simple examples suggest. Under FCC regulations, stations do not have to take the full schedule of the network that they are affiliated with. This severely limits the scope of affiliation agreements by prohibiting contracts of the form: station A receives X dollars of compensation if it transmits all of network N's programs.

The prohibition creates problems for the networks, because the networks' profits are tied to the size of the national audience of their shows. These revenues vary directly with audience size, while average costs per viewer for a given program vary inversely with size—the larger the audience, the larger the profits. The tendency of viewers not to switch channels without severe provocation means that adjacency effects exist among programs. A local station might elect to show a program appealing to a local small but desirable audience. Although this may be profitable for the local station, it could have adverse effects on the network. The small size of the local program's select audience means that there is a smaller lead-in audience to the following network show, and hence, smaller network audience and profits.

The prohibition of all-or-nothing contracts between networks and affiliates forces the networks to use compensation schemes that encourage local affiliates to carry the weaker network programs and the ones of limited local appeal. Although the networks compensate stations for most of the hours that the stations carry, they do not share the revenue for some programs (Besen and Soligo [71]). Some of the network shows that happen to have great local appeal in a particular area will be especially profitable to affiliates, because the stations can earn large revenues from the announcement time and spot commercials in those programs. If the profits on such shows exceed what the station can earn by using local or syndicated programming, then the station will carry them, with or without compensation. In our previous one-network, two-station example, the network's optimal strategy consists in part of determining such locally popular programs, and then not compensating the affiliate for them. For the remaining programs the network need only provide adequate marginal compensation per program to induce the station to carry the network program. That amount will be just large enough to exceed the profits on locally originated or syndicated material. The network will provide this marginal inducement if its profits are increased by the process. If the necessary inducement is too large, the network will be forced to let the affiliate do its own programming. The process probably benefits the station. Instead of settling for a lump sum just sufficient to induce affiliation, the affiliate receives the very popular shows free, and can receive inducements for the other programs.

The cases of one- and two-station markets are interesting, because they reverse the relative power positions of the local stations and the networks. For simplicity consider the one-station, two-network market. Since network average costs per viewer vary inversely with audience size, both networks want as many shows cleared as possible, as long as their profits from affiliation are positive. If a local affiliate of Network A also affiliates with Network B, A has no credible threat of dropping the station's affiliation—it would lose potential profits on the remaining programs by doing so. The station can bargain for the best shows of both networks and receive compensation from both. This example explains the viability of multiple affiliates in smaller markets, as well as ABC's attempts to clear some of its programs on NBC and CBS affiliates in markets where ABC does not have an affiliate.

In sum, the networks must be responsive to the needs and interests of their affiliated stations. The networks are "protected" from affiliates only to the extent that licensees are protected by the FCC from going out of business, so that they can choose to let the networks make decisions for them even though those decisions do not always result in the highest possible profit.

The Government

Network television is subject to many direct and indirect pressures from the federal government. Leaving aside those pressures regarding news and public-affairs programs and those which arise because of the FCC's version of content regulation (see the fairness doctrine discussion in Chapter 8), many purely economic constraints on network behavior remain. Often, these are imposed in response to pressures from interest groups. Examples outside our immediate concern include the banning of cigarette advertising on television, proposed rules restricting the content and commercialism of children's television, laws governing the maximum charges that may be made for political announcements, the Federal Trade Commission's "counter-advertising" proposals, and the FCC's own more or less explicit requirements regarding minimum levels of certain types of uneconomic programming, such as news and public affairs.

Certain program producers, Hollywood unions, public-interest groups, independent TV stations, and the U.S. Department of Justice believe that network monopoly is significant and is exercised to the end of reducing competition. Most of the independent program suppliers believe that the networks exert their power in the programming market, and several have banded together to bring private antitrust action. The Antitrust Division brought a similar action in 1972, but neither case has come to trial at this writing. Meanwhile, the FCC has enacted its prime time access rule, and the Hollywood unions have petitioned the FCC to restrict network reruns to no more than 25 percent of the annual prime-time schedule, a reduction of about 15 percentage points below present levels.

Theories of Network Behavior

It is difficult to analyze, let alone solve, the issues described above without some understanding of the motivation and behavior of the networks. Do the networks possess monopoly power, either individually or as a result of oligopolistic coordination among themselves? In what ways could this power, if it exists, be exercised? To answer these questions, we need to construct a theory of behavior that "explains" observed phenomena, and is capable of being tested. Any such theory must possess certain features. First, the networks are only three in number, and no oligopolists could possibly be more aware than these of their interdependence. The evidence for the networks' recognition of their interdependence includes these facts: they pay thousands of dollars for overnight ratings of their own and their rivals' program audiences; they are all located within a few blocks of each other in New York; they all participate in NAB code decisions about advertising practices (including the number of commercial minutes in prime time), discuss the role of sex and violence on television, rotate coverage of such affairs as the Watergate and impeachment hearings, jockey over the fall schedule and midseason changes, and constantly trade personnel. Second, the variables with which the networks can compete with each other include, among others: (1) the type, quality, and scheduling of their programming; (2) prices charged to advertisers; and (3) payments made to affiliated stations. Items (2) and (3) are variables that are rather highly visible to everyone in the industry, while variable (1) is less easily defined or described quantitatively. Unlike older theories, we will suggest that rivalry occurs largely in terms of quality, and in this rivalry the networks recognize explicitly their interdependence.

Models of Program Choices

The oldest model of the behavior of broadcasters is Steiner's theory of program patterns [523]. A number of subsequent writers have extended and modified Steiner's analysis. Chapter 3 contained a critical evaluation and extension of Steiner's theory.

In these models, competition under advertiser support tends to produce less diversity and more "wasteful duplication" than is socially optimal. This is a direct parallel to Hotelling's famous spatial competition example of "excessive sameness" (Hotelling [257]). This duplication occurs because there is a tendency for a decentralized system of broadcasting, with limited channel capacity, to produce rivalry for large blocks of the audience with programs that are, if not identical, at least close substitutes. There is a tendency, in our case, for the three networks to produce the same kind of programming.

Crandall's and Park's Theories

A. Cournot [148] developed in 1838 a model of duopoly behavior in which (1) the sellers chose the quantities they supplied; (2) the two sellers were aware of each other's existence; but (3) each assumed that the other would not react to its changing output—that is, the rival's output was assumed fixed. Robert Crandall and R.E. Park have each constructed models of network behavior based on a static Cournot interaction among the networks. Crandall [152, 153] attempted to show that the FCC's prime-time access rule is based on implausible assumptions about network economics. Park [430] used his model to test the economic viability of various methods of constructing and maintaining a fourth national network.

In each model networks compete for audiences by varying their expenditures on programming inputs. Both models assume that each network ignores its impact on the other networks; that is, each network expects the others not to react to its programming decisions. But is the assumption of ignorance of interdependence realistic? We think not. Park [430, p. 6] notes that the "assumption [no expected interaction] is harder to defend. There is certainly an incentive for the networks to collude; if they could agree to hold down program expenditure within some reasonable range, they could all increase their profits."

Having assumed no expected interaction, Crandall and Park have defined away the problem of rivalry.[c] The point, of course, is that when there are only three buyers of a commodity, or when there are only three sellers, one generally expects to find awareness of interdependence and some degree of tacit or implicit cooperation. Myopic behavior is implausible. Accordingly, if one wishes to argue that this is not the case, then one must produce evidence of conditions that make cooperation or "conscious parallelism" impossible or ineffective.

Crandall ([153], p. 493) suggests two reasons for Cournot behavior. First, the time lag from conception of a series to its first broadcast is on the order of eighteen months. The price for the series is thus fixed far in advance of the scheduling decision. Second, continuing series comprise the majority of each season's scheduling. He claims that the reluctance of each network to move successful series makes them insensitive to their rivals' decisions on new programs.

Crandall's two arguments are weak justification for myopic behavior. The time-lag argument is a non sequitur. All the time lag does is make interdependent action more attenuated. Does the similar time lag between the initiation of a new auto design and the sale of the new model mean that Ford and General Motors act as Cournot oligopolists?

---

[c]Park's use of the Cournot assumption does not affect his conclusions. If a fourth network cannot survive in a placid Cournot world, it will be unlikely to survive the rivalrous reaction of ABC, CBS, and NBC as it enters the industry. Crandall's conclusion (that the networks have paid their suppliers the economic value of nonnetwork rights) is probably due to the nature of the supply side of programming. In Chapter 2, we argued that the supply is competitive and elastic. Under these circumstances, the networks, whether they be three or thirty, need only pay the opportunity cost of inputs in order to elicit an adequate supply of programs and pilots (see also Besen and Soligo, [72]). By worrying about the price paid, Crandall also misses other areas of interdependence: quantity and scheduling of programs and reruns, prices paid by advertisers, and payments to affiliates.

The presence of continued series does not guarantee Cournot behavior. Thirty to 40 percent of the fall schedule is new series. By scheduling decisions and midyear replacements of failing series the networks can interact in a manner obvious to each. Despite Crandall's assertion that continued series are reluctantly moved, the networks do shift continued series. The jockeying over the fall schedule and midseason changes demonstrates the networks' recognition of their interdependence.

It appears that the problem of the economic behavior of the television networks is very much more complex than Crandall has made it out to be. The assumption of a static Cournot model is most troubling, since it is precisely by examining the nature and effects of conjectural responses in program inputs in a dynamic setting that a more powerful model of network behavior can be constructed, as we shall see below.

A Model of Dynamic Interdependence

The models of Chapter 3 are concerned with predicting (or explaining) program patterns; Crandall's approach is concerned with the problem of network monopsony power in programming markets; and Park is concerned with the viability of a fourth network. (Technically, "monopsony" occurs when there is only one *buyer* of a commodity. The term is sometimes used for cases where the number of buyers is so small that each can affect the price he has to pay.) In constructing our own model of network behavior we need not assume that the networks possess monopsony power (although we can treat this as a special case), but it will be helpful to use the Chapter 3 result that under more or less plausible circumstances the networks will tend to produce the same types of programming.

The networks clearly constitute a small-group oligopoly with only very marginal external competition from the syndication market and independent stations. They are protected from entry, albeit indirectly, by the FCC's spectrum allocation policies.[d] Hence we expect them to engage in some sort of oligopoly "game" with an ever-present tension between the rewards to be gained from cooperation, and the rewards to be gained from "cheating" on any agreement— tacit or otherwise—that might arise. The rivalry is complicated by the existence of a fairly wide variety of factors, which can be varied in order either to cooperate or to compete. These variables include the price of advertising time; the number of minutes of commercials per hour; the quality, type, and scheduling of programming offered; the quantity of programming (hours per day, week, or year); and payments to affiliates.

---

[d]For instance, the FCC might allocate more spectrum to television at the expense of other services, or it might have chosen to set up powerful regional stations instead of relatively weak local ones. See Chapters 5 and 6 *infra*. For an empirical estimate of the viability of further networks see Park [430].

The networks are most likely to agree in dimensions that are so visible that cheating is easily detected and responded to, and where outside conditions do not constrain their ability to reach agreement (Stigler [531]). The price and quantity of advertising time is relatively easy to agree upon, because the market is well organized and well informed, and because cheating can quickly be detected. Also, the NAB code limits on the number of commercial minutes per hour provide a convenient process for agreement, which has the tacit sanction of the FCC. It is unlikely that the NAB limits maximize total network profits. The cost of not perfectly maximizing industry profits is probably less than that of three oligopolists groping toward an equilibrium of their own. On the other hand, it is doubtful that the prices and quantities thus set depart very far from competitive levels, simply because most advertisers have other alternatives (e.g., close substitutes for network advertising).

Similarly, compensation payments by the networks to their affiliates could be used as a device to compete. This variable appears to be of only minor importance. ABC does attempt to use the device of higher compensation payments to increase its access to the nation's audience, but this source of competition is limited to the fringe of small one- and two-station markets. Of course, networks might try to attract affiliates on a program-by-program basis, instead of for an exclusive two-year period. Their failure to do so extensively can be explained as well by the high transaction costs and audience flow problems this would involve as by collusive behavior. However, any attempt to compete more than marginally in this way would be easily detected and would invite retaliation, so there are good reasons for the absence of such a phenomenon.

Finally, we come to the problem of program "quality" (or "audience appeal") and quantity. Here it is very important to remember that the audience behaves, or is believed to behave, in a rather peculiar way. That is, it is generally assumed that the *total* audience for all three networks combined at any time is determined almost entirely by exogenous factors. Thus, a very successful program, such as *All in the Family* is successful in that it has a large share of the usual Saturday evening audience, and not in that the total Saturday evening audience is increased, although it may be increased slightly in this and similar exceptional cases. (The Watergate and impeachment hearings were exceptional cases.) What one network produces usually comes at the expense of the others. An increase in the audience for one network (speaking now of whole schedules, not individual programs) comes about if the level of inputs for that network is raised above that of its rivals. We should not rely unduly on the assumption about audience behavior, because one suspects that it fails to be valid for program choices far outside the range actually found in network programming.

Rivalry in such a model can be characterized in game-theoretic terms. In producing revenue, the network rivalry game is constant sum *in audience*. The fixed aggregate audience and the NAB restrictions on the number of network commercials implies a fixed number of advertising commercials, and hence a fixed aggregate advertising revenue. Although the size of the revenue pie is fixed, the individual slices can be changed by varying program input levels relative to other players. In order to gain a larger share of advertising revenues, a network must increase its programming costs. The resulting pay-off matrix for network *profits* is a nonconstant sum game of the "prisoner's dilemma" type.[e] An example of this is given in Table 4-1 for the two network case, under the assumption that there are only two possible input levels: "high" and "low." (Of course, in practice, the input levels can be varied continuously and audience size is stochastic rather than deterministic.)

The basic workings of oligopolistic rivalry are captured by this illustration. The implication clearly is that failure to enter into a successful cooperative arrangement, or failure to enforce such an arrangement, will result in a tendency toward higher input levels, higher costs, and lower profits for *both* networks. The presence of three rivals aggravates the prisoner's-dilemma aspects of network rivalry. As above, it will be difficult for three networks to agree to use low inputs. In addition, it may not even pay for any two networks to agree to use low inputs (see Rapaport [457], pp. 79-86). For instance, if Network 2 believes that Network 1 will choose the low input strategy, then Network 2 has higher profits by choosing the high input level than by choosing the low level. If 2 believes 1 will follow the high input strategy, Network 2 protects its profits by following the high input strategy. By similar reasoning Network 1 chooses the high input strategy. The upper left outcome in Table 4-1, which is mutually advantageous to both networks, only occurs if both players know that cheating will be successfully detected and effective retaliation will follow. In a one-period model, trust plays an important role, because there is no second period for retaliation to occur. In a dynamic game trusting each other is of little economic importance. Either the profitability of cheating dominates or the threat of retaliation will be sufficient to prevent the high input-high input result.

Payoff matrices of the prisoner's-dilemma type do not always lead to the same result. Oligopolistic pricing behavior frequently has the characteristics exhibited in Table 4-1. If prices are public information the oligopolists can frequently avoid the dilemma result, because any potential price competitor knows that detection and retaliation are quick and certain—each rival knows that the off-diagonal states are unstable, and that the effective choices are like the diagonal ones in Table 4-1.

---

[e]The theory of games is a set of analytical tools for studying situations of conflict among individuals. A constant sum game is one where the sum of all payoffs to all participants is a fixed amount. Since the size of the pie is fixed, one rival can gain more only at the expense of another rival. Nonconstant sum games do not have this property. The "prisoner's-dilemma" is a special kind of game named after the following example: Two criminal accomplices are separated for interrogation. The district attorney offers each the opportunity to cop a plea. If both resist the offer, there will be insufficient evidence for conviction. If only one resists, he will face a heavy sentence. The situation is rich in possibilities, and the outcome depends on many factors, but the structure of the game is the same as that faced by oligopolistic rivals who cannot communicate or collude directly. See Luce and Raiffa [340], and Rapaport [457].

Table 4-1

An Example of Network Rivalry Strategies and Payoffs

(A = audience [and advertising revenue], C = cost, π = profit)

		Network 2	
		Low Input Level	*High Input Level*
	Low Input Level	A 50, 50 C 25, 25 π 25, 25	A 0, 100 C 25, 50 π −25, 50
Network 1			
	High Input Level	A 100, 0 C 50, 25 π 50, −25	A 50, 50 C 50, 50 π 0, 0

Source: See text.

Note: If Network 1 selects the low input level while 2 chooses the high (upper right corner), then:

Network 1 has no advertising revenue, costs of 25 and profits of −25;

Network 2 has advertising revenue of 100, costs of 50, and profits of 50.

Other combinations can be read in a similar manner.

The prisoner's-dilemma result occurs only if detection and/or retaliation are difficult. Uncertainty and risk play prominent roles in the process, as they do in Stigler's [531] theory of oligopoly. A common example is advertising. In any advertising campaign the outcome is very uncertain. If the campaign is successful, rivals may not be able to make an effective countermove, because of lag times and the random nature of advertising success. Consequently, advertisers may sense that the off-diagonal states are potentially viable, and that the more they spend the more likely they are to have a successful campaign. The result is that a noncooperative solution occurs where profits for all rivals are lower than if an enforceable agreement exists. Oligopoly games of this sort are common. Some of the more prominent examples are automobile style changes, cigarette and detergent advertising, airline schedules, and team-quality competition in professional sports.

The popularity and success of television schedules exhibits the same kind of unpredictability that we associate with advertising. Unlike price cuts, which are visible and easily responded to, we do not expect to see viable agreements on program quality. Nothing in this model of network behavior requires myopia or ignorance of the process or its implications on the part of the players. Quite the contrary; the participants' understanding of the nature of the game gives the process additional impetus. In the absence of a mechanism for successful collusion, the players are helpless; they always end up in the lower right corner.

If the preceding description of network rivalry is accurate, we should expect to see an increased level of general program quality, measured in terms of program costs and of quantities of inputs to programming. Historically, each will have avoided large increases in inputs because of the unpredictable audience response and the fear of massive retaliation. Consequently, each year the networks will find themselves in the low-input-level state. In replacing cancelled series and altering continued ones, each network faces a choice between continuing present input levels or increasing inputs. Its incentives are to increase input levels, either in the hope of getting an edge on its rivals or in the expectation that they will try to do so. Each will try to increase its quality the minimum amount necessary to keep even or get slightly ahead.

Faced with this dynamic rivalry, the networks will seek mechanisms for limiting the adverse effects on their profits. If agreement on program quality is impossible or unenforceable, they will seek other tools. The switch from kinescope to film in the late fifties made it possible for the networks to rerun episodes, and one tool that appears to have been employed with some success is the use of reruns throughout a larger proportion of the year. (One would expect some increase in reruns to result from this technical change in our model, in collusive models or in Cournot models.) The number of weeks of the year in which reruns are scheduled (or, alternatively, the number of original programs purchased) is a highly visible variable. If a tacit agreement, perhaps through "rerun leadership," is reached to increase the level of reruns, cheating can be easily detected. The quality of the reruns is fully determined by the quality of the original programs. If all three networks have the same or nearly the same rerun "season," their respective shares of the audience will not be altered. Thus, tacit or explicit cooperation on increased reruns can help, at least, to offset the effects of rivalry in raising the costs of original programs, because reruns cost only about 25 percent as much to broadcast as do original programs (OTP [599], p. 5).

There is nothing inherent or necessary about this process of adjusting reruns upward as original programs increase in cost and quality. It is simply one effective mechanism for mitigating the effects of rivalry in other dimensions. It would certainly be possible—and initially profitable—for any one network to "cheat" by running original episodes in rerun season. (This assumes that original programs have audiences larger than reruns, *ceteris paribus*. This plausible assumption can be tested.) But cheating would be immediately visible, and its consequence in the succeeding year predictable. It is not necessary, however, that the networks go in lock-step in pursuing this policy. That is, reruns need not always be programmed opposite reruns, particularly in the early weeks of the season. Still, since each network buys about the same number of new episodes per year in each series program, the effect is on average the same.

For several reasons, the number of reruns has an upper bound, and can only be increased gradually. First, there must be original programs to rerun, and if programs are not to be rerun more than once in a year, this implies at most an equal number of originals and reruns. (In fact, this point has now been reached, or nearly reached, for series programs.) Second, "excessive" reruns (or at least large sudden jumps in the quantity of reruns) will cause public criticism and possible regulatory pressure. (This too is now occurring, as the Hollywood unions are attempting to organize public opinion in favor of a rule limiting reruns.) Third, as the number of reruns is increased, their costs relative to original costs will increase; otherwise original episodes (which are now generally priced at a loss, which is made up later in syndication) will not be forthcoming, because there will be too few episodes for successful syndication "strips." Off-network series are customarily sold for "stripping," or *daily* showing for a period of 13, 26, or 39 weeks. Since networks series are customarily shown once a week, a successful run of several years on the network is required before enough episodes are available to "strip" series in syndication. The fewer original episodes the networks order per year, the longer the period before the syndicator has accumulated enough episodes. Episode prices may also increase, because packagers must recoup pilot costs over a smaller number of episodes. Thus, there are natural reasons to suppose that reruns will increase gradually as they have done, rather than "all at once." As Table 4-2 indicates, reruns have increased fairly steadily over the past decade. We have no data on the period before 1962, but we assume that increased reruns became a technically acceptable source of cooperative behavior when the networks were changing from kinescope to film production in the late 1950s.

ABC's position as the weakest of the three networks enhances its bargaining strength with the other two networks. As noted in Table 4-2, ABC has programmed the smallest percentage of reruns, while the opposite has been true for CBS. CBS and NBC will permit ABC to program more original episodes, because ABC's survival is of great value to them. Given ABC's smaller number of affiliates, it is quite possible that ABC would suffer heavy losses if it programmed the same number of reruns as CBS and NBC. If ABC should go out of business, the Justice Department would probably prosecute the other two networks for antitrust violations. An antitrust suit and adverse decision would be more costly to CBS and NBC than allowing ABC to "cheat" on reruns. For similar reasons, General Motors and Ford seem to permit American Motors to behave with more independence than they permit one another.

The picture that emerges is this: The networks are caught, with respect to program quality, in a prisoner's dilemma which leads to a continuous increase over time in the quantity of program inputs and a consequent increase in cost per program. They are unable to agree on any collusive or cooperative solution to this dilemma, because there is no easy way to define or measure program quality *ex ante.* Reruns, however, are highly visible, and the networks have been

Table 4-2
Network Original Programming by Year (prime time)

		Percent Original Programming	
Season	ABC	CBS	NBC
1961/62	NA	NA	71
1962/63	69	71	NA
1963/64	72	73	NA
1964/65	70	72	NA
1965/66	70	71	NA
1966/67	71	69	NA
1967/68	65	63	NA
1968/69	70	62	NA
1969/70	63	61	NA
1970/71	65	56	NA
1971/72	65	56	59

NA = Not Available.
Source: *OTP Report*, [599], Appendix Table 1.

able to grope toward a cooperative equilibrium of increased reruns. The savings from increased reruns have partially offset the increased cost of original programming.

Individuals familiar with network revenues and expenses may feel that the high network profits are inconsistent with this model of network behavior. The potential profits of the three networks are quite large because they distribute programs and can thus exploit simultaneous networking and transactions economies. As we noted in the discussion of affiliates, the networks' potential profits are enhanced by their bargaining position relative to affiliates in the large, highly profitable markets with four or more stations. In part the networks are indeed able to earn these profits. The preceding model only suggests that these potential profits are not completely realized because the networks are unable to effectively agree in the area of program quality and cost.

It is the essence of scientific method to make hypotheses that are capable of predicting results of experiments or observations not yet made. Unfortunately most of the social sciences cannot be fit into this mold, partly because experiments are seldom possible or replicable and partly because we tend to use up all of the little data at our disposal in order to construct theories which explain the behavior of those data. Much of the empirical evidence reported here is consistent with the theory expounded above precisely because the theory was formulated to explain the behavior observed. There are no contrary data. The data are not, therefore, of great interest. To test our model properly against its rivals would probably require the equivalent of what happened in the airline industry when as a result of the energy crisis the CAB allowed airlines to cooperate in cutting back excess flights generated by their own version of quality rivalry. One can make predictions about the effects of alternative policies or policy changes, and these predictions (or at least one of them) can indeed be "tested" as a result of the policy-making process. We will return to the policy issues below.

The crucial empirical facts are these: (1) Reruns have increased substantially over at least the past decade. (2) The prices paid for programs by the networks have increased faster than the increase in the prices of inputs to program production (see Tables 4-2 and 4-3). The first fact is of course consistent with our hypothesis. The second is crucial to distinguishing our hypothesis from alternative hypotheses, such as the perfectly collusive or Cournot models, in which reruns and program costs might both increase as a result of factor price increases.

Perfect collusion and *increasingly* perfect collusion can explain the increase in reruns, but cannot explain the evidence of increased levels of factor inputs in programming indicated by: (1) a significant shift away from "game shows" and to "drama/adventure" shows, with obvious increased input levels; (2) the shift from black-and-white to color programming, requiring much more expensive and elaborate sets and costumes; (3) a significant shift from studio to "on location" shooting; (4) a significant increase in the average number of days required to film one episode of a series; and (5) a large increase in the proportion of first-run or "made-for-television" motion pictures (see Tables 2-2 and 2-3).[f] Given constant returns to scale in program production, program prices should have risen no faster than input prices. However, between 1961 and 1971, program costs rose 89 percent, while input prices rose about 40 percent, as shown in Table 4-3.

Cournot models, like Crandall's, have significant weaknesses. First, as we suggested earlier, the use of the Cournot assumption to typify network behavior is either a supreme leap of faith or the confusion of mathematical tractability with economic reality. Second, Cournot models suggest that as the potential aggregate revenue grows the individual network demand curves shift outward, leading to an increase in both original programming and in quality. Using Park's approximation to a Cournot model in his equation 8 [430, p. 7], and data contained in Table 4-3 and OTP [599] appendix table 31, one can calculate that

---

[f]These phenomena could be explained by massive changes in viewer choice behavior. Although tastes have changed, we do not think the effects have been significant. First, it seems unlikely that tastes have changed so much that the networks would have to increase the quality of their programs to prevent viewers from turning off their sets. Second, it seems very improbable that viewers would strongly demand higher-quality programs and simultaneously be insensitive to the level of reruns. Third, if tastes did radically change, then it would be a sheer accident for the profit-maximizing percentage of homes viewing to remain as constant as it has. Thus, by the principle of Occam's razor we can dismiss the argument for massive changes in viewers' preferences.

Table 4-3
Cost Indices

Year	Network Price Per Hour for New Series Programs[a]	Craft Unions Wage Rates[b]	Actors' Minimum Scale[b]
1962	100	100	100
1963	104	110	100
1964	109	110	100
1965	113	116	100
1966	125	116	100
1967	138	121	112
1968	140	121	112
1969	147	135	120
1970	159	135	120
1971	189	142	138

[a]The dollar increase is approximately from $115,000 per hour to $225,000 for regular entertainment series.
[b]Hollywood only.
Source: *OTP Report*, [599], Appendix Table 22. (1962=100)

program cost inflation in the 1967-71 period should have been *slightly more than half what it actually was*. Third, in order to explain the increase in reruns in the face of expanding aggregate revenue, Cournot models have to rely on the networks' taking fifteen years to adjust to the cost savings that the switch from kinescope to film made possible.

A potential alibi for the Cournot and collusive models as alternative explanations is "increasing scarcity of talent." If "good" talent became increasingly scarce over the 1961-71 period, then that talent's income would be bid up. The rising price for scarce talent would increase program costs faster than that suggested by craft union rates and talent union floors.

The increased-scarcity argument appears inadequate for two reasons. First, if the argument held, then the above-the-line (talent) expenses would rise faster than below-the-line (production) costs. The evidence on this point is ambiguous. The OTP investigation found that some program producers had above-the-line cost increasing faster than below-the-line, while others had the opposite experience (OTP [599], pp. 14-16). Second, with low transcontinental air fares, a scarcity of "good" talent in Hollywood would be accompanied by a scarcity of such talent in New York. There is no evidence of such a scarcity on the New York stage. Thus, the popularity of existing talent appears to be as much a function of marketing and of successful combinations of talent as of individual talent.

Regulatory Issues

The FCC, the Congress, program producers, actors, and the public all have at least one thing in common—concern for the extent of "network power." We have seen that the networks' own interdependence, which is an aspect of their fewness and market power, leads them into difficulties that are only partially avoided by their ability to cooperate on other variables. Indeed, to the extent that cooperative solutions to the oligopoly game in some dimensions are barely sufficient to offset the degenerative rivalry in others, it is questionable whether the networks in fact possess much "power," beyond the value of their dominance of scarce spectrum. The picture may be different in other areas, however, and the FCC has a right to be concerned with power from the First Amendment viewpoint.

For instance, it may be that for any given input cost there is available a range of ideological viewpoints of the same audience-producing capacity. This would give the networks discretionary power. Alternatively, it might be that the most efficient set of inputs for any given level of output always produces a consistent ideological or cultural bias. More likely, catering to an audience with preferences heavily weighted toward mass programs may lead naturally to programs that appear ideologically or culturally similar, because minorities may not be actively sought as audiences.

Thus, even if one does not believe in the existence of network monopsony power, and even if in addition one believes that the networks are largely unable to cooperate in setting quality levels and advertising prices, there still remains a legitimate concern over their fewness, and it is not unreasonable to explore policies that might offset the effects of fewness.

The Prime Time Access Rule

The FCC became increasingly concerned in the fifties and sixties about the network control of programming. In particular, the Commission was disturbed by:

1. The decrease in advertiser-supplied programs and the increase in packager-supplied series;

2. The expansion of network profit and equity rights in packager-supplied programs;

3. The increased reliance of network affiliates on the networks for their prime-time programming; and

4. The decline of the syndication market.

The Commissioners perceived the first two trends as evidence of network market power. They believed that the networks were extorting profit and equity rights in packagers' programs as a quid pro quo for purchase. The third phenomenon ran counter to the FCC's goal of local control of programming decisions. Simultaneously, the decline in first-run syndication supposedly weakened the affiliates' ability to choose nonnetwork programming.

After a long investigation, in 1970 the FCC adopted the prime time access rule. The rule placed two restrictions on the networks and their affiliates: First, the networks could not own equity and profit rights in packager-supplied series; and second, stations in the top fifty markets were prohibited from carrying more than three hours of network programming (other than public affairs and news) between 7 and 11 PM. (Federal Communications Commission, "Amendment of Part 73: Commission's Rules and Regulations with Respect to Competition and Responsibility in Network Television," Report and Order #12782, May 4, 1970.)

Crandall [152, 153] has argued that the prime time access rule, in forbidding network participation in the ownership of programs at any rate lower than 100 percent, is unnecessary, because there is no monopsony power anyway. If so, the rule merely constrains the range of possible bargaining schemes, and in general makes the program market less efficient. As to barring network programs from 7:30 to 8:00 PM every day, that should indeed increase the demand for syndicated programming, which is necessarily more costly for the system as a whole, and the result can only be to produce lower-quality programs. Still, this might be a reasonable price to pay for an increase in the diversity of control over program sources, an objective perhaps motivated by First Amendment concerns.

The prime time access rule is important not so much in itself or because of its effects, which are probably small, but because debate about its goals is intense, and likely to continue for the next year or two. In the course of this debate, those who argue that the rule is ineffective in dealing with the problem of network power, or too costly even if effective, will have to propose alternatives. Possible alternatives will be discussed in Chapter 5.

Limiting Reruns

The Hollywood unions, both craft and talent, which have felt themselves disadvantaged by the increase in reruns, have called on the FCC to limit the decline in original programming. They have been encouraged in this request by a substantial portion of the California congressional delegation, by the California state legislature, and by the White House. What would be the effect of such an FCC rule? Clearly the immediate effect would be a sharp increase in the quantity of original programming ordered from Hollywood, an increase in employment, and a significant decline in network profits. In the longer term, *according to the networks themselves*, the effect would be to change the sources of programming from Hollywood to New York and overseas, and to alter significantly the *type* of programming, away from, say, drama/adventure types, and toward game shows, quiz shows, situation comedies, and similar low-cost programs.[g] Whether this would actually happen is unclear, since it would amount to a new cooperative oligopoly solution centered around program types and sources rather than reruns and advertising practices. Nevertheless, the prophecy may be self-fulfilling, as the networks use the occasion of public debate about reruns to signal each other for the contingency that might result from a new FCC regulation. The remaining effect would be a heavy intrusion by the FCC into program content regulation, as it attempted to sort out on a case by case basis the merits of requests for "waivers" of a rerun rule, just as it is now doing with the Prime Time Access Rule.

An FCC restriction on network reruns would make it harder for the networks to seek a cooperative solution to their oligopoly problem, but it would probably not make a solution impossible. Depending on the nature of the ultimate solution, viewers, program producers, and talent might or might not be helped by such a rule. The only certainty is that federal regulation of mass-media content would be significantly increased in extent and intensity, and that the FCC would be treating a symptom of network power rather than the underlying problem.

[g]Robert D. Wood, "Facts and Fallacies About First Runs and Reruns," Remarks to the Hollywood Radio and Television Society, September 12, 1972. Mr. Wood is president of CBS.

Appendix:
The Model Resurrected
Mathematically

In case the model of network behavior is not precisely clear by this point, it may be helpful to write down a formal characterization of the objective function of a network. Unfortunately, mathematics are not particularly helpful beyond that point, but they may lend some precision to the basic concepts of Chapter 4.

The model we propose can be written in a form which is comparable with Park's and Crandall's objective functions. We assume that each network attempts to maximize the following expression in each season, s:

$$E_i(\pi_{is}) \cong P_s E_i(A_{is}) - X_{is} \sum_j P_{js} t_{ijs} - (52 - X_{is}) \alpha_s \sum_j P_{js} t_{ijs} \quad (1)$$

where,

$E_i(\pi_{is})$ = The ith network's expectation of its own profit in season s.

P_s = The price paid per viewer in season s by advertisers.

$E_i(A_{is})$ = The expectation of network i as to its own audience in season s. A_{is} is a function of the quality of the programs offered by all three networks: $A_{is} = f(Q_{1s}, Q_{2s}, Q_{3s})$, where quality is a function of input and rerun levels: $Q_{is}(t_{is}, X_{is})$.

X_{is} = The number of original programs aired by network i in season s.

α_{is} = The (more or less) constant factor which relates the price of reruns to the price of original programs: $0 \leqslant \alpha_s \leqslant 1$.

P_{js} = The price paid for factor input j in season s.

t_{ijs} = The amount of factor j used by network i in season s in an original program episode.

Equation (1) is to be maximized with respect to all inputs t_{ijs} and with respect to the number of original programs X_{is} in a dynamic gaming context (in which the rivals' reactions are not expected to be zero), subject to the constraint (among others) that $\sum_i A_{is} = \overline{A}_s$, a fixed quantity in any season. Our model suggests that $E_i(Q_{js}) \geqslant Q_{j,s-1}$, or that each network expects its rivals will not decrease quality levels in each round of the game. This is a discrete, stochastic, partly cooperative, three-person differential game. (See M. Intrilligator [269], pp. 320-325 for a brief description of differential games.) The game is stochastic in several dimensions: the relationship between input levels and program quality; the strategies of rivals; and one's own strategies. The difficulty in characterizing solutions to such games is akin to the three-body problem in physics.

Even though it is not possible to produce a formal "solution" to this game (indeed, there may exist many "solutions," or equilibria, or none at all), it is possible to suggest that the process proceeds in the way we have described it. That is, $Q_{i,s} \geqslant Q_{i,s-1}$ for each network in each season (assuming that X_{is} is given) as a result of increases in input levels upon which it is impossible to collude. Since this would lead to increased cost and lower profits, the networks seek out and use the variable X_{is} to offset the process. X_{is} is fairly easy to agree on and fairly difficult to cheat on successfully. So, $X_{i,s} \leqslant X_{i,s-1}$, while $t_{i,s} \geqslant t_{i,s-1}$.

Part II:
Public Policy Toward Television

Introduction to Part II

The preceding chapters have been concerned with issues of theory, structure, and behavior in television markets. Those that follow will be concerned with policy. Because of the heavy involvement of government in television, policy is not merely an important part of the framework of television in the United States, but one of the most important potential sources of change and innovation.

Much of the discussion that follows is predicated on the objectives—economic efficiency and freedom of expression—that were set out in Chapter 1, and draws on the analysis of television program markets in Part I. But the reader should not be misled into thinking that our policy conclusions are all derived directly from the analysis. Much in the following chapters has no other basis than our own intuition and experience. Policy prescriptions are plentiful and cheap in the world of television regulation. Many of these prescriptions come from vested interests, and too many of the remainder derive from well-meant but often excessively naïve efforts to reform the present system without taking account of the incentives facing the industry and its regulators. The latter are subject to the drawback, among others, that there is no such thing as a free lunch. We bring to this active battlefield only two special things: some analysis, and a lot of the unique perspective of economics.

It is one thing to discuss policy and another thing to make it. Federal policy toward television is "made" in a highly complex interaction among Congress, the FCC, the White House, the industry, and the public. In this process "the press" (itself directly affected) plays a critical role. Since everyone's interests are affected by the performance and attitudes of the media, there is hardly anyone in the process who can lay claim to disinterest and objectivity. Every congressman seeks favor with the media in his district; the relationship between the media and the last two presidents of the United States, Nixon and Johnson, amply demonstrate the point.

Even within the "independent" regulatory agency, the FCC, there are complex and far from disinterested motives at work (Geller [215]).

For these and other reasons policy changes slowly. Incremental changes are common; large movements rare (Owen [418]). The industry does not respond to new technology with the rapidity that characterizes most other industries, especially when vested interests are at stake.

At the heart of the difficulty in the television policy-making process are two facts. The first is that, as a result of previous policy decisions, much of the industry enjoys various degrees of monopoly power and profits. The second is that every politician cares very much what the press thinks of him and how it treats him.[a] These two facts give rise to certain natural, understandable, and

---

[a]"The press" here includes not just TV stations and networks, but the many newspapers which either own or compete with TV stations.

inevitable incentives on both sides. One consequence of these incentives is that the industry has generally succeeded in protecting its equity in the status quo from new technology, such as cable television, which might benefit the public considerably.[b] On the other hand, the arrival of new technology offers one of those rare occasions when the regulatory agency has an *opportunity* to alter the status quo with improved policies. Regulatory agencies often fail to take advantage of this opportunity, and instead simply encompass the new technology with a view toward avoiding disastrous equity effects in the old. This has certainly happened, for instance, in surface transportation and in telegraphy. Still it is the arrival of new technologies that gives us the best opportunity to remedy structural defects in the present system, since a regulated industry threatened with technological obsolescence and massive new competition may be quite willing to reach compromises.

All of this is relevant to the following chapters, particularly in explaining the motivation of present policies and in evaluating the feasibility of alternatives. One of the themes that we hope to bring out in these chapters is the point that true improvement in the performance of the industry requires *structural* change that removes the *incentives* for present behavior. It is both unrealistic and unfair to blame the people who make decisions in the government and the industry for behavior that is entirely rational under present incentive structures. This kind of criticism is at present all too common. What is needed instead is a set of constructive suggestions for alterations in the set of incentives. Difficult as they may be to achieve, we will at least be addressing the problem, instead of its symptoms.

A final word of introduction: The FCC's decision-making policies can scarcely be understood in standard economic terms, at least if one accepts the nominal (stated) "objectives" of the agency. That is, the rules and procedures promulgated by the Commission are seldom an effective or efficient means of attaining the Commission's stated objectives. This could be the result of poor information, lack of expertise, or poor judgment; or it could be the result of a divergence between "real" agency objectives and those stated in public documents. We are inclined to the view that the latter explanation is usually the more valid, and that real agency objectives lie more in the direction of compromise, stability, and a quiet life than in the direction of "maximum diversity, access, competition" or "maximum" anything.

[b]As one example of the considerable political power of the broadcast industry, we note that the Senate version of a bill to establish an office of consumer advocacy within the federal government contained (in July 1974) just two exemptions: the consumer advocate would be forbidden to attack labor unions and television licensees.

5

Improving Television Performance with Limited Channels

Introduction

This chapter is devoted to an examination of a number of schemes for improving television performance with the FCC's present spectrum allocation for television. The reason why television performance might stand improvement can be inferred directly from the analysis of the preceding three chapters. Oligopolistic control of networking, the absence of any direct market link between the supply of programs and the demand for those programs by viewers, the tendency of competing, audience-maximizing broadcasters to "duplicate" programming—all contribute to a suspicion that both economic efficiency and freedom of expression could be more closely approximated than they are now.

We have already said, in Chapter 1, that our objectives were to be economic efficiency and freedom of expression. It seems self-evident that an increase in the number of persons or firms controlling broadcast content is consistent with if not essential to a better approximation to the First Amendment objective. In Chapter 3 we have already made the case, as well as economic theory will permit, that an increase in the number of competitors and pay TV are consistent with increased viewer economic welfare, both because of the likely increase in diversity and because viewers are likely to value programs more highly than advertisers do. From this point on, and without further apologies for lack of rigor, we shall assume that an increase in the diversity of program control is, other things equal, likely to improve the performance of the television industry in terms of both of our original objectives.

There are, of course, definitions of performance that go beyond (and therefore compromise) the notions we have in mind. For instance, the Congress and the FCC have for many years regarded the "public interest, convenience, and necessity" as a sufficient criterion for their actions in this field. The phrase by itself is obviously bereft of meaning. Among the objectives sought by the FCC over the years in serving the public interest have been localism in program content control, fairness in the treatment of controversial issues, and the airing of various program types thought by the FCC to be in the public interest but not profitable to broadcasters.

Early decisions of the FCC regarding spectrum allocation and broadcast regulation have resulted in a relative scarcity of VHF broadcast licenses and "supra-normal" profits for those who hold them. These profits are no doubt capitalized in the value of the licenses or stations. The effect has been to create an interest group with considerable political power which quite naturally desires to protect the value of its investment. Partly as a result, the FCC and Congress have also very clearly taken "public interest, convenience, and necessity," to mean protection of the vested interests of powerful broadcasters, sometimes at the expense of what others would call consumer or viewer welfare. For our purposes, "public interest, convenience, and necessity" as presently used is not an "operative" criterion.

There are a number of ways in which this power of the industry might be dealt with directly, such as the use of license fees that capture for the public the monopoly profits earned by broadcasters. But reforms of this sort are subject to the same political barriers that plague all efforts to improve television performance through structural reform. It would be politically as difficult to take away broadcast monopoly profits as to take away station licenses. It is not clear, what effect, if any, this would have on television program content.

In this chapter we shall be concerned with ways of changing the structure of the television industry in such a manner as to improve its likely performance *under the constraint* that the supply of spectrum available for television cannot be changed. If there is no change in the technical configuration of TV stations, this means keeping the present number of channels. If the technical configuration can be altered, either more or fewer channels can, as we shall see, become available within the same overall spectrum allocation. The proposals that are examined below include: more effective use of the UHF band; the creation of powerful regional stations; low-power local stations and VHF "drop-ins"; over-the-air pay television; and new networks and the FCC's prime-time access rule. In each case, after describing the options, we shall examine the likely consequences of the proposal in terms of our objectives and in terms of its political feasibility. As we shall see, political feasibility is an enormously important barrier to reform.

UHF Television

The FCC once thought it had solved the problems engendered by its limited allocation of VHF channels, by allocating some seventy additional channels in the UHF band. Although a number of stations are in fact operating in this band, the solution must be regarded as a financial failure. Part of the reason for the failure of UHF lies in tuning difficulties and the technical limitations of the UHF band in comparison with VHF. These have been serious handicaps in attracting audiences. Another problem with UHF is the FCC's continued insistence on localism, each station being allocated only enough power to serve a relatively small area. In the absence of network service for most UHF stations, this severely limits the advertising demand for UHF audiences and, of course, the weakness of UHF stations in turn retards the development of a fourth network.

This "chicken-and-egg" problem means that independent UHF stations cannot take advantage of the economies of transactions costs and large audiences that network-affiliates enjoy, with the result that they are not able to afford very attractive programs. While a few UHF stations now are profitable, the group as a whole has consistently lost money. (See the FCC's *Annual Report* for statistics on UHF finances. For background, see Note [401], Webbink [606].)

There have been a number of attempts to estimate the magnitude of the UHF "handicap" due to tuning difficulties (Besen [69], Park [423]). The handicap does seem to be declining, partly because of the growth of cable (which puts UHF and VHF on a par so far as reception is concerned), and partly because the FCC has ordered all television-set manufacturers to begin making "detent" (click-stop) UHF tuning dials. As the handicap declines, UHF stations and a fourth network become simultaneously more viable, but this may happen after cable has rendered the issue inconsequential.

One way in which the viability of UHF stations can be improved is through "deintermixture"—that is, by making sure that the stations in a given market are either all VHF or all UHF, or even by moving all stations everywhere to the UHF band (see Besen [69]). The FCC struggled with this proposal some years ago, but eventually caved in to pressure from VHF broadcasters (who, naturally, fought to avoid the resulting increase in competition).

In terms of cost and disruption, deintermixture may well be the cheapest and fastest way to achieve a large-scale improvement in television performance. It probably outranks all of the other proposals in this chapter in that sense, although it is by no means the most feasible in the political sense. The resulting increase in channels would probably rival the effect of cable television, and at far less cost. Indeed, this idea would be more attractive than cable altogether were it not for cable's potential "two-way" capability. One can speculate that UHF deintermixture, if the FCC had been able to go through with it, would have resulted in the absence of any significant demand for cable television.

Since deintermixture now seems to have been permanently dismissed as a policy alternative, the only remaining hope for UHF is that its relative "handicap" will gradually be reduced to the point where it provides a somewhat more effective alternative to VHF television. This does not seem likely to happen anytime soon, because cable and detent tuners are diffusing at a fairly slow rate.

Regional Stations

We have already seen that the economies of scale in sharing program costs put strong pressure on the broadcast industry to use national or network programs. There will be a tendency in this direction in any event, and it will be stronger the more homogeneous are tastes across the nation. (If people in Peoria never liked anything liked by people in New York, and vice versa, there would be no national or network programming.) If it were not for the FCC's TV allocation plan, which created low-power, local stations, we could all have access to a great many more channels. The same spectrum could be used for powerful regional stations, no one of which could serve a small community.[a] This is called the "Du Mont Plan," and has been explored at some length elsewhere (Noll, Peck, and McGowan [394]). The essence of the Du Mont Plan was to have fewer cities with TV stations, but to have each station cover a large geographical area, spanning a number of cities. Such a plan would permit the creation of new networks and increase the number of choices available to each viewer. As we have seen (Chapter 3), such an increase in the number of channels may increase diversity of programming, and certainly increases competition. The practical difficulty with recommending the Du Mont plan now, of course, is that hundreds of broadcast licenses would have to be revoked, at considerable financial loss to their present holders. This is an insurmountable difficulty, given the political power of this group. But consideration of the Du Mont plan does point up the choice that was before the FCC in the early years of television—a greater range of diversity of programming and competition versus localism in program decision-making.

A belief in the benefits of localism is more or less endemic in the American political scheme, and in First Amendment terms there is much to recommend it. The difficulty with the goal in this particular context is that it implies that a rather high degree of local monopoly power is preferable to a rather high degree of competition on a regional or national level. Are we better off as a result? Any answer requires a rather subtle value judgment. It is nice that some small cities can have their "own" TV station, but it would also be nice if the people there and elsewhere could have six or more real program alternatives rather than one or two or three. The other problem with the doctrine of localism in television is that it has little practical effect. With the perhaps important exception of local news shows, most stations do the minimum amount of local programming required to keep their licenses. For reasons that have been brought out in Chapters 2 and 4, this programming is of relatively low quality, and in fact does not get much of an audience. We are inclined to think that localism has not been worth its cost, and that the Du Mont plan might well have been a superior alternative to the present system.[b]

---

[a]The reason for this is that if all cities had stations on all twelve VHF channels they would interfere with each other intolerably. So Channel 4, for instance, can only be allocated to cities a certain minimum distance apart.

[b]We say this for commercial television. In Chapter 7 we shall argue that local *decision-making* is an important goal for *public* television. The apparent conflict is reconciled by the fact that the major argument for decentralization in public broadcasting is independence from federal political influence, given federal subsidies.

Low-Power Local Stations and
VHF "Drop-Ins"

The logical inverse of the Du Mont Plan is to create a number of very-low-power broadcast stations, each serving very small neighborhood areas. If these stations have sufficiently low power they could be fit into the present allocation structure without interfering with stations in other communities on the same frequencies. Indeed, it has been suggested (OTP [602]) that a good many more *standard* power broadcast stations could be fit into the present allocation plan; these are called VHF "drop-ins." (Any new station that is added to the FCC's Table of Allocations is called a "drop-in." The OTP suggestion resulted from new engineering estimates of tolerable interference levels given new technology.) The effect in either case is to increase the number of channels and therefore choices available within the existing spectrum allocation, given sufficient advertising support to support this increase, and provided that the new stations do not simply displace existing UHF affiliates. It seems unlikely, however, that very many additional choices would be available to any given viewer under the most optimistic of circumstances. VHF drop-ins would, it is true, increase the viability of a fourth commercial network, and vice versa, but not very much (Park [430]).

Any scheme that increases the number of channels must be welcomed, provided advertiser demand is sufficient to bear the cost. But a plan that fails to take advantage of economies of scale in program exhibition is bound to be unattractive. So is a plan, such as drop-ins, that makes only a marginal change when there are available alternatives with much more far-reaching effects. Still, precisely because it is only a slight change, the drop-in plan may be the most politically feasible of the alternatives we are considering.

Pay Television with Limited Channels

Our theoretical discussion of the effects of pay television appeared in Chapter 3. Here we want to examine the effects of relaxing the present FCC rules (which effectively bar most popular programming from over-the-air pay-TV exhibition) in the context of limited channels. (We shall pick up the discussion again in Chapter 6, in the context of cable television.) Our discussion below can be briefly summarized: Pay TV, by its nature, makes broadcast program choice sensitive to viewers' preferences—much more so than under advertiser support. As a consequence, it is likely that *some* viewers would be better off with pay TV. But it is just as likely that other viewers would be worse off, either as a result of having to pay for programs that are now "free," or because their preferred programs would disappear. Another important consequence of pay TV with *limited* channels would be a transfer of money—probably quite a large amount—from viewers to broadcasters and the program production industry. It does not take much insight to see the political implications of this, and to understand the long-standing aversion displayed by the FCC and the Congress toward pay television.

Not unexpectedly, the Hollywood program production industry has favored pay TV, while movie-theater owners have fought it. Some insight into the problem can be gained by imagining the passage of a bill that forbids charging people for movies or magazines. The number of each would probably decline if only advertising support were available, and as a result some consumers would be worse off. But other consumers would continue to get what they got before, or something close to it, "for free." While it is difficult to imagine the Congress passing such a law, the historical-technological accident that resulted in "free" TV makes the passage of a pro-pay-TV law or rule equally unlikely.

There have been several pay-TV "experiments" over the past two decades. The best known and documented of these is the RKO-General subscription television system, using Zenith equipment, in Hartford. This system used a UHF station to broadcast programs over the air. Television sets of subscribing households were fitted with "descramblers."[c] Besides an annual hookup charge, viewers were charged directly for each program that they viewed. Other pay-TV systems have been developed with signals sent by cable. The largest of these were in Los Angeles, San Francisco, and Etobicoke, a suburb of Toronto. These systems are well documented elsewhere. (For information on the Hartford and other experiments, see U.S. Congress [564], Blank [76], and Chapter 5 in Noll, Peck and McGowan [394]. See Johnson [274] for a discussion of the costs of descrambling and billing for over-the-air pay TV.)

What is the attraction of pay TV with limited channels? At first glance one suspects that he will merely be paying for programs that he now receives "free." There is certainly some truth in this contention, and we shall explore it with an example. However, the argument in favor of pay TV centers on the fact that the programs offered viewers *may* be very different from those offered under advertiser-supported TV. The analysis in Chapter 3 showed that a price system for programs will give guidance to producers regarding which programs to produce. Both the quantity of resources devoted to television and the relative profitability of different programs will depend on the intensity of viewer preferences as expressed by the amounts viewers are willing to pay. This is very different from advertiser-supported TV, which registers the intensity of advertiser demand for viewers.

---

[c]A descrambler is a device that mechanically accepts money or keeps track of accumulated charges and electronically renders the signal visible to the television user. The signal if sent "scrambled" over the air, so that a descrambler is required for viewing. Obviously if descramblers are standard and widespread, a potentially lucrative market for illegal descramblers will develop. Coping with this problem may be expensive. This is a natural hazard of over-the-air pay TV.

Chapter 3 showed that with pay TV and unlimited channels it is at least theoretically possible that the allocation of resources in television might approach efficiency. Although one cannot prove that the strict conditions for optimal allocation will be met, one suspects from the analysis in Chapter 3 that pay TV would come closer to an efficient allocation of resources than advertiser-supported TV. (Since neither allocation is necessarily efficient, one must resort to "second-best" comparisons—comparisons as to which allocation comes closest to efficiency. Such comparisons are usually very difficult. This is the question to which Minasian addressed himself [364].) If channel capacity is limited, however, then this conclusion becomes more hazardous, for it is highly questionable that pay-TV would approach efficiency. We can speculate, however, that even with limited channels the quantity of resources devoted to television production will be more responsive to viewer desires under subscriber support than under advertiser support.

If the quantity of resources devoted to television and the resulting programs are more responsive to viewer desires under pay-TV, will viewers necessarily be "better off" with pay-TV? This is the question of *consumer surplus* raised in Chapter 3. (Consumer surplus is the difference between the amount a consumer pays for an item and what it is worth to him. For total consumer surplus, the assumption is made that individual consumer surpluses can be added.) It turns out that one cannot say a priori whether consumers on the whole will have a greater consumer surplus under pay-TV than under advertiser-supported TV. The following example will illustrate the hazards that *can* arise in attempting to show that viewers will necessarily be better off with advertiser or subscriber-supported TV.

The first three lines of Table 5-1 are similar to tables in Chapter 3. There are four groups of viewers, each internally homogeneous, with group sizes and program preferences as shown. (For simplicity we have omitted second and

Table 5-1
Pay-TV Example (in dollars, except for lines 1-3)

		1	2	3	4
1.	Group	1	2	3	4
2.	Size	60,000	20,000	15,000	5,000
3.	Preferred program	A	B	C	D
4.	Maximum value each	.05	.10	.25	.50
5.	Aggregate value	3,000	2,000	3,750	2,500
6.	Program cost	100	100	100	100
7.	Advertising price	.01	.01	.01	.01
8.	Pay TV price	.01	.05	.06	.15
9.	Advertising revenue	600	200	150	50
10.	Pay TV revenue	600	1,000	900	750

Source: See text.

lesser choices, although this is highly unrealistic.) Line 4 of the table gives the maximum amount of money each viewer would be willing to pay for his preferred program. Line 5 is simply line 4 multiplied by line 2. Line 6 is the cost of producing the program, and line 7 shows that all viewers are worth 1¢ each to advertisers.

On line 8 we have inserted hypothetical prices that are to be charged for these programs with pay-TV; how these are in fact to be determined relative to the values on line 4 is a serious question. Line 9 is the product of lines 7 and 2, while 10 is the product of lines 8 and 2, giving respectively potential advertising and pay-TV revenue of each program.

Since we are concerned with the pay-TV question in the context of over-the-air TV, let us assume that there are three stations. The resulting program patterns are easily derived by inspection. Under advertiser support, we get two stations broadcasting program A and one broadcasting B, (or all three broadcasting A). Under pay TV, we get the program pattern B, C, D. What has happened to viewer welfare? To find out, we will look at consumer surplus, the difference between what viewers would be willing to pay and what they do pay. The result is contained in Table 5-2. Two things stand out in this table. First, viewers as a group are better off with pay TV, since the total viewer surplus is $5600 rather than the $5000 under advertiser support. Second, 80 percent of the viewers are individually *worse* off under pay TV! All of the viewers in Group 1 are clearly worse off, since they have no program at all. Group 2, which still gets its program, now has to pay for it. (Also, note that broadcast industry profits have gone from $500 to $2350.)

This is rather unsettling. We are asked to make a choice among alternatives. If there were some way to transfer benefit among groups, then pay TV is better, since there is enough surplus to make everyone better off. But such transfers are difficult at best. (Furthermore, it is easy to construct the example so that total consumer surplus is greater under advertiser support.)

We have not taken account of any "savings" to viewers under pay TV due to the absence of advertising costs in the purchase of consumer goods. This effect is

Table 5-2
Consumer Surplus in Pay-TV Example (dollars)

	Advertiser Support	Pay TV
Group 1	3,000	0
Group 2	2,000	1,000
Group 3	0	2,850
Group 4	0	1,750
Total	5,000	5,600

Source: Calculated from Table 5-1.

small,[d] and it is most unlikely that the cost of consumer products would decline significantly if there were no TV advertising; other kinds of advertising would probably takes its place. And finally, it is unlikely that advertising would in fact be absent from pay-TV, unless that were a legal requirement! Audiences generated by pay-TV programs would likely be extremely valuable to advertisers, and program producers would be anxious to sell the audiences, unless it turned out that viewers were willing to pay quite a lot more for commercial-free programs.

The common argument heard against pay TV is that advertiser-supported TV is "free," and that viewers would be worse off if pay TV were allowed. The example has shown that this may indeed be the case for some viewers, while others may gain. Without reliable estimates of viewer demand for programs (the "values" in the example) it is impossible to prove or disprove contentions regarding consumer surplus. A few attempts have been made to derive implicit measures of the consumer surplus that viewers receive from "free" TV. The estimates are subject to wide margins of error and the studies suffer from some methodological problems. (See Nathan [374] and Chapter 2 in Noll, Peck and McGowan [394] with comments by Besen and Mitchell [70].) These studies suggest, however, that the annual surplus in dollars might be quite high.

In the absence of reliable empirical estimates of consumer demand for pay-TV programs, one can only guess as to the overall effects on performance of a move to pay TV with limited channels. We are persuaded, almost entirely on intuitive grounds, that programs would be much "better" in every category. Competition for viewers and the promise of increased revenues per viewer would almost certainly bid up the production cost per viewer. But surely *some* persons would be worse off, for with limited channels, a pay-TV program must displace another existing (presumably advertiser-supported) program. Whether the people who will be worse off are rich or poor, highbrow or lowbrow, avid viewers or light viewers, is very difficult to predict. What *is* easy to predict is continued political opposition to pay TV, and continued severe restrictions on it by the FCC. This opposition and restriction may be due in part to uncertainty as to which kinds of viewers will be hurt by pay TV (an uncertainty that presumably also exists in the minds of viewers contemplating the change). But it is also due to the immense difficulty in any democratic system of making a change that benefits some at the expense of others. If television had only just been invented, we would almost certainly favor pay TV, and oppose restrictions upon it. But we are stuck with "free TV" now, and such a judgment is vastly more difficult, precisely for the same reason that it is politically difficult to threaten broadcasters' profits: some viewers, conceivably most viewers, have a vested interest in the status quo.

---

[d]Total U.S. advertising expenditure is about 3 percent of total consumption expenditure, and television accounts for only 17 percent of the 3 percent, or about one-half of one percent of consumption expenditures.

New Networks

There are a number of ways in which new networks might be created within the existing allocation of spectrum to television, but there has been a serious question whether a new fourth commercial network would be financially viable. Even if it were, one must doubt whether the result would be a dramatic improvement in television performance. (In most of the models of Chapter 3, adding just one new, advertiser-supported channel does not help matters very much.) This section is devoted to a brief review of some research by R.E. Park [430] on the economic feasibility of a fourth network, and to a few somewhat whimsical (because of their political infeasibility) proposals of our own for decreasing concentration of control or increasing diversity of programming within the present three-network system.

The traditional road to a fourth network is the use of existing VHF independent stations, plus some UHF stations to create access to a national audience. This approach suffers from the UHF "handicap" problem discussed earlier in this chapter. Variations on the theme include use of VHF drop-ins, new UHF stations, use of cable-television systems, and so on. Park's analysis takes these and other proposed approaches and evaluates their financial viability, taking account of network competitive behavior in a way that biases the results in favor of the viability of a new network. (Park also ignores the question of the viability of stations affiliated with the fourth network.) Only two proposals seem likely to be viable: divestiture of present network affiliates to create four equally handicapped networks (a political impossibility), and the use of cable television under the assumption that anti-pay-TV rules are relaxed and that cable grows rather rapidly. The assumptions about cable are optimistic at best. Of the other alternatives (Park considers more than seventeen) the most nearly viable of the traditional approaches involves the use of existing independents plus VHF drop-ins plus new UHF stations, under the assumption that the present UHF handicap is considerably reduced through the growth of cable and detent tuning.

Park's results, in sum, are not very comforting for people who think that a fourth network is just over the horizon. It seems likely that cable will have to grow for many years before much of anything along that line becomes feasible, either economically or politically.

If we are stuck, for the moment, with three commercial, advertiser-supported networks, is there anything we can do about *their* structure to improve television performance? There are in fact several possible answers to this question, although we do not think the answers would be very attractive to political decision-makers. The first and most obvious alternative is simply to diversify control of program selection on the networks. This could be done by making the networks (considered as systems integral with their affiliated stations) into common carriers. This would in effect require program producers, or more likely advertisers, to buy program time on the networks at published and conceivably regulated prices, possibly through brokers. The advantages of such a structure, presumably, would be in the First Amendment area, since far more people would have a hand in determining television content and viewpoint. But there are several practical difficulties. First, the relationship between adjacent programs could not be taken account of "internally" by a single firm, resulting in an unknown effect on viewer welfare. Second, there would still be only three channels, and there is therefore no reason to believe diversity of content would be improved. Third, although the government could use the opportunity to get out of content regulation, it would be more likely that the opposite would occur, because of the continued need to regulate the common carriers' use of their monopoly power. Finally, there are certain practical problems associated with the affiliate-network relationship, which might be difficult to resolve. Of these disadvantages, the most serious is probably the program adjacency problem. We will suggest a remedy for this in a moment. But it is important to say here that common carrier television might well be, on balance, a system preferable to the present one. This would almost certainly be true if a real deconcentration of control resulted, if program producers did not become tied to single large advertisers, and if the government did not regulate content.

A somewhat more modest proposal, designed to deal with the program adjacency or audience flow problem, is the "rotating control" approach. In this structure, control of the facilities and stations of each network would change every day of the week, but repeat itself weekly. Thus, there would be in effect a Monday NBC, a Tuesday NBC, a Wednesday NBC, etc., each a separate firm, and similarly with the other networks. This would create twenty-one "networks" per week, and over the course of each week the audience would have access to twenty-one potentially different points of view.

This proposal has most of the advantages and fewer of the infirmities of the previous proposal, and it does not seem wildly impractical. One consequence, of course, would probably be the creation of entirely independent services for television news, since none of our twenty-one networks would want to maintain a full-time news staff. How many of these new news services there might be is problematical. Presumably there would be at least three, but if there were only three we would not have gained much in the First Amendment area. Still, if there were only three news services, there would still be twenty-one competing buyers of news services, and this might serve as some check on their power. Overall, this proposal seems slightly preferable to the common-carrier approach, although it too is likely to be politically infeasible, given the power of the owners of the present system.

Having gone this far, we will present a generalization of the last proposal, which does seem to have some promise of actually increasing program diversity as well as decreasing concentration of control. The rest of this section will be devoted to the details of this proposal, which is called "temporal monopoly." The reader is warned that we will do so in a fairly formalistic way, consistent with the analysis in Chapter 3.

Temporal Monopoly

Chapter 3 showed that under limited channels, we cannot say for certain whether monopoly or competition will yield greater program diversity. Duplication under competition displaces programs for minority audiences; but the monopolist's search for "common-denominator" programming does not ensure the production of preferred programs. In a world with limited channels, can we conceive of a structure under which networks might avoid both of these tendencies—one in which they avoid duplication at a point in time *and* produce programs that are valued highly by viewers? It is possible that there *is* such a structure. In the "temporal monopoly" structure each network is allowed to have a monopoly over all channels during any single time period, but then must turn control of all channels over to another network in the next time period. In this sense, each network is a monopolist at a point in time, but competes over time with other networks for audiences. Thus, the structure is (rather awkwardly, we fear) referred to as "temporal monopoly." (See Figure 5-1 for a diagram of the alternative structures.)

Let us examine one example of some program choices offered viewers under

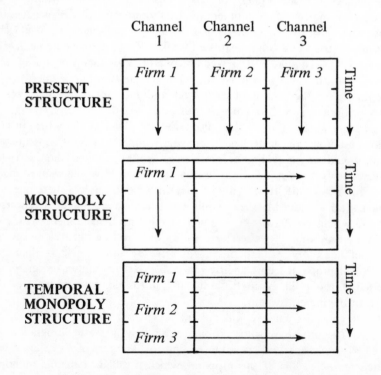

Figure 5-1. Alternative Structures for Television

the structure of temporal monopoly, and compare these to what viewers would receive under monopoly, where one network controls all of the channels all of the time, and competition, where each network controls only one channel all of the time. To do this we need to extend the single-period model of Chapter 3 by adding a time dimension. We also need to add time to viewer preferences. Then we can use the extended model to compare some possible program choices under temporal monopoly, simple monopoly, and competition. The interesting result is that it is at least possible that viewers will prefer temporal monopoly to both monopoly and competition. Depending on viewer behavior and preferences for programs, temporal monopolists might avoid program duplication *and* produce preferred programs, rather than common denominator programs.

Consider how this result comes about. The following assumptions will extend the single-period model of Chapter 3.

Assumptions

1. There is a multiperiod "time span" of fixed length that is divided into "program periods," each of equal length. (For example, think of the time span as an evening three hours in length and each program period as one hour within the evening.)

2. Each viewer or group of viewers has some upper limit to the time watching television in the relevant time span, and this limit is *less* than the time span. (For example, a group will watch no more than two hours out of the three-hour evening.) Certainly some such limit must exist for most viewers.

3. The upper limit that a group will spend watching television in the time span is independent of which programs are actually offered in that time span.

4. Viewers are indifferent as to the program periods in which they allocate their viewing within the time span.

5. Viewers are expected to view with equal probability any options that offer equal satisfaction, whether the options occur at a point in time or over time.

The first assumption is definitional in nature. The second is absolutely crucial to the results. The third, fourth, and fifth may not be necessary, but simplify the model considerably.

Each viewer looks at the total program offerings in the time span, chooses that program in each period which he prefers, and then chooses those periods for viewing which provide choices preferred to those offered in other periods such that his total time allocation is no greater than his upper limit. (He is expected to view with equal probability any options that offer equal satisfaction.) If he finds no option that he prefers to nonviewing, then he turns his set off.

We can allow as many temporal monopolists as there are time periods in the time span. We assume also that there is some positive cost associated with purchasing a program (assumed equal for all programs), but that it costs nothing extra for a broadcaster, once he has purchased the program, to show the program in more than one time period. (For simplicity, costs are treated implicitly in the example.) The following example will illustrate the proposition that temporal monopolists *may* produce over the time span both a diverse program mix (which competitors won't do) and preferred choices (which a monopolist won't do). The preferences below are very similar to those depicted in Chapter 3:

Viewer group	1	2	3
Group size	60	25	15
Maximum viewing	2	2	1
Program preferences:			
First choice	A	B	C
Second choice	E	F	none
Third choice	D	D	none

Take the monopoly case first. The profit-maximizing menu of programs is described by the following table for three program periods and three channels:

	Period	Channel 1	Channel 2	Channel 3
	1	D	C	dark
Monopoly	2	D	C (or dark)	dark
	3	D (or dark)	C (or dark)	dark

Given viewer preferences, the monopolist can capture the entire audience for its maximum viewing limit merely by offering program D for two hours and program C for one. (Since the marginal cost of rebroadcasting is assumed to be zero, we have included the option that he continues to show these programs for three periods. The same option appears in the outcome for competition.) The monopolist attains 185 viewer hours—120 hours from group 1 (60 viewers times 2 hours), 50 hours from group 2 (25 times 2), and 15 hours from group 3. He can get these viewer hours with other programs, but he will have to purchase more than two programs to do so.

Compare the above result to what occurs when the networks are competitively structured as at present:

	Period	Channel 1	Channel 2	Channel 3
	1	A	A	B
Competition	2	A	A	B
	3	A	A	B (or dark)

How this program pattern comes about is slightly harder to see. Suppose one firm finds that it can obtain 170 viewer hours by showing program D for two (or three) hours. Another firm finds that it can get *all* of group 1 for two hours (120 viewer hours) by showing either program A or E. Suppose it shows A. Then the producer of program D finds himself left with group 2 only (50 viewer hours). He will clearly reach a larger audience if he duplicates program A, thereby getting 60 viewer hours (half of 120). Now the third firm enters. It can show (1) program A, receiving 40 viewer hours (a third of 120); (2) program B, F, or D, getting 50 viewer hours (group 2 for 2 hours); or (3) program C, reaching 15 viewer hours. He is indifferent between B, F, and D, but let us assume he chooses B (a choice biased against our results). The final result of competition is then two channels of A and one of B.

Groups 1 and 2 prefer this structure to monopoly, but group 3 is now clearly worse off. The "minority" program never appears. (This is the typical result of competitive duplication under constrained channel capacity in Chapter 3.)

Now consider the program pattern under the structure of "temporal monopoly":

	Period	Channel 1	Channel 2	Channel 3
	1	A	B	C
Temporal monopoly	2	A	B	C
	3	A	B	C

To see how this occurs, suppose there is only one time period and one firm. What will this firm offer viewers? He will show what the monopolist earlier showed—programs D and C. Ignoring the other two time periods for the moment, he will get the whole audience (100 viewers) with only two programs. Now if there are two time periods and two temporal monopolists, what will the second firm do? He will also show D and C! Since group 3 will watch only one hour, however, each of the two firms will split group 3 and expect 92.5 viewers during its hour. Because groups 1 and 2 will watch the full two hours, there is no incentive for either firm to offer these groups a program preferred to D. (To do so, would cost the firms more without increasing viewers.)

Now add a third time period and a third firm. It also will show program C, splitting group 3 equally with the other two firms. But will it produce program D also? No! Because groups 1 and 2 will view only two of the three hours, *all* *three* of the firms must now offer these groups their preferred choices, in order to entice them away from the other two firms. The reader can trace through how groups 1 and 2 end up with their first choices, so long as they refuse to watch the full three periods. (The importance of assumption 2 is now apparent.)

We can now rank these outcomes in terms of which structures are preferred by viewers: Groups 1 and 2 prefer temporal monopoly and competition to monopoly, but are indifferent between temporal monopoly and competition; group 3 prefers temporal monopoly and monopoly to competition, but is indifferent between temporal monopoly and monopoly.

We can rank temporal monopoly as preferable to monopoly in this example since a vote between the two would favor temporal monopoly. We can rank it preferable to competition for the same reason. Everyone is at least as well off with temporal monopoly as with any other structure. So long as viewers will not watch the full time span and common-denominator lesser choices exist the vote is likely to come out in favor of temporal monopoly over monopoly. So long as considerable duplication occurs under competition (due to the skewed distribution of viewer preferences), the vote will tend to come out in favor of temporal monopoly over competition. The reasons are twofold: the temporal monopolists will always avoid duplication within their own time periods; and at the same time, if viewers limit their total viewing, the temporal monopolists must compete for viewers (over time) by offering preferred choices.

Under the conditions of the model, the institutional structure of temporal monopoly provides an economic incentive to producers to lessen both competitive duplication and monopolistic production of common-denominator programming. Such a structure is not all that farfetched. One might give many networks each successive one-hour blocks throughout the day, allowing each network in turn to program all three channels. Or one might allow each network one evening, rotating networks in succession, as discussed earlier. Note that there is no limit to the total number of possible networks, so that this approach could also be used to increase the number of viewpoints, and thus serve First Amendment objectives.

The success of any such proposal depends critically on the nature of viewer preferences. If viewers will always watch the full time span, then the institution of successive monopolists will produce programming no "better" than that of monopoly, and may provide programming inferior to competition.

An immediate objection is that this scheme ignores the effects of economies in networking *over* time—that is, the problem of "audience flow" on a particular channel. The network controlling one time period must take into account the character of the audience built up on each channel over preceding periods, and this interrelationship, if it really is important, may lead to inefficiency. The answer to this objection is merely that the units in which time is allocated must be sufficiently long to optimize the amount of externality in view of the other objectives. For instance, audience flow between successive days is probably insignificant. In any event, program patterns would likely change enough so that "passive" audience behavior would not be a problem.

Another objection is that such a scheme could not work within the existing affiliate structure, since some stations would have an incentive not to clear less popular programs. Thus, the approach requires reformulation of the affiliate structure, or at least appropriate changes in the compensation arrangements. It is not difficult to imagine ways of accomplishing this, but the details are sufficiently boring to warrant omission here.

It must be admitted, however, that an alteration of this magnitude in the structure of television would encounter serious opposition, some of it rightly related to its practical difficulties. Some improvement in viewer welfare can be expected even if the number of networks is not increased; this should maintain or even increase network and station profits. Thus, a modest version of the temporal monopolist proposal might be worth its transitional adjustment costs, and could possibly be found to lack a significant political opposition from the industry. However, it is essential to point out that the "temporal monopoly" feature of this proposal is one step beyond what one might wish *merely on First Amendment grounds*. A minimum policy designed to increase diversity of sources of control over programming, given the relative passivity of affiliates, is to adopt the twenty-one networks proposal outlined earlier in this section. It may be that this is the most technically feasible, practical, and efficacious way in which to create new networks within the current spectrum allocation. It is, however, a proposal that the networks would violently oppose, and for that reason must be of interest mainly to the antitrust authorities and the courts.

Government Policy and Network Dominance

In the 1950s, network television time was sold in half-hour or hour chunks directly to sponsors, who supplied both program material and commercials. The system ended for reasons discussed in Chapter 2. The vast majority of television advertising accounts now involve advance purchase of packages of commercial minutes spread over a dozen or more programs. The consequence of this change, of course, was increased network control of program content, and a reduction in the number of buyers of programming and controllers of content. The FCC became increasingly concerned about this, as did sellers of programs. After a long investigation the FCC in 1970 adopted the prime time access rule, which was discussed in Chapter 4. The intent of the rule is twofold: To reduce network monopsony power in the program market, and to beef up the degree of "localism" in station prime-time program decisions. The prime time access rule is economically ill conceived. Its effect is to induce stations to purchase second-rate syndicated programs, mostly game shows, to replace the lost network programming.

Not long after the FCC instituted the prime time access rule, the Antitrust Division brought the three networks into court, seeking an antitrust decree to prevent the networks from producing any of their own programming. The networks have argued that the logical consequence of the Antitrust Division's suit is to turn them into common carriers—in effect to return to the 1950s. In that era, there was great concern that sponsor-provided program content was too sensitive to the narrow economic interests of its sponsors. It is unlikely that advertisers would wish to reassume the risk of financing whole programs,[e] but there really is no particular reason why the present system could not continue with entities other than the networks supplying (choosing) programs and performing the brokerage function, as we suggested in the last section in discussing common-carrier television. The benefit of this approach could only lie in its contribution to First Amendment objectives, since it seems unlikely that much change in economic performance could result. The structure of incentives to produce the present program patterns would not be significantly altered.

With respect to programming demanded by a national audience, as opposed to a local or regional audience, a solution to the problem of network dominance must rely either on the creation of new channels or on some *time* partition of existing channels. The former policy would rely on VHF drop-ins, regional stations, or cable television. The latter requires structures of the sort discussed in the previous section, which are the only ones that could conceivably be reached through antitrust action. The other structures require regulatory action and Congressional approval, either tacit or statutory. Given its incentives and constraints, it is not surprising that the FCC has not been able to deal efficiently with network dominance, but the antitrust authorities have different incentives and fewer constraints. One might hope for more imaginative approaches from the antitrust quarter.

Conclusion

There are a number of ways in which television performance might be improved by structural and institutional changes in the present system. In most cases, however, the emphasis must be put on "might." Indeed, with the possible exceptions of the temporal-monopoly scheme and UHF deintermixture, none of these proposals is guaranteed to improve matters in terms of our original objectives, or to be enough of an improvement to justify the effort and cost involved in undertaking it. To be sure, some of the proposals have considerable

---

[e]There has however been some increase in "barter" in the syndication market. Barter is the practice of an advertiser supplying a program (with his commercials) to a station free of charge. Some spaces are left in the program for commercial spots to be sold by the station.

hope of improving matters, but one would want to do a great deal of research and experimentation before becoming committed to any of them. And then there is the practical political problem—the violence done to powerful vested economic interests by structural reform. Perhaps the worst evil of the present system, and the most serious mistake of public policy since the passage of the Radio Act of 1927, has been the creation of scarcity rents in broadcast licenses through government allocation of the spectrum. As a result, the broadcast industry has very great economic and political power. This phenomenon, certainly foreign to the intentions of the drafters of our early communications policy, plagues reform at every turn, and places nearly insuperable barriers in the path of efforts to improve the performance of the television industry. Accordingly, one must place a very high value on efforts, however quixotic, to introduce private markets into the spectrum allocation process, or to increase license fees to very high levels, and/or encourage countervailing vested interests, such as those now emerging in the cable-television field.

6

Improving Television Performance with Unlimited Channels

Introduction

In Chapter 5 we were concerned with alternative reforms of television under conditions of channel scarcity, by which we essentially mean a limited supply of VHF-TV allocations. This chapter is concerned with television in the context of "unlimited" channels, where the supply of channels is elastic, and not subject to determination by the FCC, but instead determined by economic forces. The most promising technology of unlimited channels at the moment is cable television, but our discussion would also be applicable to other technologies wherein the supply of channels is responsive to the demand for them. Indeed, a good case can be made for the proposition that a different policy approach to over-the-air broadcasting would never have called forth cable at all. Either UHF deintermixture (see Chapter 5) or a free market in spectrum might have denied to cable its present ability to alleviate the artificial scarcity of channels. Less restrictive FCC rules regarding over-the-air pay TV might then have removed the remaining source of demand for cable, since the technical equipment costs associated with over-the-air pay TV, while high, are probably not as high as the capital costs of cable television. (The latter are on the order of $200 per subscribing household.)

A very great deal has already been written about cable television, and we will not try to duplicate this work (see Smith [510], Sloan Commission [508], White [601]). In this chapter we will first describe briefly the technology and regulatory history of cable, then sketch what seems to us to be the appropriate policy environment, and finally examine some of the implications of that policy and the technology for the economic performance of the future industry, under both pay TV and advertiser support.

FCC Policies Toward Cable

Cable television is simply television delivered by wire instead of over the air. The innovation of sending TV signals by wire occurred about 1950, not because it was cheaper than over-the-air transmission (which it still is not), but because some areas could not receive over-the-air transmission very well, or could not obtain FCC licences. Its original purpose was simply to enhance clarity of reception of already existing TV signals, and this is still one of cable's principal selling points. Cable is not less expensive than additional over-the-air broadcasts, but FCC spectrum allocation policies have prevented the installation of addi-

141

tional broadcast capacity. For this reason people who believe that an increase in the number of channels of communication is important (see Chapter 3) have been very interested in cable.

There are two reasons why cable is more important than its early role as an adjunct to broadcast television would seem to indicate. The first is that the number of channels that can be carried on a cable is very large (new systems have twenty or thirty channels), and is not limited by FCC spectrum allocation policies. The second reason is that the technology of cable lends itself to two-way communication, in contrast to the one-way communication of a standard TV broadcast. The economic importance of two-way communication lies in its potential for the exercise of choice by subscribers among programs, and the possibility of monitoring that choice for billing purposes. Viewer program choices can, with cable, be monitored and billed much like long-distance phone calls. In a word, pay television is more economical with cable technology than with over-the-air technology, and so are many other services requiring two-way communication. Both an increase in the number of channels and a decrease in the transactions cost of pay TV greatly increase the potential for a more responsive television industry.

The regulatory history of cable exemplifies the behavioral pattern of regulatory agencies faced with a technological or economic threat to their client industries. (For a fascinating parallel, see the description of the British experience with radio broadcasting by wire in Coase [125], Chapter 4. Railroads and trucking provide an earlier example.) Throughout the 1950s, the FCC denied that it had any regulatory jurisdiction over cable. But toward the end of that decade, cable systems began to realize that the demand for their service could be increased if they supplied additional TV signals, and to obtain these signals they "imported" stations from "distant" cities. Cable operators chose distant signal importation as a means of increasing demand because it was the cheapest means of providing additional programming. Additional programming is necessary if cable is to attract subscribers in areas where over-the-air TV reception is already good. Under a Supreme Court interpretation [209] of the 1909 copyright act, cable operators were not required to pay royalties to the stations originating the signals. Accordingly, importation was cheaper than simply purchasing program materials directly. But the effect of distant signal importation was to increase competition for viewers in each broadcast market, since local stations had to compete for viewers who faced a greater number of choices. The effect was the same, given the degree to which cable had penetrated the market, as the creation of new TV stations in the market. With the rapid growth of cable (0.15 million subscribers in 1955, 0.65 in 1960, 1.28 in 1965, 4.5 in 1970, and 7.0 million in 1974), this threatened to eventually reduce the profitability of virtually every VHF-TV station in the nation. The reason, of course, is that an increased number of viewing choices "fragments" the local audience, reducing advertising revenues for local TV stations. This does not affect the networks much, and may considerably add to the profits of independent VHF stations in large cities, which are the ones that tend to get exported to other areas by cable operators. The effect on most UHF stations is to improve reception and to reduce the difficulty of tuning for viewers, and thus to increase UHF audiences. But VHF network affiliates have little to gain from cable, and it is this group that is most powerful politically and economically. Accordingly, broadcasters began a campaign of active opposition to cable, and especially to distant signal importation.

The response of the FCC was, first, to assert regulatory jurisdiction over cable (eventually upheld by a closely divided Supreme Court in *Midwest Video* [361]), and second, to freeze the growth of cable from 1968 to 1972 by banning distant-signal importation in the hundred largest TV markets. The first step was justified by the doctrine that regulation of cable was "ancillary" to television regulation. The second move was frankly protectionist, justified by an assumed threat by cable to the FCC's UHF expansion policy. It turned out upon analysis (Park [423]) that cable helped rather than hurt UHF stations, by improving their reception, except in those areas where the FCC had *not* forbidden signal importation; that is, in the smaller markets. (For a history of cable regulation to 1972, see Barnett [42]. Besen [68] provides an analysis of the famous cable "compromise" of 1971.) It is difficult to avoid the conclusion that the FCC acted to protect the wealthiest and most powerful stations against increased competition, and in doing so denied millions of viewers in larger markets a greater range of choice among broadcast signals.

During the period of the freeze, cable systems began to organize their own political lobby, and eventually a compromise was reached that allowed some importation of distant signals. This compromise was embodied in a massive set of FCC rules for cable, promulgated in 1972. (This set of FCC rules is reprinted as an appendix to the Cabinet Committee Report [99].) In addition to full regulatory jurisdiction, the FCC embarked on a program of requiring public-service obligations from cable systems, including the donation of free channels to civic purposes. This "taxation by regulation" (Posner [449]) has always been the quid pro quo for regulatory protectionism, and had been an important part of broadcast regulation since the *Carroll* case (see Chapter 1).

The FCC's 1972 cable decision left three major issues undecided. The first was the question of federal regulation of cable program content, and the closely related issue of the degree of the cable-system owner's control of access and content. The second was the issue of pay television on the cable. And finally there was the question of cable's copyright liability. These issues were addressed in the President's Cabinet Committee Report on Cable Television [99], and indeed, these are the crucial issues for the future of television. We will examine them in depth in the next section.

The principal question to ask about the FCC's behavior with respect to cable television is whether it is in any way justified by its own public-interest considerations. Cable is a technology of communications that is nothing more than a different means of delivering TV signals, and has the potential of increasing the number of channels of communication. Having more channels available can hardly make viewers worse off, at least in the context of the model developed in Chapter 3. And from the discussion in Chapter 2, we know that the supply of programming to fill the new channels is elastic. All that is wanting is information about the demand for cable by advertisers and subscribers.

What public interest was served by the FCC's "freeze" on cable growth from 1968 to 1972, and the current set of only slightly less stringent rules? There are several answers to this question: (1) Under the *Fortnightly* [209] decision, cable systems in some sense competed "unfairly" with broadcasters by using programming for which no copyright payment was made. (2) Any increase in competition for existing TV stations would reduce their profits, and hence their ability in the eyes of the FCC to do public-service programming. (3) A significant increase in competition facing broadcast stations could drive some of them into bankruptcy, leaving some viewers (those who were not cable subscribers) without TV service, or with fewer choices. (4) As a result of (3), some viewers might in effect be forced to pay directly for services they previously received free of charge.

In order to suppose that the effect of cable television is injury to the public interest, one must believe that the economic process here, in which each individual consumer freely chooses whether or not to subscribe to cable service, has the cumulative effect of leaving consumers as a whole worse off, or of leaving some large body of consumers worse off. It is true that *some* consumers will be worse off as a result of cable—particularly consumers who place no value on additional TV program choices and consumers who would never be offered cable because of their uneconomic physical locations. At least some people can be hurt if some marginal TV stations really are driven off the air. Although this argument usually runs in terms of rural areas, it is interesting to note that it is precisely in such areas (Wyoming and Vermont, for instance) that cable penetration is highest. This is due to the scarcity of local over-the-air signals in such areas under the FCC's spectrum allocation scheme.

It does not necessarily follow that because some people are hurt by cable it is in the public interest to freeze cable growth, or to regulate its growth. After all, this may be helping the few at the expense of the many. There are several alternatives. One is to do nothing, which is generally the policy followed in unregulated industries when technological or economic change alters industry structure.[a] Another is to compensate the consumers who are harmed, for instance through government subsidies. But the traditional regulatory approach is to preserve the technologically obsolete industry artificially ("uneconomically"), by regulatory restrictions on the ability of the new technology to

---

[a]The growth of the automobile trade drove some blacksmiths out of business. Should auto growth have been "frozen" in order to protect consumers who still owned horses from the consequences of this trend? The Blacksmith Control Commission might have answered Yes.

compete. This is the pattern regulators have followed, for instance, in railroads and telegraph service. This approach can have enormous costs to society, and one suspects that it is usually motivated more by a desire to protect the profits of a group of businessmen (the owners of the obsolete technology) than by a desire to prevent harm to some group of consumers. One of the tasks of economic analysis in such cases is to estimate the costs of a protectionist policy. (See Park's paper in Park [428].) (The benefits will be emphasized by those who are being protected.) We do not have sufficient data to estimate here the consumer welfare lost to households who have been and are being denied access to additional TV program choices as a result of the FCC's regulations. We are confident, however, that the welfare loss is considerable, and that it is considerably greater than the sum of profits saved by broadcasters and welfare saved by those consumers who would be disadvantaged by cable.

The information required to make such measures is discussed in Chapter 3. Noll, Peck, and McGowan [394] have made some calculations along these lines, but see Besen and Mitchell's criticism [70]. To give the reader some idea of what is involved, suppose the average household would be willing to pay up to $10 per month above cost for three additional TV signals which cable could provide. Then if the effect of the FCC's freeze on cable is to deny these signals to ten million subscribers, the "welfare loss" becomes $1.2 billion per year. Although this number is merely an illustration, it is probably about the right order of magnitude—far in excess of the broadcaster profits that were "protected."

The epitome of the Commission's approach to cable is captured in paragraph 76.251, subparagraph (8) of its *Rules and Regulations* (the so-called "N+1" rule):

Whenever all the channels described in subparagraphs (4) through (7) of this paragraph are in use during 80 percent of the weekdays (Monday-Friday) for 80 percent of the time during any consecutive 3-hour period for 6 consecutive weeks, such system shall have six months in which to make a new channel available for any or all of the above-described purposes.

This is supposed to guarantee adequate channel capacity. The next paragraph goes on to order that the channels in question be made available free of charge! This kind of regulation is not merely silly, it exemplifies the FCC's inability to think of cable in terms of its own possibilities and potential, but instead to think of it as a sort of telephone company which broadcasts TV signals, categories the Commission is used to dealing with.

The most important indictment of the FCC's regulation of cable, however, has been its extreme myopia. It has seen cable successively as an insignificant nuisance, a vague threat to its cherished UHF-TV plans, a major threat to TV station profitability, poor people, and others, and an opportunity to mandate some of its favorite public-service objectives, such as educational programming.

It has never seen cable as what it really is—a chance to expand viewer choice, a chance to increase freedom of expression, and a chance to reduce the intrusion of government into the marketplace of ideas. This vision was left to the Cabinet Committee on Cable Communications.

The Whitehead Report

In 1971 President Nixon appointed a Cabinet Committee on Cable Communications. This committee, whose chairman, Clay T. Whitehead, was Director of the Office of Telecommunications Policy, published its *Report to the President* in January 1974.[b]

The approach taken in the Whitehead Report had many of the virtues lacking in the FCC's approach. The Committee recommended that freedom of expression in cable communications be maximized. This is to be accomplished by not allowing the cable operator (a local monopolist)[c] to control program content on his channels, but instead to lease capacity to others in the manner of a common carrier. Given the increase in competition in program and opinion supply which this portends, there remains no rationale for government regulation or licensing of program content, and the Committee recommended its eventual abolition. The third major recommendation of the report was the eventual loosening of most of the rules against pay television, the rationale being that consumers should not be denied the freedom to purchase whatever programming they want. This is a key recommendation, since it seems highly unlikely that cable will offer much increase in diversity or even grow to significant size under advertising support. Pay TV is an essential source of revenue. All of these recommendations are to take effect when cable becomes a "mature" industry, defined as that point when 50 percent of the nation's homes are wired. Meanwhile, a set of "transition policies," essentially the present FCC rules, would be in effect.

These are the highlights of the report. There are other recommendations, some of which have the effect of more or less qualifying the purity of the basic recommendations. These are "political" compromises, designed to increase the chances that the report will eventually be acted upon by Congress, since the major recommendations should be laws, not FCC regulations. The political compromises in the Whitehead Report (of which the "transition period" and its policies may be the most fatal) are another unfortunate reflection of the

---

[b]Mr. Whitehead was also instrumental in reaching a "compromise" on the copyright and distant signal issues which led to the 1972 FCC rules criticized above and in Besen [68].

[c]In a local area a cable-television system has many of the characteristics of a "natural monopoly." That is, it is unlikely that two or more systems could compete indefinitely on the same streets, and it would probably be inefficient to do so. In this respect, cable resembles water, electricity, and gas companies. The geographical extent of the natural monopoly is probably limited, and a reasonably large city might have two or three systems serving different neighborhoods.

political power in Washington of broadcasters and even cable operators. If the interests of viewers were represented with a force equally proportionate to their stake in the matter, such compromises would be unthinkable. As it is, the legislation required to implement the report in its present form is far from imminent. Still, the Whitehead Report stands as one of the more far-sighted government documents on this or any other regulated industry.

The economic reasoning behind the recommendations in the Whitehead Report is straightforward. The local cable-television system, if it leases channels in the manner of a common carrier, will be incapable of extending its "natural" monopoly of transmission backward into an "unnatural" control of program selection or production. Instead, there can be competing suppliers of programming, each using the cable system in the way a magazine or book publisher uses the postal service. The analysis in Chapter 2 tells us that competition in the production of programs is likely to continue. Then the only place there could be any concentration of control of content is in the function that corresponds to networking in present-day television or distribution in the motion-picture trade. While the evidence on this point is less conclusive, there does not seem to be any reason to expect significant concentration of economic power in this function (see Chapter 2). Entry will be enhanced by the expansive capacity of cable and the principle of common-carrier access. Expansion of the number of competing channels is at least consistent with better performance in satisfying consumer preferences, as is pay TV (see Chapter 3).

With pay television and common-carrier access, cable systems will be very much like magazines and the postal service. The cable will serve as a delivery conduit for all sorts of diverse programming, some highly specialized, some of mass appeal. As with magazines and books, there would be only the most minimal content regulation by the state, and the First Amendment would apply with its original force. Neither the cable operator nor anyone else would have significant monopoly power in the marketplace of ideas. This potential, while not impossible in theory for over-the-air television, has been denied by the history of broadcast regulation, and cable provides the opportunity to achieve it in the electronic media.

The problem of how to regulate the transmission rates of the cable operator is a difficult one. The Whitehead Report suggests that this should be avoided as long as possible. There are two reasons for this. The first is that for a long time cable will not have very much monopoly power, because of continued competition with TV stations and other media. The second is that our experience in this country with rate-of-return regulation of public utilities is not a happy one. From the point of view of economic efficiency it is by no means clear that public-utility regulation is always preferable to unfettered monopoly. This is so partly because regulation seems to introduce distortions in the incentives facing regulated firms (Bailey [29], Kahn [289]), and partly because regulators end up retarding technological innovations that threaten the position of their client industries. Whatever is done with regulation of the prices charged by cable operators for transmission service, it is both unnecessary and harmful to regulate the prices charged viewers for program content (pay-TV prices). The effects of such regulation are discussed in Chapter 3.

The long-term recommendations of the Whitehead Report are by any reasonable standard extremely libertarian and laissez-faire, and reflect an understanding of the economics of television markets. The policies recommended are consistent both with economic efficiency and First Amendment objectives.

Before continuing with a discussion of advertising and pay TV on cable, we must raise one question about the preceding policy conclusion and how it might be achieved: If common-carrier-access obligations for cable are desirable at that point when cable obtains a local monopoly of transmission, is it desirable to impose these obligations at an earlier stage in the development of cable? The problem is that if common-carrier status when it comes reduces the profits of the monopoly cable operator, it may be politically infeasible to impose such obligations on a mature industry. We have too many examples of the influence of regulated industries on their regulators to be naïve about this process, especially in broadcasting. On the other hand, early imposition of common-carrier obligations could have the effect of retarding cable growth. The reason for this perverse possibility is as follows. A person renting a channel from a cable operator receives income from the use of that channel (either advertising revenue or pay-TV revenue). But in making use of the channel, the programmer also adds to the value of the cable system, and thus causes additional people to subscribe. This increases revenue to the cable operator, both from additional subscriber rents and from increased channel-leasing value. The independent programmer has no incentive to take this effect into account in setting his own prices and in making programming decisions. If the cable owner were in control of programming decisions, he would "internalize" this external effect. If he does not have this control, the independent programmer has a smaller incentive to engage in the programming business than does a cable operator.

The effect described in the preceding paragraph is of absolutely no moment so long as the cable operator can adjust the price at which he rents capacity to programmers in such a way as to reflect the benefits to him of additional services on his system, and so long as the price that does take this effect into account is positive. A problem arises, however, when the optimal lease price is negative— that is, when the cable operator, in order to maximize profits, would like to *pay others* to supply programming. (This is not dissimilar to the start-up losses often associated with a new business.) Since paying others is equivalent to choosing his own programming,[d] a negative price is inconsistent with the common-carrier

---

[d]At least, it is equivalent so long as there exists more than one profit-maximizing menu of program content. Since the relevant issue here is "political slant" or ideological bias, which may be very subtle, it seems likely that more than one profit maximizing choice does exist.

principle. We do not know whether the optimal price is negative, but we do know it is more likely to be negative in the early years of cable growth, and is certainly not going to be negative when all or nearly all of the households in a service area have become subscribers to the basic system. One can imagine *regulations* to deal with this problem, but that throws the baby out with the bath. One can also imagine solving the problem by setting channel lease rates in proportion to audience size, but that would lead inevitably to highly complex rate schedules and charges of discriminatory pricing; these in turn would lead to more detailed regulation.

This final point has perhaps taken more space than it deserves, but it does serve (in a slightly different form) as the principal objection to common-carrier status by cable operators. On the other hand, the common stocks of cable television firms generally rose in price about the time the report was released, albeit temporarily.

Sources of Revenue for Cable

Most cable subscribers pay about six dollars per month for the service, plus an installation charge. This amount seems sufficient to pay for the costs of the cable system itself, plus the very cheap programming provided by over-the-air and imported signals, for which no copyright payment is at present made. But this programming does not fill very many channels, compared to cable's potential, and is almost certainly insufficiently attractive to produce a "wired nation."

There are two additional sources of revenue that cable can tap in order to fill its vacant channels with the programming it needs to attract new subscribers. The first is advertising. The second is to charge viewers directly (pay TV) an amount sufficient to pay for the program, but not so great that the price exceeds the program's value to the viewer.

There are a number of reasons why advertising alone is almost certainly not going to be a sufficient source of revenue to make cable into a significant medium. We shall explore these reasons before turning to a discussion of paying by the program.

As noted earlier, networks and television stations essentially perform a brokerage function. They acquire audiences by broadcasting free shows. They then sell commercial time to advertisers who want access to those audiences. Thus, network and station demand for programming is a derived demand. The interaction of advertising demand, the ability of programming to generate audiences, and the supply of programming jointly determine the actual programming broadcast. The same would be true for cable.

It is unlikely that cable-system operators or channel lessees will find the use of the existing syndication market as a direct source of programming profitable in the near future. (For an example of how an advertiser-supported cable channel might operate, see the story of UHF-TV station WGNO in *Variety*, February 6, 1974, p. 29.)

Cable operators are now so small that syndicated material would be quite costly to them. Under present FCC rules and with franchising carried out on a town-by-town basis, a system of 10,000 homes is large. For a system of that size the acquisition cost of syndicated programming per half-hour would be at least $32 to $42 (see Table 2-14 in the appendix to Chapter 2), or in this case $3.20 to $4.20 per thousand subscribers. However, for homes *delivered* the cost will be even higher, because many viewers will continue to watch network affiliates and local independents. Even if the show could gain one-fifth of the potential audience, the cost per home delivered per half-hour would be 1.6¢ to 2.2¢. The experience of independent television stations suggests that 10 percent is a much more realistic upper bound; this gives a delivered cost of 3.2¢ to 4.4¢ or higher per home delivered, compared to 0.8¢ per half-hour for network prime-time programming. (See the appendix to Chapter 2.) These costs are in excess of likely revenues from national advertisers. Consequently, programs with quality levels similar to off-network fare are probably too expensive at present for cable systems, unless the local advertising market can be tapped.

As for local advertising revenue, any increase in cable programming will tend to fragment the audiences into small groups with more select local characteristics. This will give cable television access to the geographically specialized audiences that have traditionally been the targets of local advertisers through newspapers and throwaways. Such access should raise the revenue per viewer earned by cable operators. The advertising increase may mitigate the program cost disadvantages of the size of cable operators. Local advertising prices per thousand "exposures" are much higher than national advertising rates.

Territorial exclusivity will cause further problems for cable operators who could otherwise afford syndicated material (see Park [424]). At the moment, syndication contracts give the leaseholder exclusive rights to a program in his market area, and that leaseholder is typically a TV station. (Suburban newspapers have similar problems in obtaining syndicated feature material licensed to big-city dailies under territorial exclusivity.) Even if an area were saturated with cable, a syndicator would have to sell a show to many cable systems in order to earn revenues equaling a lease to a single station, resulting in lower profits because of increased transactions costs. For both of these reasons, cable operators may be left with the dregs of the syndication market.

One hope for avoiding these two problems is the creation of cable networks. Such networks would have affiliates (channel lessees) similar to TV network affiliates. The reasons that a cable-system operator or lessee might affiliate include all of the reasons that local television stations find it profitable to affiliate with networks.

A cable network would still face disadvantages. It would have to affiliate with nearly all of the many cable systems in any area in order to arrive at audiences similar to those of a single TV station, leading to higher transmission and transaction costs. Even satellite interconnection would not significantly alter this picture. Thus, a cable network might well be at a competitive cost disadvantage vis-à-vis the existing TV networks, quite aside from the fact that for a long time not all TV homes will subscribe to cable. (Park's analysis [430] discussed in Chapter 5 ranks advertiser-supported cable networks among the least viable ways to create a fourth network.)

We are in the end highly skeptical that the introduction of widespread cable usage will lead to large increases in network quality programming if the FCC forces cable operators to rely solely on advertiser support, or vice versa. The existence of town-by-town franchising prevents the cable operators from exploiting economies of scale in audiences inherent in the syndication market. This seems unlikely to be offset any time soon by increased access to local advertising markets or the prospects for a fourth advertiser-supported network.

If advertising revenue is unlikely to be a viable source of support for cable expansion, what about pay TV? We do know, both from intuition and from the prices paid for cable service, that viewers value programs more than advertisers value viewers. What are the implications of removing the present FCC restrictions on cable pay TV? (The present restrictions forbid charges for most sports programming, many movies, and all "series" programs; they also forbid the use of advertising in pay-programs.)

There are two questions to ask about pay TV with unlimited channels. The first is whether this would support cable expansion, and the second concerns the economic efficiency of such a system. The first can be dealt with quickly: it is almost impossible to believe that direct viewer payment would not result in a vast expansion of demand for cable programming. There is, admittedly, only indirect empirical evidence on this point, but that evidence is quite convincing. (The evidence is from pay-TV experiments of the sort described in Chapter 5. The results have to be "scaled up" to national levels because of the economies of scale in producing programs for larger audiences. See Noll, Peck and McGowan [394].) The question of economic efficiency is deeper and, to us, at least, more interesting.

The structure of competitive, multichannel television systems in the absence of restrictions on pay TV would probably closely resemble our present magazine and movie industries. That is, there would be a wide range of program types, some quite specialized, some quite "popular," with varying degrees of income from advertising and subscription revenues. As shown in Chapter 3, to the extent that viewers are able to vote with dollars, and to express the *intensity* of their preferences for particular programs, programs would more nearly reflect viewer desires than those under advertiser support. In particular, programs that are valued very highly by a comparatively small audience may become profitable. It does seem very likely that multichannel pay-cable will make most consumers better off than limited-channel advertiser-supported TV. The hypothesis is put forth on pp. 78-80 that as product differentiation increases in the monopolistically competitive production of public goods (such as programming), the effect is to gradually eliminate inefficiencies due to the use of price as an exclusion mechanism. That is, the tastes of customers who purchase individual products are increasingly homogeneous, and the price charged to each group will tend less and less to exclude consumers whose valuation of the good is positive but less than the price. In a sense, this is equivalent to price discrimination through product differentiation. Perfect price discrimination has long been known to be consistent with efficient private production of public goods.

Increasing specialization need not take the form of increasingly recondite content. It can also take the form of increasingly "tailor-made" content which, although covering a wide variety of subjects, is the "right" mix for a relatively small audience.

Supposing that the cable industry is organized along the lines of the Whitehead Report, each program (or more broadly, message) will be differentiated by content and by "quality" and will be protected by copyright. We take magazine, book, and movie production (creation, not transmission) as evidence supplementary to that in Chapter 2 that the efficient firm size in *creating* these messages is quite small, that entry costs are low, and that numbers will be large. Metering, billing, copyright, and other devices are available to deal with the exclusion and appropriability problems under cable technology.

But the analogy suggests that the very structure of the cable industry proposed in the Whitehead Report may supply a close approach to efficiency. By ensuring sufficiently large numbers of competitors each specializing extensively, one can perhaps come close to efficient production of programs in a way that preserves both consumer sovereignty and producer incentive. Whether the ultimate constellation of products produced is the "right" one is a deeper and more difficult question.[e]

Cable and the Future

Cable is not going to revolutionize the communication media overnight. On the other hand, it is clearly going to be extremely important in the future. With such inventions as xerography and computer typesetting, it seems clear that the technologies of the present media are converging on electronic delivery. We are at the beginning of the end of the Gutenberg revolution. At the same time the demands of modern society for communication, both mass and private, seem to grow very rapidly indeed. (Such demand is almost certainly highly income

[e]Some preliminary work by Professor A. Michael Spence suggests that there will still be a tendency to exclude products with low price elasticities of demand, relative to the optimum. But this problem is worse under advertiser support.

elastic. In addition, because of the public-good aspect, mass communication demand grows simply with population.) Advertising demand is not going to decline. Subscription television opens up a whole new source of revenue.

While all these things cause pressure for better media performance, over-the-air television has come to seem a dead end. The present structure of television and radio spectrum regulation is far too inflexible to adjust to these growing demands. It may also be true that the basic technology of over-the-air broadcasting is inferior in the end to wired delivery with its two-way capability, and its capacity for selective access to information-storage devices by individuals, e.g., electronic program libraries and data banks, from which viewers can call up material on demand for display on their TV sets. It does not seem excessively rash to predict the eventual emergence of the most ambitious of the blue-sky promises of the cable enthusiasts: electronic voting, electronic libraries, electronic education. These things are all terribly expensive now, but may well become viable when built as marginal increments to a system whose original viability is due to more prosaic stuff, such as pay-TV sports and movies. But we should also, no doubt, expect electronic demagogues, electronic shoplifting, electronic hate letters, and electronic snooping. The cable and its technological successors do seem likely to be the communication highways of the future, at least so long as "meddling ad-hocery" is absent from our government's policies in this area.

But the first fruits that we are likely to see of this "revolution" will be unspeakably banal: channel after channel of movies, rerun endlessly; programming not much higher in its aesthetic standards than most pulp paperbacks. Giving sovereignty to the consumer in any market has sometimes disappointing results for those with proudly uncommon tastes. But as these mass tastes are satisfied, eventually there will come the less popular programming and services that those who write about cable hope to see. If they can't wait, they should turn to the discussion of public television in the next chapter. Meanwhile we will go on to discuss some broader implications of the growth of cable.

What are the social and cultural implications of the cable revolution? It is very hard to foresee much of this. Probably communication will become an even better substitute for transportation of people and things. As the cost of direct access by consumers to original sources of information falls, perhaps we shall see an increase in the quality and sophistication of such editorial services as newspapers and journals. The same effect may result in increasing specialization of skills and knowledge. Will access to a greater variety of programming material on the "tube" increase passivity and reduce social and family interaction? Possibly. But cable is *two*-way; in this respect at least it is fundamentally different from the "tube." The implication of two-way cable may be a *decrease* in passivity. At least that outcome will be possible; it is not with present-day television.

Cable will undoubtedly cause many new social problems and political issues to arise, just as it "solves" old ones. One should not rely overmuch on technology to solve social and cultural problems. The important point about cable is that it presents an opportunity to alter certain institutional deficiencies in our present system, deficiencies that if they had never existed might never have called forth cable. In every important sense, these deficiencies are due to social, political, and economic forces, not technological constraints. The task of setting things right is an entirely human endeavor, for which the march of technology provides only a convenient opportunity.

Public Television

Overview

Public television has been this country's answer to complaints about the performance of the commercial advertiser-supported system. Most European countries place great emphasis on the use of government-run or -supported systems of broadcasting. Our own experience with this approach is much more recent, and reflects an earlier commitment to the use of private enterprise that is almost unique in the world. Still, many people have admired the performance of such systems as the BBC.

This chapter is concerned with the following set of questions: (1) What ought to be the goals or objectives of public television in the United States? (2) Given these objectives, what is the best institutional structure for decision-making (program choice) within the public broadcasting system? (3) How should we go about deciding how much money to spend on public television?

Before we can address these issues, it will be necessary to describe briefly the history of educational and public television, and to recite the nature of its recent political troubles. We end the chapter with some discussion of the future prospects for public television.

Historical Background

When the FCC set out its table of spectrum allocation for television service in 1952, it reserved a large number of channels for "educational" use (Noll, Peck, and McGowan [394]). These channels were supposed to be used by educational institutions as a supplement to the traditional instructional media. (Many of these channels are valuable VHF assignments in large cities, channels that could otherwise be devoted to commercial broadcasting.) There was great hope that this would revolutionize American education, and many people expected that this would be the principal contribution of television to society. The result did not justify this hope. Educational institutions either did not see much benefit for themselves from using the new medium, or had no funds to make use of it. The Educational Broadcasting Facilities Act of 1962 channeled funds to these institutions for equipment to utilize their generous spectrum allocations, but money for programming was not available from federal sources. The result was, as one might have predicted, disappointing at best, and many of the channels never were activated, or were highly ineffective as instructional tools.

In 1967 the Carnegie Commission on Public Television [102] recommended, and the federal government accepted, a new concept: public television. Public television was to be a medium of excellence in programming; instructional programs would be a distinct subset of the content of the new medium. Emphasis was placed on culture, "quality entertainment," public affairs, and similar programming. In the same year, Congress created the Corporation for Public Broadcasting (CPB), an organization meant to channel federal funds to local public-TV stations for programming, to implement this new vision, and to guide its development. (The board of directors of the CPB is appointed by the President, with the advice and consent of the Senate.) The CPB created what is in effect a television network, the Public Broadcasting Service (PBS), to distribute programs to the 250-odd public-television stations.

The reasons for Congress's establishment of the Corporation for Public Broadcasting are, as in most public decisions, complex. One motivation certainly was a widespread intellectual dissatisfaction with commercial programming, epitomized by Newton Minow's "vast wasteland [365]." This motivation has two distinct levels. First, there existed a literate, vocal, and influential group of people who were not themselves well satisfied by the performance of commercial television. This "elitist"[a] group wanted more culture, more public affairs, more "serious" TV programs available for their own viewing. Second, an overlapping group of television critics saw commercial television's menu of "banal" programming as harmful to the public at large; they wished to have a means to present "uplifting" program choices to other people—the people who do not have access to the culture of the big cities or the universities. The BBC model was much admired. Another motivation may have been the desire to subsidize that group of artists whose work would presumably be viewed on public television, as a gesture of Congressional patronage, not unrelated to the creation of the National Endowments for the Arts and Humanities.[b] The broadcasting industry generally welcomed the idea, perhaps because it would reduce some of the pressure on itself to produce unprofitable public-interest programming.

There are now (1974) about two-hundred-fifty local public television stations, and these are overwhelmingly licensed to state or local school systems or universities. Only about sixty are "community" stations—but this type of station dominates most policy debate, and indeed, most actual decision-making within the public-broadcasting community.

Sources of funding for public television are numerous. The federal govern-

---

[a]We shall use this word extensively in this chapter simply because it seems to us the most appropriate to our point. Unfortunately, since former Vice President Agnew, the word has acquired a nasty reputation. We wish to emphasize that this connotation is not intended; we have nothing against elitists.

[b]The National Endowments are designed to funnel federal subsidies to the arts and humanities, including the performing arts. Started on a modest scale in the 1960s, these funds were increased substantially during the Nixon administration—budget authority in fiscal year 1973 was about $90 million, six times the 1969 level.

ment supplied about 21 percent of all funds in fiscal 1971, partly through a $23 million grant to CPB, partly through grants totaling $10 million directly to stations for the purchase of equipment under the Educational Broadcasting Facilities Act, and partly by direct funding of certain programs, such as *Sesame Street*. State and local governments provided nearly half of all public-television income, or $75 million, in fiscal 1971. The remaining money came from private foundations and businesses (15 percent) and individual contributions (8 percent). Since 1971, the contribution of the federal government has substantially increased in terms of Congressional *authorizations*, but Presidential vetoes (all but one unrelated to issues of public broadcasting itself) have frozen the actual appropriations to a level of $35 million for CPB.

The Corporation for Public Broadcasting was a major monument of the Kennedy-Johnson administration. Not surprisingly, it came under fire almost immediately when the Nixon administration took office. The issue that set off the controversy was long-range financing. CPB wanted an end to the annual appropriations process, which it felt provided insufficient insulation from political influence. At the same time, CPB wanted a large increase in the amount of federal money flowing into programming. The Nixon administration perceived the programs, personnel, and policies of the public-broadcasting establishment as biased at least against a conservative view of the world, if not against the administration itself. The resulting conflict nearly destroyed public broadcasting.

The administration's substantive criticisms of public broadcasting were (1) that it had created a national network with centralized program decisions (PBS), against the express intent of Congress and the Carnegie Commission, both of which had emphasized local station sovereignty; (2) that it was attempting to emulate the commercial networks by choosing programs on the basis of popularity, by hiring away commercial-network personalities, and by imitating the format of commercial television, including obtrusive announcements between programs; and (3) that it improperly engaged in politically sensitive public affairs programs that were constitutionally inappropriate uses of federal money, at least in a centralized system.

In an attempt to resolve these conflicts, the Corporation and the administration negotiated on the issue of "decentralized decision-making" within the system. In return for long-term funding and an increase in funding, the corporation was to pass on a large share of these funds directly to local stations, which in turn could, *if they chose*, purchase national (PBS network) programming. Subsequently the administration broke off negotiations, and in a dramatic move the President in June 1972 vetoed the fiscal year 1973 budget authorization bill for public broadcasting. This precipitated the resignations of top CPB officials, who were promptly replaced with Nixon appointees. Two years of uncertainty, conflict, and confusion followed, after which a compromise appeared to have been reached on long-term funding with a formula for a "flow-through" of funds to local stations.

At this writing, the administration and the public broadcasting community seem to have agreed on the following formula: (1) There will be five-year funding by means of five-year Congressional authorizations and appropriations. (2) The level of federal funding will be tied to private donations on a matching basis. (3) Between 40 and 50 percent of the federal funds will be channeled directly to local stations (press release, Office of Telecommunications Policy, July 16, 1974). The *level* of funding, however, has not been agreed upon.

The ideological (and essentially partisan) conflicts that set off the controversy over public broadcasting should not be allowed to obscure the substantive issues that still plague this institution. It is these issues that we will try to assess in this chapter. However, the ideological conflict should be remembered as an illustration of why it is dangerous to have the hand of government involved in the machinery of the media. There are even more ominous illustrations to be found in the European experience.

The Goals of Public Television

The point of public television was supposed to be its independence from commercial pressures—that is, independence from the need to compete in selling audiences to advertisers for a profit. One reason for wanting to do this should be clear from the discussion in Chapter 3: There are some programs that an advertiser-supported television industry with limited channels may not be able to produce. There are other reasons as well for public television, which we shall explore below. The price that has to be paid for independence from commercial processes—though not from economic pressure—is that public television is dependent on public money, and the appropriation and allocation of public money is, and should be, a political process. The relationship between the political process and the structure of public-television program choice constitutes the most interesting set of issues concerning public television.

The difficulty with public broadcasting from the point of view of economics is that it is not clear how to characterize the *objectives* of the system in any concrete, measurable way. How are we to know if the programs actually selected for public broadcasting are the "right ones," in terms of some objective criterion? In one sense this is an easy problem: if we accept the notion that public broadcasting is an institution created to serve the needs of a small cultural elite, and is run by representatives of that elite, then the problem goes away, or at least ceases to be interesting from an economic point of view. The problem also goes away if we see public television as a means of force-feeding the masses with culturally uplifting or informative programming—in this case the educational establishment can run the system in the same way they run their university curricula. Such programs would be "merit goods"—services provided by the state simply because the polity decides such services ought to be available as government enterprises. Other examples of merit goods include public health and education. (See Musgrave [371].)

But if the purpose of public television is to remedy the defects in a commercial system with limited channels, the defects alluded to in Chapter 3 and 5, then we have to ask some hard questions: What programs should be produced? How much money should be allocated to these programs? Who should make these decisions? Based on what information? It was these questions that forced a crisis in public television in 1971, and they have not yet been answered in any very satisfactory way.

All of this is a natural consequence of the absence of a set of objective performance criteria for noncommercial television. It is entirely possible that such criteria are incapable of being defined in a way that everyone agrees is correct. (This vagueness may be essential to the maintenance of the coalition that supports public television.) For present purposes, we will put forth some criteria of our own that seem to make economic sense.

First, we shall assume that the purpose of noncommercial, government-subsidized television is to supply programs that a commercial system with limited channels fails to produce, either because of "duplication" (in the sense of Chapter 3) or because the program draws an audience too small to be supported by advertising revenue, even though its value to viewers exceeds its cost of production. In the presence of both budget and channel constraints, the system should choose from among these programs those which are "most valuable" to consumers. Next, we shall assume that audience tastes differ in different regions of the country. (If this is not true, there is very little rationale for the decentralized system proposed below.) Finally, we shall assert that it is important to "insulate" the selection of programs (though not the overall budget) from political influence.

In the absence of pay TV and unlimited channels, it is presumably the task of public television to supply the "first" programs that such a system would provide, if it had all the right incentives to satisfy consumer demand, given the programs available on commercial television. The effect of the second assumption is to suggest that these program choices might be different in different cities. The effect of the last assumption is to suggest that centralized program choice is politically undesirable because it is most easily influenced by national political pressure.

We have chosen to make the assumption that the public-television system should maximize the net (of program costs) value to consumers of its program choices, for the simple reason that this objective is the only one that makes much sense to an economist. (Because this is the most efficient thing to do, and because this criterion reflects the public's choices directly.) It is also the one that makes the most sense if the rationale for public television is the necessity of remedying defects in the commercial system brought about by the barriers to channel expansion and pay TV. Table 7-1 illustrates the rationale we have adopted with a concrete example.

Table 7-1

Failure of Advertiser-Supported Commercial TV as a Rationale for Public Broadcasting

Group	1	2	3
Size	40	35	10
First choice program	A	B	C
Second choice program	D	D	–
Value of program (group) to:			
Advertisers	40	35	10
Viewers	20	50	20
Cost of program	10	10	10
4 station program pattern: AABB (see Chapter 3).			

Source: See text.

In the table, group 3 may suffer the absence of program C, even though its benefits exceed its costs, (1) because of "wasteful duplication" among available channels under commercial broadcasting, (2) because there are insufficient channels, or (3) because group 3 and its program are only of indifference to commercial broadcasters in any case, given advertising revenues and program costs. Even if there were monopoly control of channels, given the existence of less-preferred programs of the common-denominator type (program D), the monopolist would still be indifferent about program C, and would not produce A or B at all. C is the type of program that might be offered by public television. Note that programs suitable for public television under this approach are defined by the structure of viewer preferences, not by program content per se.

The difficulty that may arise is that the program choices called for by this criterion might seem highly inappropriate to "public" television—such as soap operas. (On the other hand, Galsworthy's *Forsythe Saga*, immensely popular on public television, may properly be put into this classification.) The reader who rejects this result must also reject this particular objective for public television.

If a system of *local* program choices is to characterize decision-making, in order to avoid the political sensitivity of centralized decision-making, one must still take account of program costs and the related public-good aspect of programs. That is, with a limited budget, each local station must make a trade-off between the diverse and peculiar tastes of its local audience and the economies that may be achieved by sharing programs and program costs with other stations. If every local audience had the same tastes, this would dictate a national network with all public television stations having the same programs, and it would not matter whether decision-making were centralized or not.

Here and below, "decentralized" decision-making means that local stations have all the money, and can choose to purchase *either* local or national (PBS) programming, or both. Thus, there *could* be two hundred and fifty different programs produced each hour. "Centralized" means that all the money is spent by PBS on national programs, which all local stations must carry (or effectively go dark). In practice, of course, the local stations would have some funds for local programming from local sources, but not very much.

If local tastes were always unique, there would be no national or shared programming at all. National programming can be justified if each community has a unique *ranking* of the same set of programs, but not if every city wants to see, for instance, its own high-school football games. The latter constitutes "unique" tastes in our sense. For a given national budget, more programs can be produced for a national system than for a localized diverse system, unless local-interest programs cost much less than national-interest programs to produce, which they apparently do not. Somewhere between these two extremes lies the right combination of locally unique and shared programming.

Two questions now come to the fore: How should each local station determine the demand for possible programs by its audience? Will a decentralized decision-making system pick the "right" or nearly the right programs?

Centralization vs. Decentralization in Program Choice

We have assumed that decentralized (station) program choice is preferable to centralized (network or CPB) program choice in public television, in order to insulate program choices from political pressure from the federal government, which supplies the money for programming—and, perhaps as important, to avoid giving any single, centralized group the political power that goes with the power to select programs.[c] This is the First Amendment objective in this context. The question addressed in this section is whether this is also an acceptable institutional structure on economic efficiency grounds. Do we have to make a trade-off between the First Amendment and economic efficiency? Is a system in which local stations have the funds with the option of spending them on national or "shared" programming likely to be inferior to a system that is *constrained* to have one channel of national programming? The problem here is similar in principle to the commercial-TV problem: someone is acting as a proxy for the viewer in making program choices. In commercial television this choice is made on the basis of a nose count, and that is one of the defects of the commercial system. Public broadcasters must try to take into account the intensity of viewer preferences.

The local public-television station might ask itself, "Given the present

[c]For discussion of this and related issues in public broadcasting, see Alexander [6], Blakely [75], Coase and Barrett [132], Dirlam and Kahn [164], Hull [259], Macy [348], Noll, Peck and McGowan [394], Schramm [492] [494] [496], and White [609].

commercial TV programs, what program would the profit-seeking owner of a pay-TV channel put on?" The answer to this will depend both on the tastes of the local audience and on program costs. If the local audience has highly unique and intense preferences, it may be most profitable (and efficient) to put on a locally produced program. If their tastes are not so unique (or not so intense), it will be more profitable or efficient to buy regionally or nationally shared programs. Measurement of tastes is exceedingly difficult, particularly when the only feedback is the stream of voluntary donations, which may reflect nothing more than the preferences of local philanthropists for what *other* people ought to see! This raises certain problems for the matching-grant approach to federal funding. More important, there is the "free-rider" problem; viewers have no incentive to give in proportion to their true valuation of the programs. Nevertheless, some measurement of tastes must be attempted.

In Table 7-2, we illustrate some of the effects of moving from centralized to decentralized decision-making. The numbers at the top of the table give the money values of various programs to viewers in each of two communities, and the cost of producing those programs. In Case 1, we consider the choice among programs A, B, and C only, on the assumption that each decision-maker maximizes the difference between benefit and cost. In this case, decentralized decision-making results in the greatest net benefit. The reasons, of course, are that we have assumed that "local" programs (A and B) cost less to produce than "national" programs (C), and are valued rather highly in their respective communities, and that the decentralized system has two channels (one in each community) to the centralized system's single common channel. (Of course, we can imagine a "central" system taking into account local preferences—or not—and dictating *different* programs for each community. We ignore this possibility for what should by now be obvious reasons.) In Case 2, adding program D to the choices available to decision-makers, both systems produce the same benefits. In Case 3, we consider the choice among programs A, B, C, and E. Here, centralization produces greater net benefit than decentralization, *but only at the cost of making one community better off at the expense of the other*, given our allocation of program costs. Hence centralization is not preferred to decentralization by both communities in this case. One could also construct cases in which centralization was preferred in both communities. Two tendencies stand out in these illustrations (and they are only that). First, there may exist *some* real-world situations for which decentralization is better than centralization, despite the strong economies of scale of a centralized system. Second, decentralization seems to result in an efficient solution provided that there exists a mechanism for sharing costs—that is, a market for programs, which lets decentralized decision-makers know what prices for programs will be if they share them. This may not require anything more than a competitive program-supply market, although the public-good problem remains potentially troublesome. (The assumption in Table 7-2 that program costs are divided equally is not realistic. The point is that the decentralized system has an element of flexibility

Table 7-2
Centralization vs. Decentralization In Noncommercial Television

Program	Cost	Benefit to Viewers		
		Community 1	Community 2	Total
A	25	100	0	100
B	25	0	100	100
C	50	90	90	180
D	50	110	110	220
E	50	110	95	205

	Programs	Benefit to Viewers			Total Cost	Net Benefit
		Community 1	Community 2	Total		
Case 1: Consider only Programs A, B, C						
Centralization	C	90	90	180	50	130
Decentralization	A, B	100	100	200	50[a]	150
Case 2: Add Program D						
Centralization	D	110	110	220	50	170
Decentralization	D	110	110	220	50[a]	170
Case 3: Add Program E instead of D						
Centralization	E	110	95	205	50	155
Decentralization	A, B	100	100	200	50[a]	150

[a]25 each.

Note: The illustrations assume a single time period, one channel in each community, and an overall budget of 50.

Source: See text.

that is lacking in the centralized alternative, even though true efficiency may be impossible because of the public-good problem.) The supply side of this market (Chapter 2) is surely competitive, and with two hundred fifty-odd public-TV stations, so is the demand side of this market, at least for national programming. Thus, the principal barrier to efficient program choice in decentralized public television lies in the difficulty of obtaining information on viewer preferences, rather than in the decentralized decision-making process itself.

There is just no question that the economies of scale effects are very important in programming. On the other hand we have ample evidence from other media, such as newspapers, that strong preferences for local content can sometimes offset these scale economies in program supply. (Still, local news-papers do buy a lot of national "programming": AP, UPI, syndicated features, and the like.) That it is manifestly not offset in commercial television should not blind us to the possibility that it may be for public television operating under our objective function. Only if transactions costs in a decentralized system are very high—which they need not be if the PBS network always provides an option for a high degree of sharing—does it seem likely that a constraint limiting every station to nationally supplied programs results in a more efficient system. The important point is that decentralization of decision-making does not seem to exclude the possibility of sharing costs if that is best, while flexibility in the opposite direction is absent with the centralized system.

We have omitted two issues that may be of considerable importance. The first is that program choice for a public-television station operating under our rules may be highly interactive with the choices of local commercial stations. (The same would apply on the network level.) Indeed, unless there exists some rather small group of viewers with very strong demands, such interaction is virtually inevitable. Public-broadcast programs would, or could, change the programs offered by commercial stations. To deal with this problem one would have to rework the models of Chapters 3 and 4, with one station maximizing "esti-mated" pay-TV profits (on the grounds, mentioned earlier, that this will lead in the direction of efficient choices, equivalent to those which would arise from consumer surplus maximization, see Chapter 3), and the rest maximizing advertising profits. The second issue has already been mentioned: How is the station to estimate the intensity of preferences for various programs?

One possibility for measuring the demand for programs is to examine programming that is not available on commercial TV for institutional or economic reasons, but *is* available in other places. Unfortunately, this suggests X-rated movies as a likely possibility. But other possibilities include certain sports events, and also the types of programming that warm the heart of every elitist: opera, legitimate theater, and ballet. Public-television stations would do well to examine the results and implications of those pay-TV experiments which have taken place, in order to arrive at some idea of the intensity of demand for this type of programming.

Determination of System-Wide Budget Levels

We turn now to consideration of overall budget levels, a discussion that will be carried out with the aid of Table 7-3. There are three types of programs, A, B, and C, corresponding roughly to those in Table 7-2, but for each we now have a range of program "qualities," measured respectively by Q_A, Q_B, and Q_C. (This example assumes that the program pattern problem is solved. We also ignore fixed costs.) If one is in possession of information on viewer preferences, one can write down marginal benefit schedules, such as those illustrated in Table 7-3, for each program in each community. Efficiency requires that, for each program produced, the quality be chosen in such a way that the sum of marginal benefits across communities equals the marginal cost of program quality. (This is a necessary condition for efficient production of a public good.) For program C, for instance, we require

$$2(80 - 2Q_C) = 4Q_C, \text{ or } Q_C = 20.$$

Table 7-3
Determining Efficient Funding Level and Structure

| Program | Marginal Benefit | | Marginal Cost |
	Community 1	Community 2	
A	$100 - 2Q_A$	0	$2Q_A$
B	0	$100 - 2Q_B$	$2Q_B$
C	$80 - 2Q_C$	$80 - 2Q_C$	$4Q_C$

(Q is the "level" or "quality" of the program)

Optimal Levels (one period, one channel per community)

	Program	Level (Q)	Total Benefit	Total Cost	Net Benefit	
Decentralization	A	25	1875	625	1250	2500
	B	25	1875	625	1250	
Centralization	C	20	2400	800	1600	

Net benefit is greater for decentralization, but so is cost. Suppose the decentralized system had only $800 to spend. Then,

$$Q_A, Q_B = 20$$

$$\text{Total benefit} = 3200$$
$$\text{Total cost} = 800$$
$$\text{Net benefit} = 2400$$

Source: See text.

Having chosen the right levels of quality, we can calculate the total budget requirements (total cost). For instance, the total cost of producing program A is Q_A^2, while the total cost of producing program C is $2Q_C^2$.

A decentralized system of public broadcasting, producing programs A and B, would in this example have to spend $1250 in order to achieve the optimal quality level, achieving net benefits of $2500. The centralized system with only one program, C, shown in both communities, spends only $800, producing net benefits of $1600. The decentralized system costs more, but produces more net benefit. If one wanted to move from a centralized system to a decentralized system in this example, without increasing the budget, Q_A and Q_B would be set at 20, and net benefits would be $2400, which still exceed the net benefits of the centralized system with the same $800 budget.

The case for decentralization of decision-making in public broadcasting thus need not rest solely on its greater insensitivity to political manipulation. It is at least possible that decentralization, even with the same budget, is as efficient as centralization. There is no a priori way in which to prove this, or the converse. It all depends on the structure of costs and the degree of local diversity of tastes.

In practice it will be difficult or impossible to estimate marginal-benefit functions for individual program quality levels. This is one of the deficiencies of any system of central planning—that it requires access to information that is extremely difficult to get, and that a competitive market system with prices provides automatically, at least for private goods. But since in justifying a public-television system we have assumed away the possibility of an efficient competitive market, we must face the issue squarely. A possibility that comes to mind is the use of data from cable television demand studies and pay-TV experiments (see pp. 86-88). Studies of cable demand attempt to explain the demand for subscriptions in terms of the subscription price, the number and quality of existing over-the-air systems, and the number and type of signals available on the cable. These studies have almost uniformly concluded that a public-TV channel with present-day programming has a nil or even negative effect on subscriptions, other things equal. This is disquieting. The results suggest that people place a very low value on present public-broadcasting programs. Still, this suggests that these studies may provide a method for measuring the response to public-broadcasting program choice, and in principle an objective measure of marginal benefit in making budget decisions.

Public Television and the Future

Even at its best in terms of the objectives *we* have set out for it, public television may be inferior to cable television, and especially pay television on cable, in its ability to increase consumer welfare. Whatever its usefulness as an interim measure while we await the arrival of cable's promise, public television must then either disappear or have some different goal. It is difficult to imagine deficiencies in the structure and performance of cable (assuming the right policies) that would justify continued federal subsidization of a public broadcast system of the kind we have today. On the other hand, one might wish to use a "merit good" argument to support continued subsidization of certain cultural programs for which the demand was "insufficient" even with pay TV. (Even pay TV with unlimited channels may have a tendency to produce too few programs of low price elasticity—programs valued highly by a small group.) But an institution like the National Endowment, not a network of stations, would best serve this purpose. Perhaps the concept of a network of *stations* is the most important failing of the present system. One can imagine a public-broadcast institution, still local, which simply bought time on local commercial stations (or combined resources to buy network time) for programs that fit our selection criteria. This would have at least three advantages. First, the heavy capital and overhead cost of maintaining 225 local stations would be saved. Second, public-broadcast programs would not be confined to the ghetto of a channel that many people have come to associate with "boring" programs. Third, a number of useful VHF television assignments would be opened up for commercial use—either as independents or as affiliates of a new fourth network, options that viewers *would* value highly.[d] Of course, the FCC might have to exert some coercion to get commercial stations to accept this programming at their usual time rates. While probably out of the question as a political matter now, this model of public television may be useful in the future.

The long-range future of the public-television system is therefore gloomy. We may perhaps regret that it has not been in existence since the beginning of television, rather than created more than halfway through that period whose conditions may justify its existence. We hope that the creative talent that produces so much that is excellent in public television today can and will make an easy transition to the opportunity and challenge of the new media.

In the meantime we would argue that the experiment with decentralization—local-station sovereignty in making program choices—should be continued, with the condition that the PBS network and its national program choices remain available in order to minimize the transaction costs of sharing programs. We would also urge that public-television stations, if not the system as a whole, begin to think systematically about their objectives and goals, if only in order to be able to measure their own performance against some objective standard. If they don't, Congress will have the duty to do it for them, under whatever funding rules eventually emerge. We do not see why large sums of public funds should be guaranteed to this system indefinitely until these objectives have been defined.

---

[d]We are indebted to Robert Crandall for this idea of using the assignments for commercial purposes.

Related Policy Issues

Introduction

The preceding chapters have already dealt with a wide range of major structural policy issues in television broadcasting: network power, reruns, the prime-time access rule, pay TV, diversity, program duplication, antitrust, new networks, UHF policy, VHF "drop-ins," spectrum allocation policy, cable television, and public broadcasting. This chapter is devoted principally to a few less sweeping issues: children's programs and violence, access questions, the license-renewal process, cross-media ownership, and communication satellites. Finally, we provide a brief perspective on television economics and television policy. This summary of the state of television policy today is rather dismal. For properly qualified proposals to reform the system, we refer the reader to previous chapters.

Children's Television and Violence

Many people seem to feel that the quality of children's programming, its commercialization, and the degree of violence on television in general are serious problems. (See Baker and Ball [30], Melody [358]; for a contrary view, see Milgram and Shotland [362].) We are not in a position to debate this issue, except to note that children's programming is one area where public television has more than lived up to its expectations.

The question we want to address is this: Assuming that violence and commercialization are a problem in children's programs (or in general), what can or should be done about it? Under the current theory of broadcast regulation, TV licensees are fiduciaries of the public, and their use of the spectrum is predicated on service to the public interest. One might therefore expect them to yield to moral exhortation on a point such as this, especially since it seems likely that any reduction in violence and in the degree of commercialization of children's programming would not decrease profits, so long as all stations (or networks) undertook it simultaneously. That children's television can be produced on a level that is higher than the networks' Saturday morning mayhem, and that is sufficiently popular to be profitable, is demonstrated by *Sesame Street* and the other public-television offerings. The degree of commercialization (both the ratio of commercial minutes to program minutes, and actual commercial content in the programming) is high, possibly because the networks have not operated in this field long enough for cooperative patterns of behavior to emerge, as they have in prime time (see Chapter 4, and Brown [92]), and possibly because children's attitudes toward commercials differ from adult attitudes. Concern in Washington with these issues may make cooperation easier, at least with respect to "commercialization," which is easy to define and monitor, compared to program content.

The issue of violence is more difficult. One assumes from the historical behavior of the industry that violent programs are more popular than others of equal cost, or cheaper than others of equal popularity. Any attempt to regulate violence out of programming would run smack into the problem of how to define the elements of program quality, not to mention the enforcement problems that would arise. It is precisely the difficulty of defining program "quality" (in the sense of Chapter 4) that leads the networks into rivalry in the program market. Moreover, it is impossible to imagine that regulators can do much about violence without edging over into very dangerous content regulation.

This has led several people, including Senator Pastore, to suggest the construction of a "violence index" to measure and monitor violence on television. The usefulness of such an index is clear—under the present structure of broadcast regulation, stations or networks with high violence indexes could be threatened or cowed into submission by the FCC through its license-renewal process. But while violence may be a problem, we do not see any hope in the violence-index approach. No one is competent to construct such an index, since no one knows what effects violence on television has on people. Without this knowledge one is reduced to the utterly silly task of counting killings, stabbings, etc., without being able to weigh these events by their contextual sociological or psychological implications. In its psychological effect one murder is not always a perfect substitute for another. (This has not stopped people from constructing violence indices. See Comstock and Rubinstein [141, Vol. 1], pp. 29-34, and Owen [414].) The effect of proceeding in this way is to give the networks an incentive to reduce not violence, nor its harmful effects (if any), but simply to reduce the "violence index," which need bear no relation to either. Such effects are already apparent. Network programming has recently (1973-74) begun to de-emphasize violent death, and in its place has substituted endless "chases."[a] Are suspenseful chases less psychologically harmful to impressionable children than brutal slayings? No one seems to know, but it is at least possible that they are worse.

When one goes beyond the context of the current structure of broadcast regulation, into a postcable world, these problems seem both better and worse. Federal regulation of content will presumably be impossible in such an environment, and we can expect such nasty things as violence and sex to

[a]We are indebted to Marc Roberts for this observation.

flourish. At the same time, viewers will presumably have greater choice in the range of programs offered, choices whose range approximates that of the print media. Parents will then only have the problem of making sure that their children's choices are properly structured. As things now stand, their only choice is to use the off switch on their sets, and this is sometimes inconvenient. Despite the distaste with which any sensitive person must view much of the program content in question, effective remedies seem to us to imply a still more distasteful degree of government paternalism.

Access Questions

Much has been written about the problem of access to the media, especially television and newspapers (Rucker [480], Barron [45]). Except for political campaigns, where Section 315 of the Communications Act does give candidates equal-time access, there is no right of access to television. (In its famous 1974 *Tornillo* decision, the Supreme Court held that there can be no government-mandated right of access to newspapers.) The FCC has chosen to use the "fairness doctrine" as a substitute for access in the case of television. The fairness doctrine requires that a station give both, or all, sides of controversial issues balanced treatment. This is not a right of reply, since the station itself is responsible for presenting the issues, but the station may choose to give air time to others if it wishes. The difficulty with the fairness doctrine is that it imposes restrictions on the content of public affairs programming that make advocacy journalism impossible, and puts the FCC in the position of being the umpire of the content when there is a dispute about a program's fairness. When this results in case-by-case FCC review of individual program content in the public-affairs area, as it has done with increasing frequency, it is tantamount to direct regulation of content. In a decision that is very revealing in its illustration of the Supreme Court's naïveté in matters of technology, the Supreme Court upheld this use of the fairness doctrine in 1969. The *Red Lion* [459] decision in effect put the First Amendment into the straitjacket of the 1934 Communications Act and the FCC's table of spectrum allocations. The case involved an appeal by a radio station from an FCC order requiring it to present the other side of an issue upon which the station had broadcast an opinion. (For background on the Fairness Doctrine, see Botein [81], Robinson [465], and Thomas [543].)

The logic of the *Red Lion* decision is deceptively simple: (1) There is a limited supply of spectrum; (2) the spectrum is a public resource, allocated by the government; (3) there is concentration of control of access to the airwaves by broadcast licensees. Therefore government regulation of content (in particular, the fairness doctrine and its enforcement) are necessary in order to preserve balance in the media, and in order to reach First Amendment objectives. This logic is entirely faulty. First, the premises are all either false or only one of several alternatives, alternatives which the Court could have changed. Premise (1) is false. Spectrum is *technically* neither more nor less limited than land, water, paper, ink, or printing presses. This is true *especially* of that part of spectrum used for broadcasting. (Of course, the FCC has chosen as a matter of *policy* to limit the number of channels.) Premise (2) is true, but not necessary. The spectrum *could* be a private resource, allocated by the market. (See Coase [130], De Vany, et al. [160].) Premise (3) is false in the sense that broadcasters are more plentiful for most of the population than newspapers. This is true of television and especially of radio, which was the issue in *Red Lion*. Even granting concentration of control, that concentration is the result of FCC policies to limit the number of licensees, not any technical constraint on numbers.

Moreover, the premises do not justify the conclusion. A conclusion more in line with the spirit of the First Amendment, given the premises, would be an order turning all TV stations into common carriers, with FCC regulation of prices and profits of stations, but no regulation of content (see Chapter 5).

Thus, the Court could have avoided its strained conclusion in any of several ways, but it chose not to. Apparently one must look to cable, the Whitehead Report, and Congress for a return to freedom from government regulation of media content. Meanwhile, many people think that the *Red Lion* decision's logic should not only be accepted, but extended to newspapers (Barron [45]).

The access issue has arisen in a slightly different guise in recent years. In 1971 it was suggested that there should be a "right of paid access" to broadcast stations (Whitehead [611]). This implies something like common-carrier status, at least for advertising time. Then in 1972 various groups sought to buy, and were denied, airtime for "editorial announcements." In the BEM case [98], the Supreme Court said that stations could not arbitrarily refuse to sell time for such purposes, but otherwise left the issue unresolved.

Also in 1971, Miles Kirkpatrick, Federal Trade Commission chairman, suggested that the FCC force stations to accept "counteradvertising." (See Scanlon [490] for a review of this proposal.) An example of "counteradvertising" is the anticigarette ads that appeared before cigarette advertising was banned from television. The Kirkpatrick suggestion would have forced stations to accept announcements questioning the safety, quality, or environmental effects of products advertised on regular commercials. The FCC turned the idea down flat, on the grounds that it would destroy the existing economic basis for broadcasting; unpaid commercials equal in number to paid commercials would considerably reduce revenues.

It is our view that cable, properly structured, will resolve the access issue in time. If cable is delayed or if we are too impatient, some of the approaches suggested in Chapter 5 are well suited to increase access without government content regulation, and thus without doing violence to either the letter or spirit of the First Amendment, which says, after all, "Congress shall make no law . . . abridging the freedom of speech, or of the press."

The License-Renewal Process

The license-renewal process has always been the heart of the FCC mechanism of program-content regulation. Its purpose is to ensure that the stations will broadcast the "right" set of programs from the FCC's public-interest point of view. It is a highly inefficient substitute for the economic incentives provided by direct price signals in a market system, since it attempts to dictate or constrain behavior in ways that run counter to the interests of the stations under present economic incentives. Even if the FCC feels that the "right" programs are not those that would be produced by market incentives in the context of a more rational industry structure (see Chapters 5 and 6), there may still be more efficient ways than the license-renewal process to introduce economic incentives to produce those programs.

The licenses are, however, only very rarely not renewed, and then only in extraordinary circumstances, no doubt in part because television licensees have an enormous incentive not to do things that will endanger their licenses. It is interesting to compare this situation with that prevailing in radio, where competition among stations is much keener, and scarcity rents are presumably smaller. License revocations are much more common in radio than in television (*Annual Report* of the FCC, 1971, p. 148). Radio stations have less to lose from license revocation, and perhaps more to gain from license-endangering behavior.

The process of license renewal is usually pro forma. The station hires a Washington attorney, a member of the communications bar, who helps to prepare a license-renewal application reciting all the good things the station has done over the past three years, and especially all the good things it expects to do in the next three. (For samples of the extensive reporting required, see 43 FCC 2nd 1 (1973). Note that the renewal is usually pro forma only after the licensee has spent thousands of dollars in attorney's fees. The probability of renewal without these expenditures may be much lower, but few dare to find out.) The performance of the station in the eyes of the FCC can hardly be evaluated in any other way than through program content, so stations are very anxious to know what program-content criteria the Commission has in mind as the minimum necessary standard for renewal. Formally or informally, the station's lawyers obtain estimates of these (unpublished) standards from the Commission or its staff, and the station takes care to supply the relevant programming (see Robinson [465], Goldberg [223], Krasnow and Longley [311]). There is a controversial proposal that the FCC actually publish these standards as renewal criteria.

Since such standards consist of percentages of *time* devoted to certain program *types* (such as public affairs or religious programming) rather than expenditure minima or audience sizes, the quality standards of such programming are generally low. Also, the "sustaining" programming, as it is called, is broadcast in obscure time periods, such as Sunday morning.

It has been a favorite sport for license challengers to appear before the FCC by filing a petition to deny renewal of the existing license, and then to try to obtain the license themselves. The object of this game is simply the hope of getting the license for a price (in attorney fees) less than its scarcity value. The challenged station is of course willing to spend a similar amount to defend its license. Since the process of awarding a new license or a revoked license involves comparative hearings in which the claimants for the license compete in their promises of good behavior, and since such hearings are difficult for the FCC to resolve, there has always been a more or less explicit assumption at the Commission that existing licenses would be renewed unless really extraordinary circumstances prevailed.

Recently, there has been a trend toward license challenges by public-interest groups. These groups usually wish to protest the absence of minority-group or public-interest programming, or the employment practices of the station. The FCC at first was inclined to ignore such challenges entirely, but court decisions have forced the Commission to take them more seriously, eventually denying renewal of some public television licenses in Alabama. This has led to pressure on Congress to change the law in a way that better protects existing licenses. Both in the case of a challenge for pure monetary gain and in the public-interest challenge, it is not uncommon for the station to try to buy off the challenger, either by paying a sum of money (disguised as reimbursement for legal expenses) or by caving in to the demands of the public-interest group for more programming of whatever type it wants.

Since the Commission is the ultimate arbiter, its standards of program performance are very important in this process. Thus, the license-renewal process is in effect a process by which the FCC acquires regulatory control over content. We regard FCC content regulation as dangerous in principle, on First Amendment grounds. Given the current structure of broadcasting some degree of indirect content control is inevitable, but it could at least be limited to structural regulation with only implied program content consequences.

Television licensees, of course, view the renewal process with alarm, and have always sought to have it changed. Hundreds of bills have been introduced in Congress that would have the effect of protecting existing licensees from challenge, but none has as yet passed both houses. Such protection would enable the existing stations to retain their monopolistic profits instead of passing them on to lawyers and spending them on uneconomic program types. From the point of view of freedom of expression, and particularly in view of the growth of cable, it would seem highly desirable to make a change in this system. Perhaps the best way to go about it is simply to vest the licenses in their present holders in perpetuity, perhaps with annual fees for use of the spectrum (for the purpose of recapturing the scarcity rents for the Treasury), and the right to sell the license to others at will. If this is too extreme to be practical, the present three-year term could be lengthened as much as possible, and this would tend to have the same effect.

When one thinks about radio broadcasting, with dozens of competing stations in most large communities, the whole process of content regulation looks even less rational. In radio, there is a very strong case for deregulation, and this case is made in Chapter 6 in the context of cable television.

The important point is that it is not just the fairness doctrine or the prime time access rule that leads to intrusive federal regulation of media content. Both of these devices are grounded logically on the existence of licenses granted to stations for (in effect) the term of their "good behavior." It is this power that is ultimately dangerous, just as it would be in the print media.

Cross-Media Ownership

About 30 percent of all commercial television stations are owned by newspapers. This has resulted in a long-drawn-out controversy. Proponents of increased media competition have argued that joint newspaper-TV ownership is harmful on First Amendment and economic concentration grounds (Rucker [480]). The combination companies have argued that there are substantial benefits from joint ownership (ANPA [10]). The FCC has had a proposal pending since 1968 that if enacted would require divestiture of all existing combinations. It already has a policy, rather frequently waived, against awarding new TV licenses to newspaper firms operating in the same city. The Antitrust Division has been challenging the licenses of TV stations owned by newspapers at renewal time.

Newspapers and TV stations compete in the market for local and national spot advertising, and they may also be said to compete in the marketplace of ideas. Since most cities have only one daily newspaper firm, and three or fewer TV stations, economic concentration in both markets is already a serious issue. There is some evidence (Owen [413]) that advertising prices are higher for combination companies, implying monopoly power in advertising markets as well. Moreover, any politician endorsed for election by a joint newspaper-TV combination company is in a very advantageous position, particularly if the endorsement extends to favorable news coverage.

The arguments in favor of joint ownership are (1) that joint economies exist in operating the two media, and (2) that the revenue from a TV station may sustain a newspaper that would otherwise go bankrupt. Neither of these arguments is convincing (Rosse, Owen, and Grey [477]). The only place there could be common costs is in the news department, a very minor part of the TV operation, and one with a technology dissimilar to that of the newspaper. As for subsidization of failing newspapers, that can just as well be done by the local furniture manufacturer or candlestick maker as by the TV station.

It seems clear that joint ownership is undesirable. In a world that did not contain the promise of cable, we would want to fight very hard to see divestiture policies undertaken. With cable on the horizon this may be less important, depending on the situation in each individual city and the actual rate of growth of cable. It seems very unlikely in any event that the FCC will require divestiture of newspaper-owned stations, simply because of the enormous political power of these companies. It is interesting to note that such liberal newspapers as the *Washington Post* (owner of *Post-Newsweek* Stations) do not seem to be embarrassed by their own vigorous opposition to divestiture. On the other hand, the undesirability of joint ownership has been pointed out by such disparate politicians as Spiro Agnew and Nicholas Johnson, so that it may be unfair to characterize divestiture as a "liberal" cause.[b]

Communication Satellites

Commercial communication satellites are now a reality for U.S. domestic communications, as they have been for about ten years in international communication. The effect of this development on television will not, however, be terribly dramatic. The satellites will reduce the cost of network interconnection, which is the process of sending TV signals from their point of origination in New York to the individual broadcast stations across the country. This service is now provided mostly by AT&T microwave routes, at a price of about $20 million per network per year—a very small part (about 6 percent) of each network's expenses.

The present AT&T tariffs for television transmission will probably decline drastically as satellites become available, particularly since AT&T will face competition in this service. Also, the present structure of prices for TV transmission, which tends to discourage part-time networks, will doubtless be altered. But transmission costs are simply too small a part of a network's budget for even drastic downward revisions to make much difference to the viability of new networks. If and when cable television networks begin to appear, they will doubtless make use of satellite interconnection services. Indeed, a major builder of satellites, the Hughes Aircraft Corporation, is planning to enter the business of supplying programming to cable systems in this way.

What of "direct broadcast" satellites? (That is, satellite broadcasts which can be picked up directly by home antennae. For background, see Chayes [118], UNESCO [552].) Present technology requires large, expensive earth stations to receive signals transmitted from a satellite, which are then relayed to the home by cable or local over-the-air broadcasts. But it may not be long before increased power in the satellites will make it feasible to broadcast TV programs directly to individual homes equipped with antennae costing "only" a few hundred dollars. Does this hold promise for an improvement in our television service?

The answer is almost certainly No. In the first place, one must compare direct

---

[b]For background on this cross-ownership issue, see Anderson [13], Barnett [39] [41], Lago [315], Levin [326] [327] [329], Mathewson [351], Peterman [437], Rosse [475], and Sterling [527] [528].

broadcast satellites to cable television in order to see which technology is more viable. For the price of even a rather optimistically designed home satellite-receiving antenna, one could have access to cable service; the transmission costs are not dissimilar. But the satellite would be incapable of offering *local* programs, whereas cable could offer both local and national programs. Also, the satellite could not offer two-way service or any possibility of selective delivery to individual homes, which cable can offer. Given the same cost, cable is simply a better communication technology, at least in the environment of the United States. There is some thought that satellites broadcasting directly to community reception sites may be useful in less-developed nations, however.

The Future of Television Policy

Television policy over the years has been characterized by two major failings: the logical incompatibility of the Communications Act of 1934 and the First Amendment, and the consistent failure of the FCC to make effective use of economic analysis and economic incentives in dealing with broadcast licensees. Among the results of these failings has been the creation of a relatively small group of individuals and firms with considerable economic and political power. To protect their economic interests, this group exercises its political power to thwart structural change that, while it may leave viewers better off, threatens broadcasters with greater competition. Historically, the two best examples of the exercise of this power are the failure of UHF deintermixture and the freeze on cable television. We do not mean to imply that the broadcast industry is all-powerful. It is not. But in complex technical matters, and in issues that affect each individual viewer only slightly (however important in the aggregate), these interests are sufficient to thwart change.

The sources of the FCC's failings are numerous. Partly, they are the result of giving a regulatory agency most of the responsibilities of Congress, without accompanying that responsibility with the political power to accomplish structural changes. The regulatory agency has no natural constituency, save the industry it regulates. Some blame must be placed on the hoary practice by successive administrations of using the FCC (and the other regulatory agencies) as tools of political patronage. It is only by an occasional happy accident that able and far-sighted people are drawn into communications policy. Such talented men as former FCC Chairman Dean Burch unfortunately are rarities in this and other regulatory fields.

It is almost certainly useless to expect a regulatory commission to take sustained interest in major *structural* changes, especially those which might erode its own powers; gradual improvement—incrementalism—is the most that can be expected. One must instead depend on the Congress, the Executive

Branch, and the courts to recognize and act on the need for such reforms.[c] Since in communications both the Congress and the courts seem mesmerized by the technological mystique of the broadcasting business, extra responsibility is placed on the Executive Branch. But the Executive Branch has its own problems with communications policy. Until 1970, when the Office of Telecommunications Policy was created, there was no agency in the Executive Branch with any real responsibility in this area. And, as the experience of OTP in the Nixon years demonstrated, there is great difficulty in separating an administration's *media policy* from its *press relations.* This difficulty exists both within an administration and in the perceptions of the media themselves. The natural, necessary, and healthy antagonism that exists between government and the press is confounded and compromised by the power of government, under present law, to regulate that press, and by the role of the television media as recipients of economic largesse from that same government. There is too much power, and too many wrong incentives on both sides of this relationship.

These are difficult and ultimately dangerous conditions in which to formulate and undertake communications policy. They are in fact so difficult and so dangerous that one is driven again to the conclusion that the less government has to do with regulating the media, and the less economic concentration there is within the media, the better off we will be. So we arrive again at the First Amendment.

It is our hope that the ideas and approach in this book demonstrate that policies exist that go some way toward reducing the role of government intrusion in the media, while improving the position of viewers. Some of these policies allow a closer approximation to freedom of expression, consumer sovereignty, and efficiency in the marketplace of ideas. While we have certainly not provided all that is necessary for a repeal and revision of the Communications Act of 1934, we hope that we have provided a useful way to think about that task. The time to undertake it is long overdue.

[c]Probably most of the deficiencies of present broadcast regulation could not be remedied even by incremental changes undertaken by a firm and steady hand over a period of years. The underlying legal and economic structure is too far out of whack. New technology may, however, alleviate this condition.

Bibliography

Bibliography

The following bibliography contains not only references specifically mentioned in the text, but other works on television and related industries of interest to students of mass-media economics. We are grateful to a long line of research assistants who have helped to prepare and edit the bibliography, including Andrew Wechsler, Dennis Weller, and David Waterman.

[1]   Abbott, Lawrence, *Quality and Competition* (Columbia University Press, 1955).

[2]   Abel, J.D., C. Clift, and F.A. Weiss, "Station License Revocations and Denials of Renewal, 1934-1969," *Journal of Broadcasting*, v. 14 (Fall 1970).

[3]   Adams, W., "Dissolution, Divorcement, Divestiture: The Pyrrhic Victories of Antitrust," *Indiana Law Journal*, v. 27, (Fall 1951).

[4]   Adelman, M.A., "Effective Competition and the Antitrust Laws," *Harvard Law Review*, v. 61 (September 1948).

[5]   Adler, R., and W.S. Baer, eds., *The Electronic Box Office* (Praeger, 1974).

[6]   Alexander, S.S., "Public Television and the 'Ought' of Public Policy," *Washington University Law Quarterly*, v. 1968 (Winter 1968).

[7]   Allen, C.L., "Photographing the TV Audience," *Journal of Advertising Research*, v. 5, No. 1 (March 1965).

[8]   Allen, T.H., "Mass Media Use Patterns in a Negro Ghetto," *Journalism Quarterly*, v. 45 (Autumn 1968).

[9]   American Institute for Political Communication, *The Effects of Local Media Monopoly on the Mass Mind* (AIPC, January 1971).

[10]   American Newspaper Publishers Association, "Comments in Opposition," in Matter of Commission Rules Relating to Multiple Ownership of Standard FM and Television Broadcast Stations, Docket #18110, with professional studies and legal memoranda, 3 vols. (April 2, 1971).

[11]   American Newspaper Publishers Association, Bureau of Advertising, "Research Studies and Reports Published by Newspapers in the United States and Canada from Sept. 1, 1969 through Dec. 31, 1970" (July 1971).

[12]   American Newspaper Publishers Association Research Institute, "Newspapers and CATV—The Numbers," R.I. Bulletin #1053 (May 28, 1971).

[13]   Anderson, J., "The Alliance of Broadcast Stations and Newspapers: The Problem of Information Control," *Journal of Broadcasting*, v. 16 (Winter 1971-72).

[14]   Anderson, J., R. Coe, and J. Saunders, "Economic Issues Relating to the F.C.C.'s Proposed 'One-to-a-Customer' Rule," *Journal of Broadcasting*, v. 13 (Summer 1969).

[15] Andersson, D., "The CATV Industry: Current Subscriber Penetration, Projected Subscriber Growth, Capitalization, by 5-Year Periods, 1972-1992" (National Cable Television Association, September 1972).

[16] *Annual Review of Information Science and Technology*, C.A. Cuadra, ed. (Interscience, annual).

[17] Anthony, G., "A Regulator Looks at State CATV Regulation," *Public Utilities Fortnightly*, v. 82 (December 1968).

[18] Archibald, G.C., "Profit-Maximising and Non-Price Competition," *Economica*, (February 1964).

[19] Armstrong, W.P., Jr., "The Sherman Act and the Movies: A Supplement," *Temple Law Quarterly*, v. 26 (Summer 1952).

[20] Arrow, K.J., "The Economic Context," in *The Future of Commercial Television, 1965-1975*, ed. by S.T. Donner (Stanford University Press, 1965).

[21] Arrow, K.J., and M. Nerlove, "Optimal Advertising Policy Under Dynamic Conditions," *Economica*, v. 29 (May 1962).

[22] *Associated Press vs. U.S.* 326 U.S. 1 (1945).

[23] Austin, A., "Antitrust Proscription and the Mass Media," *Duke Law Journal*, v. 1968 (December 1968).

[24] *AV Communication Review* (Association for Educational Communications and Technology, quarterly).

[25] Backman, J., *Advertising and Competition* (NYU Press, 1967).

[26] Baer, W.S., "Cable Television: A Handbook for Decisionmaking," Report R-1133-NSF (Santa Monica: RAND Corporation, February 1973).

[27] Baer, W.S., "Interactive Television: Prospects for Two-way Services on Cable," Report R-888-MF (Santa Monica: RAND Corporation, November 1971).

[28] Bagdikian, B.H., *Information Machines: Their Impact on Men and the Media* (Harper & Row, 1971).

[29] Bailey, Elizabeth, *Economic Theory of Regulatory Constraint* (Lexington Books, D.C. Heath and Company, 1973).

[30] Baker, R., and S. Ball, "Violence and the Media," Staff Report to the National Commission on the Causes and Prevention of Violence (Government Printing Office, 1969).

[31] Baran, P., "The Future Computer Utility," *The Public Interest*, No. 8 (Summer 1967).

[32] Baran, P., "On the Impact of the New Communications Media Upon Social Values," *Law and Contemporary Problems*, v. 34 (Spring 1969).

[33] Barber, R.J., "Newspaper Monopoly in New Orleans: The Lessons for Antitrust Policy," *Louisiana Law Review*, v. 24 (April 1964).

[34] Barnett, H.J., "Economics of Television Markets," Appendix B to Peter O. Steiner and Harold J. Barnett, "Comments of Economic Consultants Dr. Peter O. Steiner and Dr. Harold J. Barnett on the MPATI Petition,"

submitted to the Federal Communications Commission in Docket 14229 (April 3, 1964).

[35] Barnett, H.J., "Resistance to the Wired City," Research Monograph #12-70 (St. Louis: Washington Uniersity, 1970).

[36] Barnett, H.J., and E. Greenberg, "On the Economics of Wired City Television," *American Economic Review*, v. 58 (June 1968).

[37] Barnett, H.J., and E. Greenberg, "A Proposal for Wired City Television," *Washington University Law Quarterly*, v. 1968 (Winter 1968).

[38] Barnett, H.J., and E. Greenberg, "Regulating CATV Systems: An Analysis of F.C.C. Policy and An Alternative," *Law and Contemporary Problems*, v. 34 (Summer 1969).

[39] Barnett, S.R., "Cable Television and Media Concentration, Part I: Control of Cable Systems by Local Broadcasters," *Stanford Law Review*, v. 22 (January 1970).

[40] Barnett, S.R., "Democracy in the Newsroom and the FCC," *Conference on Communications Policy Research, Nov. 17-18, 1972* (Office of Telecommunications Policy, 1972).

[41] Barnett, S.R., "Reply Comments before the F.C.C. to Docket #18110 (Commission's Rules Relating to Multiple Ownership of Standard, FM and Television Broadcast Stations) and Docket #18891 (Commission's Rules Relative to Diversification of Control of Community Antenna Television Systems)" (August 16, 1971).

[42] Barnett, S.R., "State, Federal, and Local Regulation of Cable Television," *Notre Dame Lawyer*, v. 47 (April 1972).

[43] Barnow, E., *A History of Broadcasting in the United States*, 3 vols. (Oxford University Press, 1966-1970).

[44] Barret, M., ed., *The Alfred I. DuPont-Columbia University Survey of Broadcast Journalism: 1968-1969* (Grosset and Dunlap, 1969).

[45] Barron, J.A., "Access to the Press—A New First Amendment Right," *Harvard Law Review*, v. 80 (June 1967).

[46] Barron, J.A., "An Emerging First Amendment Right of Access to the Media?" *George Washington Law Review*, v. 37 (March 1969).

[47] Barrow, R.L., "Antitrust and the Regulated Industry: Promoting Competition in Broadcasting," *Duke Law Journal*, v. 1964 (Spring 1964).

[48] Barrow, R.L., "Attainment of Balanced Program Service in Television," *Virginia Law Review*, v. 52 (May 1966).

[49] Barrow, R.L., "Network Broadcasting—The Report of the FCC Network Study Staff," *Law and Contemporary Problems*, v. 22 (Autumn 1957).

[50] Barrow, R.L., and D.J. Manelli, "Communications Technology—A Forecast of Change," Parts I and II, *Law and Contemporary Problems*, v. 34 (Spring and Summer 1969).

[51] Barton, R., *Media in Advertising* (McGraw-Hill, 1964).

[52] Barton, J.H., D.A. Dunn, E.B. Parker, and J.N. Rosse, "Nondiscrimi-

natory Access to Cable Television Channels," Studies in Industry Economics #17 (Department of Economics, Stanford, May 1972).

[53] Bauer, R.A., and S.A. Greyser, *Advertising in America: The Consumer View* (Harvard University, Graduate School of Business Administration, 1968).

[54] Baumol, W.J., and W.G. Bowen, *Performing Arts: The Economic Dilemma* (Twentieth Century Fund, 1966).

[55] Baxter, W.F., "Regulation and Diversity in Communications Media," *American Economic Review*, v. 64 (May 1974).

[56] Becknell, J.C., Jr., "The Influence of Newspaper Tune-In Advertising on the Size of a TV Show's Audience," *Journal of Advertising Research*, v. 1 (March 1961).

[57] Beebe, J.H., "Institutional Structure and Program Choices in Television and Cable Television Markets," Research Memorandum #131 (Stanford University: Research Center in Economic Growth, August 1972).

[58] Beebe, J.H., and B.M. Owen, "Alternative Structures for Television," U.S. Office of Telecommunications Policy, Executive Office of the President (Washington, D.C., November 1972).

[59] Belson, W.A., "The Effects of Television on the Reading and the Buying of Newspapers and Magazines," *Public Opinion Quarterly*, v. 25 (Fall 1961).

[60] Belson, W.A., *The Impact of Television* (Archon Books, 1967).

[61] Bennett, R.C., "Merger Movement in the Motion Picture Industry," *Annals of the American Academy*, v. 147 (January 1930).

[62] Bennett, R.W., "Media Concentration and the FCC: Focusing with a Section Seven Lens," *Northwestern University Law Review*, v. 66 (May/June 1971).

[63] Berelson, B., *Content Analysis in Communication Research* (Glencoe Free Press, 1952).

[64] Berg, S.V., "Copyright, Conflict, and a Theory of Property Rights," *Journal of Economic Issues*, v. 5 (June 1971).

[65] Bernstein, I., *The Economics of Television Film Production and Distribution*, A Report to the Screen Actors Guild, 1960 (S.A.G., Sherman Oaks, Calif., 1960).

[66] Bernstein, I., *Hollywood at the Crossroads: An Economic Study of the Motion Picture Industry*, (A.F.L. Film Council, Hollywood, 1957).

[67] Bernstein, M.H., *Regulating Business by Independent Commission* (Princeton University Press, 1955).

[68] Besen, S.M., "The Economics of the Cable Television 'Consensus' " in *Conference on Communication Policy Research: Papers and Proceedings Nov. 17-18, 1972* (Office of Telecommunications Policy).

[69] Besen, S.M., "The Value of Television Time and the Prospects for New Stations," RAND Report R-1328-MF (RAND Corporation, October 1973).

[70] Besen, S.M., and B.M. Mitchell, "Review of Noll, Peck, and McGowan's *Economic Aspects of Television Regulation," Bell Journal of Econ. and Mgmt. Science*, vol. 5, No. 1 (Spring 1974).

[71] Besen, S.M., and R. Soligo, "The Economics of the Network-Affiliate Relationship in the Television Broadcasting Industry," *American Economic Review*, v. 63 (June 1973).

[72] Besen, S.M., and R. Soligo, "Regulation of Television Program Production and Distribution" (Mimeo, 1974).

[73] Blair, John, and Company, *Statistical Trends in Broadcasting* (John Blair, annual).

[74] Blake, H.M., and J.A. Blum, "Network Television Rate Practices: A Case Study in the Failure of Social Control of Price Discrimination," *Yale Law Journal*, v. 74 (July 1965).

[75] Blakely, R.J., *The Peoples' Instrument: A Philosophy of Programming for Public Television*, a Charles F. Kettering Foundation report (Washington, D.C.: Public Affairs Press, 1971).

[76] Blank, D.M., "The Quest for Quantity and Diversity in Television Programming," *American Economic Review, Papers and Proceedings*, v. 56 (May 1966).

[77] Blank, D.M., "Television Advertising: The Great Discount Illusion, or Tonypandy Revisited," *Journal of Business*, v. 41 (January 1968).

[78] Blum, E., *Basic Books in the Mass Media*, (University of Illinois Press, 1972), revises *Reference Books in the Mass Media* (1962).

[79] Bogart, L., *The Age of Television* (Ungar, 1956, 1972).

[80] Bork, R., "Vertical Integration and the Sherman Act: The Legal History of An Economic Misconception," *University of Chicago Law Review*, v. 22 (Autumn 1954).

[81] Botein, Michael, "The Federal Communication Commission's Fairness Regulations: A First Step Toward Creation of a Right of Access to the Mass Media," *Cornell Law Review*, v. 54 (1969).

[82] Bowman, G.W., and J. Farley, "TV Viewing: Application of a Formal Choice Model," *Applied Economics*, v. 4 (December 1972).

[83] Brandsberg, G., *The Free Papers: A Comprehensive Study of America's Shopping Guide and Free Circulation Newspaper Industry* (Wordsmith Books, 1969).

[84] Brehm, J.W., and A.R. Cohen, *Explorations in Cognitive Dissonance* (Wiley, 1962).

[85] Bretz, R., "Communications Media: Properties and Uses," Memorandum RM-6070-NLM/PR (Santa Monica: RAND Corporation, September 1969).

[86] Bretz, R., *A Taxonomy of Communication Media*, (Educational Technology Publications, 1971), also published as Memorandum RM-6070 (Santa Monica: RAND Corporation, September 1969).

[87] Brinton, J.E., "Failure of the Western Edition of the New York Times," *Journalism Quarterly*, v. 41 (Spring 1964).

[88] *Broadcasting*, (Broadcasting Publications, weekly).

[89] *Broadcasting*, special report: "What Happened on 1,001 Movie Nights" (November 3, 1969).

[90] *Broadcasting Yearbook* (Broadcasting Publications, annual).

[91] Brown, G.H., "Measuring the Sales Effectiveness of Alternative Media," in *Proceedings of the 7th Annual Conference* (New York: Advertising Research Foundation, 1964).

[92] Brown, L., *TELEVI$ION: The Business Behind the Box* (Harcourt-Brace-Jovanovich, 1971).

[93] Brunner, J., "The Economics of Fleet Street," *Lloyd's Bank Review*, v. 68 (April 1963).

[94] Bryant, A.P., "Historical and Social Aspects of Concentration of Program Control in Television," *Law and Contemporary Problems*, v. 34 (Summer 1969).

[95] Buchanan, J.M., *The Demand and Supply of Public Goods* (Rand McNally, 1968).

[96] Buchanan, J.M., "Public Goods in Theory and Practice," *Journal of Law and Economics*, v. 10 (October 1967).

[97] Buchanan, N.S., "Advertising Expenditures: A Suggested Treatment," *Journal of Political Economy*, v. 50 (August 1942).

[98] *Business Executive's Move For Vietnam Peace vs. FCC, et al.* 41 LW 4688 (May 1973).

[99] Cabinet Committee on Cable Communications, *Report to the President* [Whitehead Report] (Washington, January 1974).

[100] Canadian Senate Committee on the Mass Media, "Mirror of the U.S.," *Columbia Journalism Review* (May/June 1971).

[101] Canadian Special Senate Committee on Mass Media, *Report on the Mass Media*, 3 vols., *The Uncertain Mirror; Words, Music, and Dollars; Good, Bad, or Simply Inevitable?* (Ottawa: Information Canada, 1970).

[102] Carnegie Commission, *Public Television, a Program for Action* (Bantam Books, 1967).

[103] *Carroll Broadcasting Co. vs. FCC*, 258 F. 2d 440 (1958).

[104] *Carter Mountain Transmission Corp. v. FCC*, 321 F. 2d 359 (D.C. Cir., 1963).

[105] Cassady, R., Jr., "Impact of the Paramount Decision on Motion Picture Distribution and Price Making," *Southern California Law Review*, v. 31 (February 1958).

[106] Cassady, R., Jr., "Monopoly in Motion Picture Production and Distribution: 1908-1915," *Southern California Law Review*, v. 32 (Summer 1959).

[107] Cassady, R., Jr., and R. Cassady, III, *The Private Antitrust Suit in American Business Competition: A Motion Picture Industry Case Analysis* (UCLA, Bureau of Business and Economic Research, 1964).

[108] Casty, A., *Mass Media and Mass Man* (Holt, Rinehart and Winston, 1968).

[109] *CATV Sourcebook* (Broadcasting Publications, Inc., annual).

[110] *CATV and Station Coverage Atlas* (1971-72 edition Washington, D.C.: Television Digest, Inc.).

[111] Celler, E., "Concentration of Ownership and the Decline of Competition in the News Media," *Antitrust Bulletin*, v. 8 (March-April 1963).

[112] Chaffee, Z., Jr., *Freedom of Speech and Press* (New York: Freedom Agenda, 1955).

[113] Chaffee, Z., Jr., *Governmental and Mass Communications* (Archon, 1965).

[114] Chamberlin, E.H., "Pure Spatial Competition," Appendix C to *The Theory of Monopolistic Competition*, 7th ed. (Harvard University Press, 1960).

[115] Chapin, R.E., *Mass Communications: A Statistical Analysis* (Michigan State University Press, 1957).

[116] Charles River Associates, Inc., "Analysis of the Demand for Cable Television," Report #78-2, prepared for Office of Telecommunications, U.S. Department of Commerce (April 1973).

[117] Charles River Associates, Inc., "The Impact of CATV on Local Television Stations: A Critique of the FCC's Staff Report," Appendix C to Twenty-One Television Stations' Comments in FCC Docket #18397-A" (December 7, 1970).

[118] Chayes, A., "The Impact of Satellites on Cable Communication," report prepared for the Sloan Commission on Cable Communications (May 1971).

[119] Chazen, L., and L. Ross, "Federal Regulation of Cable Television: The Visible Hand," *Harvard Law Review*, v. 83 (June 1970).

[120] Childs, O.W., "The FCC's Proposed CATV Regulations," *Stanford Law Review*, v. 21 (June 1969).

[121] *Citizen Publishing Co. et al. vs. U.S.* 394 U.S. 131 (1969).

[122] Clark, D.G., and Hutchison, eds., *Mass Media and the Law: Freedom and Restraint* (Wiley-Interscience, 1970).

[123] *Clay Broadcasting Corporation of Texas vs. FCC et al.*, 464 F. 2d. 1313 (1972).

[124] Clemens, E.W., and L.W. Thatcher, "The Reorganization of the FCC: A Case Study in Administration and Organization," *Land Economics*, v. 77 (August 1951).

[125] Coase, R.H., *British Broadcasting: A Study in Monopoly* (Harvard University Press, 1950).

[126] Coase, R.H., "The Economics of Broadcasting and Government Policy," *American Economic Review*, v. 56 (May 1966).

[127] Coase, R.H., "Evaluation of Public Policy Relating to Radio and Television Broadcasting: Social and Economic Issues," *Land Economics*, v. 41 (May 1965).

[128] Coase, R.H., "The Market for Goods and the Market for Ideas," *American Economic Review*, v. 64 (May 1974).

[129] Coase, R.H., "The Nature of the Firm," *Economica*, (New Series), v. 14 (1937).

[130] Coase, R.H., "The Federal Communications Commission," *Journal of Law and Economics*, v. 2 (October 1959).

[131] Coase, R.H., "The Interdepartmental Radio Advisory Committee," *Journal of Law and Economics*, v. 5 (October 1962).

[132] Coase, R.H., and E.W. Barrett, *Educational TV: Who Should Pay?* (Washington, D.C.: American Enterprise Institute for Public Policy Research, 1968).

[133] Coase, R.H., W. Meckling, and J. Minasian, "Problems of Radio Frequency Allocation," Memorandum RM-3598-NASA (Santa Monica: RAND Corporation, May 1963).

[134] Cole, B.G., and A.P. Klose, "A Selected Bibliography on the History of Broadcasting," *Journal of Broadcasting*, v. 7 (Summer 1963).

[135] Cole, J.P., Jr., "CATV, the Broadcaster Establishment, and the Federal Regulator," *American University Law Review*, v. 14 (June 1965).

[136] *Columbia Broadcasting System vs. TelePrompTer Corp.*, 251 F. Supp. 302 (1965).

[137] Comanor, W.S., and B.M. Mitchell, "Cable Television and the Impact of Regulation," *Bell Journal of Economics and Management Science*, v. 2 (Spring 1971).

[138] Comanor, W.S., and B.M. Mitchell, "The Costs of Planning: The FCC and Cable Television," *Journal of Law and Economics*, v. 15 (April 1972).

[139] Commission on Freedom of the Press, *A Free and Responsible Press: A General Report on Mass Communication: Newspapers, Radio, Motion Pictures, Magazines, and Books* (University of Chicago Press, 1947).

[140] Communication Act of 1934, 47 USC sec. 151ff.

[141] Comstock, G.A., and Eli Rubinstein, eds., *Television and Social Behavior*, Report to the Surgeon General's Advisory Committee on Television and Social Behavior (Washington, 1972).

[142] Conant, M., *Antitrust in the Motion Picture Industry: Economic & Legal Analysis* (University of California Press, 1960).

[143] Conant, M., "Consciously Parallel Action in Restraint of Trade," *Minnesota Law Review*, v. 38 (June 1954).

[144] Cooney, S., "An Annotated Bibliography of Articles on Broadcasting Law and Regulation in Law Periodicals: 1920-1955," *Journal of Broadcasting*, v. 14 (Winter 1969-70).

[145] Coons, J.E., *Freedom and Responsibility in Broadcasting* (Northwestern University Press, 1961).

[146] *Copyright Act of 1909*, 17 USC 1-215.

[147] Corden, W.M., "The Maximisation of Profit by a Newspaper," *Review of Economic Studies*, v. 20 (1952).

[148] Cournot, A., *The Mathematical Principles of the Theory of Wealth* (Irwin, 1963; originally published in French in 1838).

[149] Cox, K.A., "Competition in and Among the Broadcasting, CATV and Pay-TV Industries," *Antitrust Bulletin*, v. 13 (Fall 1968).

[150] Cox, K.A., and N. Johnson, "Broadcasting in America and the FCC's License Renewal Process," 14 FCC 2d.1 (1968).

[151] Cox, K.A., and N. Johnson, "Renewal Standards: The District of Columbia, Maryland, Virginia and West Virginia License Renewals," 21 FCC 2d 35 (1970).

[152] Crandall, R.W., "The Economic Effect of Television-Network Program 'Ownership'," *Journal of Law and Economics*, v. 14 (October 1971).

[153] Crandall, R.W., "FCC Regulation, Monopsony, and Network Television Program Costs," *Bell Journal of Economics and Management Science*, v. 3 (1972).

[154] Currier, Fred, "Economic Theory and Its Application to Newspapers," *Journalism Quarterly*, v. 37 (Spring 1960).

[155] De Fluer, M.L., *Theories of Communication*, revised ed. (McKay, 1970).

[156] Demsetz, H., "Joint Supply and Price Discrimination," *Journal of Law and Economics*, v. 16, (October 1973). Also "Reply to Professor Thompson," v. 16 (October 1973).

[157] Demsetz, H., "The Private Production of Public Goods," *The Journal of Law and Economics*, v. 13 (October 1970).

[158] Dernburg, T.F., "Consumer Response to Innovation: Television," in Thomas F. Dernburg, Richard N. Rosett, and Harold W. Watts, *Studies in Household Economic Behavior* (Yale University Press, 1958).

[159] Deutshman, P.J., and W.B. Emery, "Sale and Value of Radio Stations," *Journal of Broadcasting*, v. 5 (Summer 1961).

[160] De Vany, A.S., R. Eckert, C.J. Meyers, D.J. O'Hara, and R.C. Scott, "A Property System for Market Allocation of the Electromagnetic Spectrum: A Legal-Economic-Engineering Study," *Stanford Law Review*, v. 21 (June 1969).

[161] Devletoglou, Nicos E., "A Dissenting View of Duopoly and Spatial Competition," *Economica*, v. 32 (May 1965).

[162] Dimling, J.A., Jr., and G.E. Coffee, "The Evaluation of Alternatives for the Production, Distribution, and Financing of Television Programs" (Spindletop Research Report 219, 1967).

[163] Dingell, J.D., "The Role of Spectrum Allocation in Monopoly or Competition in Communications," *The Antitrust Bulletin*, v. 13 (Fall 1968).

[164] Dirlam, J.B., and A.E. Kahn, "The Merits of Reserving the Cost Savings from Domestic Communications Satellites for Support of Educational Television," *Yale Law Journal*, v. 77 (January 1968).

[165] Donner, S.T., ed., *The Future of Commercial Television, 1965-1975* (Stanford University Press, 1965).

[166] Doyle, P., "Economic Aspects of Advertising: A Survey," *Economic Journal*, v. 78 (September 1968).

[167] Eckert, R.D., "Spectrum Allocation and Regulatory Incentives," in *Conference on Communication Policy Research: Papers and Proceedings* (Office of Telecommunications Policy, Nov. 17-18, 1972).

[168] Edelman, J.M., *The Licensing of Radio Services in the United States 1927 to 1947: A Study in Administrative Formulation of Policy* (University of Illinois Press, 1950).

[169] *Educational Broadcasting Facilities Act*, 47 USC sec. 390ff.

[170] *Educational Broadcasting Review* (National Association of Educational Broadcasters, bi-monthly).

[171] Efron, E., *The News Twisters* (Nash Publishing, 1971).

[172] Ehrenberg, A.S.C., "Factor Analytic Search for Program Types," *Journal of Advertising Research*, v. 8 (March 1968).

[173] Electronic Industries Association, Industrial Electronics Division, "The IED/EIA Response to the FCC Docket 18397, Part V, 'The Future of Broadband Communications'," submitted to the FCC on October 29, 1969 (IED/EIA, 1969).

[174] Ellis, L.E., *Newsprint: Producers, Publishers, Political Pressures* (Rutgers University Press, 1960).

[175] Emery, E., *The Press in America: An Interpretive History of the Mass Media*, 3rd edition (Prentice-Hall, 1972).

[176] Emery, W.B., *Broadcasting and Government: Responsibilities and Regulations* (Michigan State University Press, 1971).

[177] Emery, W.B., *National and International Systems of Broadcasting: Their History, Operation, and Control* (Michigan State University Press, 1969).

[178] Epstein, E.J., *News From Nowhere: Television and the News* (Random House, 1973).

[179] Ernst, M.L., *The First Freedom* (Macmillan, 1946).

[180] *Facts, Figures and Film* (Broadcast Information Bureau, Inc., monthly).

[181] Faine, H.R., "Unions and the Arts," *American Economic Review*, v. 62 (May 1972).

[182] *Federal Communications Bar Journal* (Washington, D.C.: Federal Communication Bar Association, tri-annual).

[183] Federal Communications Commission, *An Economic Study of Standard Broadcasting* (U.S. Government Printing Office, 1947).

[184] Federal Communications Commission, *Annual Report*.

[185] Federal Communications Commission, "Cable Television Report and Order," 24 *Pike and Fisher Radio Reg* 2d 1501 (1972).

[186] Federal Communications Commission, *FCC Reports* (weekly).

[187] Federal Communications Commission, "The Economics of the TV-CATV Interface," staff report to the FCC prepared by the Research Branch of the Broadcast Bureau (July 15, 1970).

[188] Federal Communications Commission, "Fostering Expanded Use of UHF Television Channels," Docket #14229: "Fifth Report and Memorandum Opinion and Order, adopted Feb. 9, 1966," 2 FCC 2d 527 (1960).

[189] Federal Communications Commission, *Letter of Intent* (August 5, 1971), 22 *Pike and Fisher Radio Reg.* 2d 1755 (1971).

[190] Federal Communications Commission, *Network Broadcasting*, report of the Network Study Staff of the Network Study Committee, 1957. Printed as House Report 1297, 85th Cong., 2nd Sess., 1958.

[191] Federal Communications Commission, *Report on Chain Broadcasting;* Commission Order #37, Docket #5060 (May 1941).

[192] Federal Communications Commission, *Television Network Program Procurement, Part 1*, report by the Office of Network Study. Printed as House Report 281, 88th Cong. 1st Sess., 1963.

[193] Federal Communications Commission, *Television Network Program Procurement, Part II*, second interim report by the Office of Network Study (Washington, D.C.: Government Printing Office, 1965).

[194] Federal Communications Commission Network Study Staff, "Prospects for a Fourth Network in Television," *Journal of Broadcasting*, v. 2 (Winter 1957-58).

[195] Federal Communications Commission, "*En Banc* Programming Inquiry," 25 F.R. 7291 (1960).

[196] Federal Communications Commission, "Report on Editorializing by Broadcast Licenses," 13 FCC 1246 (1949).

[197] *Federal Communications Commission vs Sanders Bros.*, 309 U.S. 470 (1940).

[198] Feldman, N.E., "Cable Television and Satellites," Paper P-4171 (Santa Monica: RAND Corporation, August 1969).

[199] Festinger, L., *A Theory of Cognitive Dissonance* (Row, Peterson, 1957).

[200] Festinger, L., and N. Maccoby, "On Resistance to Persuasive Messages," *Journal of Abnormal and Social Psychology*, v. 68 (1964).

[201] *Film Daily Year Book of Motion Pictures* (Film Daily, annual).

[202] Finkelstein, H., "Copyright Revision-Music: CATV, Educational Broadcasting, and Juke Boxes," *Iowa Law Review*, v. 53 (February 1968).

[203] Fischman, L.L., "Evaluation of the FCC August 5, 1971 Distant Signal Proposals for Cable Television in Terms of their Impact on Over-the-Air Broadcasting," prepared for Covington and Burling by Economic Associates, Inc. (September 1971).

[204] Fisher, F.M., "Appendix to Reply Comments of the National Association of Broadcasters: The Fisher Report," mimeo (Washington, D.C.: October 26, 1964).

[205] Fisher, F.M., and G. Kraft, "The Impact of CATV on Local Television Stations: A Critique of the FCC's Staff Report," contained in "Joint Comments of 21 Television Broadcast Stations," in FCC Docket #18397A (December 7, 1971).

[206] Fisher, F.M., and V.E. Ferral, et al., "Community Antenna Television Systems and Local Television Stations Audiences," *Quarterly Journal of Economics*, v. 80 (May 1966).

[207] Fisher, F.M., "CATV and the Regulation of Television Broadcasting," *American Economic Review*, v. 56 (May 1966).

[208] Ford, F.W., "Economic Considerations in Licensing of Radio Broadcast Stations," *Federal Communications Bar Journal*, v. 17 (1961).

[209] *Fortnightly Corp. vs. United Artists Television, Inc.*, 392 U.S. 390 (1968).

[210] Frech, H.E., "Institutions for Allocating the Radio-TV Spectrum and the Vested Interests," *Journal of Economic Issues*, v. 4 (December 1970).

[211] Frech, H.E., "More on Efficiency in the Allocation of Radio-TV Spectrum," *Journal of Economic Issues*, v. 5 (September 1971).

[212] Friedrich, C.J., and E. Sternberg, "Congress and the Control of Radio Broadcasting," *The American Political Science Review*, v. 37 (October/December 1943).

[213] Friendly, F., *Due to Circumstances Beyond Our Control* (Random House, 1967).

[214] Friendly, H.J., "The Licensing of Radio and Television Broadcasting," in *The Federal Administrative Agencies; The Need for Better Definition of Standards* (Harvard University Press, 1962).

[215] Geller, H., "A Modest Proposal to Reform the Federal Communications Commission," RAND Paper P-5209 (RAND Corporation, 1974).

[216] Georgetown Law Journal, *Media and the First Amendment in a Free Society* (University of Massachusetts Press, 1973).

[217] Gerald, J.E., *The British Press Under Government Economic Controls* (University of Minnedota Press, 1956).

[218] Gerald, J.E., *The Social Responsibility of the Press* (University of Minnesota Press, 1963).

[219] Gerbner, G., "Mass Media and Human Communications Theory," in F.E.X. Dance, ed., *Human Communications Theory* (Holt, Rinehart and Winston, 1967).

[220] Gillmor, D.M., and J.A. Barron, *Mass Communications Law: Cases and Comment* (West, 1969; with supplement, 1971).

[221] Givens, R.A., "Refusal of Radio and Television Licenses on Economic Grounds," *Virginia Law Review*, v. 46 (November 1960).

[222] Goldberg, M.B., "Effect of Antitrust Legislation on Anticompetitive Practices of Television Networks in the Sale of Advertising Time," *University of Cincinatti Law Review*, v. 37 (Summer 1968).

[223] Goldberg, H., "A Proposal to Deregulate Broadcast Programming," *George Washington University Law Review*, v. 42, No. 1 (November 1973).

[224] Goldberg, V., "Marginal Cost Pricing, Investment Theory and CATV: Comment," *Journal of Law and Economics*, v. 14 (October 1971).

[225] Goldhamer, H., ed., "The Social Effects of Communication Technology," Report R-486-RSF (Santa Monica: RAND Corporation, May 1970).

[226] Goldin, H.H., "Economic and Regulatory Problems in the Broadcast Field," *Land Economics*, v. 30 (August 1954).

[227] Goldin, H.H., "The Economics of Broadcasting and Advertising," *American Economic Review*, v. 56 (May 1966).

[228] Goldin, H.H., "Financing Public Broadcasting," *Law and Contemporary Problems*, v. 34 (Summer 1969).

[229] Goldin, H.H., "Innovation and the Regulatory Agency: FCC's Reaction to CATV," report prepared for the Sloan Commission on Cable Communications (August 1970).

[230] Gompertz, K., "A Bibliography of Articles About Broadcasting in Law Periodicals, 1956-1968," *Journal of Broadcasting*, v. 14 (Winter 1969-70).

[231] Gordon, S., "The Cable Television Industry," report (New York: Equity Research Associates, October 1971).

[232] Great Britain, Committee on Broadcasting, *Report*, 2 vols. with appendices (Her Majesty's Stationery Office, 1962).

[233] Greenberg, B.S., and B. Dervin, *Use of the Mass Media by the Urban Poor* (Praeger, 1970).

[234] Greenberg, E., "Television Station Profitability and FCC Regulatory Policy," *Journal of Industrial Economics*, v. 17 (July 1969).

[235] Greenberg, E., "Wire Television and the FCC's Second Report and Order on CATV Systems," *Journal of Law and Economics*, v. 10 (October 1967).

[236] Greenberg, E., and H.J. Barnett, "TV Program Diversity-New Evidence and Old Theories," *American Economic Review*, v. 61 (May 1971).

[237] Grunewald, D., "Should the Comparative Hearing Process Be Retained in Television Licensing?" *American University Law Review*, v. 13 (June 1964). Reprinted in D. Grunewald and H.L. Bass, eds., *Public Policy and the Modern Corporation* (Appleton-Century-Crofts, 1966).

[238] Grunig, J.E., "The Role of Information in Economic Decision-Making," *Journalism Monographs*, No. 3 (Minneapolis: Association for Education in Journalism, December 1966).

[239] Buback, T.H., "American Interests in the British Film Industry," *The Quarterly Review of Economics and Business*, v. 7 (Summer 1967).

[240] Haiman, F.S., *Freedom of Speech* (Random House, 1965).

[241] Hale, G.E., and R.D. Hale, "Competition or Control: Radio and Television Broadcasting," *University of Pennsylvania Law Review*, v. 107 (March 1959).

[242] Hall, W.C., and R.B. Batlivala, "Market Structure and Duplication in TV Broadcasting," *Land Economics*, v. 47 (November 1971).

[243] Halloran, J.D., ed., *The Effects of Television* (Panther, 1970).

[244] Hansen, V.R', "Broadcasting and the Antitrust Laws," *Law and Contemporary Problems*, v. 22 (Autumn 1957).

[245] Harbridge House, Inc., *Copyright Fees for a Compulsory License of CATV* (an analysis of FCC "Public Dividend Plan") prepared for the Committee of Copyright Owners (n.d.).

[246] Harwood, K., "Broadcasting and the Theory of the Firm," *Law and Contemporary Problems*, v. 34 (Summer 1969).

[247] Hazard, W.R., "A Specification of Eight Television Appeals," *Journal of Broadcasting*, v. 10 (Winter 1965-66).

[248] Head, S.W., *Broadcasting in America: A Survey of Television and Radio*, revised edition (Houghton-Mifflin, 1972).

[249] Heitler, B., and K. Kalba, eds., "The Cable Fable," *Yale Review of Law and Social Action*, v. 2 (Spring 1972).

[250] Henderson, H., "Access to the Media: A Problem in Democracy," *Columbia Journalism Review*, v. 8 (Spring 1969).

[251] Herring, J.M., and G.C. Gross, *Telecommunications: Economics and Regulation* (McGraw-Hill, 1936).

[252] Herzel, Leo, "Public Interest and the Market in Color Television Regulation," *University of Chicago Law Review*, v. 18 (Summer 1951). Also: *University of Chicago Law Review*, v. 20 (Autumn 1952).

[253] Hilton, A., "The Economics of the Theater," *Lloyd's Bank Review*, v. 101 (July 1971).

[254] Hilton, G.W., "The Basic Behavior of Regulatory Commissions," *American Economic Review*, v. 62 (May 1972).

[255] Hochberg, P.R., "A Step Into the Regulatory Vacuum: Cable Television in the District of Columbia," *Catholic University Law Review*, v. 21 (Fall 1971).

[256] Horowitz, I., "Sports Broadcasting," in Roger Noll, ed., *Government and the Sports Business* (Brookings, 1974).

[257] Hotelling, H., "Stability in Competition," *The Economic Journal*, v. 34 (March 1929).

[258] Huettig, H., *Economic Control of the Motion Picture Industry: A Study in Industrial Organization* (University of Pennsylvania Press, 1944; reprinted 1971).

[259] Hull, W.H.N., "Public Control of Broadcasting: The Canadian and Australian Experiences," *Canadian Journal of Economics and Political Science*, v. 28 (1962).

[260] Hurt, R.M., and R.M. Schuchman, "The Economic Rationale of Copyright," *American Economic Review*, v. 56 (May 1966).

[261] Hyde, R.H., "The Role of Competition and Monopoly in the Communications Industries," *The Antitrust Bulletin*, v. 13 (Fall 1968).

[262] Innis, D.Q., "The Geographic Characteristics of Radio," *Canadian Journal of Economics and Political Science*, v. 20 (February 1954).

[263] Innis, H.A., *The Bias of Communication* (University of Toronto Press, 1951).

[264] Innis, H.A., *Changing Concepts of Time* (University of Toronto Press, 1952).

[265] Innis, H.A., *Empire and Communication* (Clarendon Press, 1950).

[266] Innis, H.A., "Technology and Public Opinion in the United States," *Canadian Journal of Economics and Political Science*, v. 17 (February 1951).

[267] *International Film Annual* (Doubleday, annual).

[268] *International Motion Picture Almanac* (Quigly Publications, annual).

[269] Intrilligator, M.D., *Mathematical Optimization and Economic Theory* (Prentice-Hall, 1971).

[270] Jaffe, L., "WHDH: The FCC and Broadcasting License Renewals," *Harvard Law Review*, v. 82 (January 1969).

[271] Johnson, H.G., *The Canadian Quandary*, Chapter 17: "Advertising in Today's Economy," and Chapter 18: "Apologia for Ad Men" (McGraw-Hill, 1963).

[272] Johnson, L.L., "Cable Television and Higher Education: Two Contrasting Experiences," Report R-828-MF (Santa Monica: RAND Corporation, September 1971).

[273] Johnson, L.L., "Cable Television and the Question of Protecting Local Broadcasting," Report R-595-MF (Santa Monica: RAND Corporation, October 1970).

[274] Johnson, L.L., "The Future of Cable Television: Some Problems of Federal Regulation," Memorandum RM-6199-FF (Santa Monica: RAND Corporation, January 1970).

[275] Johnson, L.L., "New Technology: Its Effect on Use and Management of the Radio Spectrum," *Washington University Law Quarterly*, v. 1967 (Fall 1967).

[276] Johnson, L.L., and M. Botein, "Cable Television: The Process of Franchising," Report R-1135-NSF (Santa Monica: RAND Corporation, March 1973).

[277] Johnson, L.L., et al., "Cable Communications in the Dayton Miami Valley: Basic Report," report R-943 KF/FF (Santa Monica: RAND Corporation, January 1972) and "Summary Report," report R-942 KF/FF (January 1972).

[278] Johnson, L.L., "The Impact of Communications Satellites on the Television Industry," paper No. P-3572 (Santa Monica: RAND Corporation, April 1967).

[279] Johnson, N., "The Public Interest and Public Broacasting: Looking at Communications as a Whole," *Washington University Law Quarterly* v. 1967 (Fall 1967).

[280] Johnson, N., *How to Talk Back to Your Television Set* (Bantam Books, 1970).

[281] Johnson, N., and J.M. Hoak, Jr., "Media Concentration: Some Observa-

tions on the United States Experience," *Iowa Law Review*, v. 56 (December 1970).

[282] Johnson, N., and T.A. Westen, "A Twentieth Century Soapbox: The Right to Purchase Radio and Television Time," *Virginia Law Review*, v. 57 (May 1971).

[283] Jones, W.K., "Licensing of Major Broadcast Facilities by the Federal Communications Commission," in Hearings on the FCC, Part 1, before the Subcommittee No. 6 of the House Select Committee on Small Business, 89th Congress, 2d Session (1966).

[284] Jones, W.K., "Regulation of Cable Television by the State of New York," report to the State of New York Public Service Commission (December 1970).

[285] Jones, W.K., "Regulation of Radio and Television Broadcasting," Chapter 10 in W.K. Jones, *Regulated Industries: Cases and Materials* (The Foundation Press, Inc., 1967).

[286] Jones, W.K., "Use and Regulation of the Radio Spectrum: Report on a Conference," *Washington University Law Quarterly*, v. 1968 (Winter 1968).

[287] Jorgensen, N.E., L. Schwartz, and R.A. Woods, "Programming Diversity in Proposals for New Broadcast Licenses," *George Washington Law Review*, v. 32 (April 1964).

[288] *Journal of Broadcasting* (Association for Professional Broadcasting Education, quarterly).

[289] Kahn, A.E., *The Economics of Regulation: Principles and Institutions*, 2 vols. (Wiley, 1971).

[290] Kahn, E., "Commercial Uses of Broadband Communications," report prepared for the Sloan Commission on Cable Communications (June 1971).

[291] Kahn, F.J., ed., *Documents of American Broadcasting* (Appleton-Century-Crofts, 1968; revised edition, 1972).

[292] Kahn, F.J., "Economic Injury and the Public Interest," *Federal Communications Bar Journal*, v. 23 (1969).

[293] Kahn, F.J., "Economic Regulation of Broadcasting as a Utility," *Journal of Broadcasting*, v. 7 (Spring 1963).

[294] Kahn, F.J., "Regulation of Intramedium 'Economic Injury' by the FCC," *Journal of Broadcasting*, v. 13 (Summer 1969).

[295] Kaldor, Nicholas, "The Economic Aspects of Advertising," *Review of Economic Studies*, v. 18 (1950-51).

[296] Kalven, H., Jr., "Broadcasting, Public Policy, and the First Amendment," *Journal of Law and Economics*, v. 10 (October 1967).

[297] Kellner, C.A., "The Rise and Fall of the Overmyer Network," *Journal of Broadcasting*, v. 13 (Spring 1969).

[298] Kelly, T., *A Competitive Cinema* (London: Institute of Economic Affairs, 1966).

[299] Kennedy, R., "Programming Content and Quality," *Law and Contemporary Problems*, v. 22 (Autumn 1957).

[300] Kennedy, W., "State and Local Taxation of Commercial Broadcasting," *Journal of Broadcasting*, v. 17 (Winter 1972-73).

[301] Kestenbaum, L., "Cable Television as a Common Carrier," in *Conference on Communications Policy Research: Papers and Proceedings* (Office of Telecommunications Policy, November 1972).

[302] Kestenbaum, L., *Common Carrier Access to Cable Communication: Regulations and Economic Issues*, report prepared for the Sloan Commission on Cable Communication (August 1971).

[303] Keyes, L.S., "The Recommendations of the Network Study Staff: A Study of Non-Price Discrimination in Broadcast Television," *George Washington Law Review*, v. 27 (January 1959).

[304] Kinter, C.V., "A Case Study in the Economics of Mass Communications," *Journalism Quarterly*, v. 25 (December 1948).

[305] Klapper, J., *The Effects of Mass Communication* (Glencoe Free Press, 1960).

[306] Kletter, R., "Cable Television: Making Public Access Effective," report R-1142-NSF (Santa Monica: RAND Corporation, 1973).

[307] Kletter, R., "TV Cassettes—A New Hardware and Its Implication," (Stanford University: Institute for Communication Research, February 1971).

[308] Knight, F.H., *Risk, Uncertainty, and Profit* (University of Chicago Press, 1971; originally published 1921).

[309] Knox, W.T., "Problems of Communication in Large Cities," a report to the Secretary, Smithsonian Institution (Washington, D.C.: Theil Press, April 1971).

[310] Koenig, A.E., *Broadcasting and Bargaining: Labor Relations in Radio and Television* (University of Wisconsin Press, 1970).

[311] Krasnow, E.G., and L.D. Longley, *The Politics of Broadcast Regulation* (St. Martin's Press, 1973).

[312] Kreps, T.J., "The Newspaper Industry," in *The Structure of American Industry*, ed. by W. Adams, 3rd. ed. (Macmillan, 1961).

[313] Krugman, H., "The Impact of Television Advertising: Learning Without Involvement," *Public Opinion Quarterly*, v. 29 (Fall 1965).

[314] Lacy, D., *Freedom and Communications* (University of Illinois Press, 1965).

[315] Lago, A.M., "The Price Effects of Joint Mass Communication Media Ownership," *Antitrust Bulletin*, v. 16 (Winter 1971).

[316] Lang, K., "Areas of Radio Preferences: A Preliminary Inquiry," *Journal of Applied Psychology*, v. 41 (February 1957).

[317] Land, Herman W. and Associates, Inc., *Television and the Wired City*, commissioned by National Association of Broadcasters, July 1968, for the use of the President's Task Force on Communication Policy.

[318] Le Duc, D.R., "The Cable Question: Evolution or Revolution in Electronic Mass Communications," *Annals of the American Academy of Political and Social Science*, (March 1972).

[319] Le Duc, D.R., "A Selective Bibliography on the Evolution of CATV: 1950-1970," *Journal of Broadcasting*, v. 15 (Spring 1971).

[320] Le Duc, D.R., and T.A. McCain, "The Federal Radio Commission in Federal Court: Origins of Broadcast Regulatory Doctrines," *Journal of Broadcasting*, v. 14 (Fall 1970).

[321] Lees, F.A., and C.Y. Yang, "The Redistributional Effect of Television Advertising," *Economic Journal*, v. 76 (June 1966).

[322] Lehmann, D.R., "Television Show Preference: Application of a Choice Model," *Journal of Marketing Research*, v. 8 (February 1971).

[323] Leonard, W.N., "Network Television Pricing: A Comment," *Journal of Business*, v. 42 (January 1969).

[324] Lerner, A.P., and H.W. Singer, "Some Notes on Duopoly and Spatial Competition," *Journal of Political Economy*, v. 65 (April 1937).

[325] Lever, E.A., *Advertising and Economic Theory* (Oxford University Press, 1947).

[326] Levin, H.J., *Broadcast Regulation and Joint Ownership of Media* (New York University Press, 1960).

[327] Levin, H.J., "Competition, Diversity, and the Television Group Ownership Rule," *Columbia Law Review*, v. 70 (May 1970).

[328] Levin, H.J., *The Invisible Resource: Use and Regulation of the Radio Spectrum* (Johns Hopkins Press, 1971).

[329] Levin, H.J., "The Policy of Joint Ownership of Newspapers and Television Stations: Some Assumptions, Objectives and Effects," reply comments to Docket #18110 before the FCC (New York Center for Policy Research, August 1971).

[330] Levin, H.J., "Program Duplication, Diversity, and Effective Viewer Choices: Some Empirical Findings," *American Economic Review*, v. 61 (May 1971).

[331] Levin, H.J., "Television's Second Choice: A Retrospective Look at the Sloan Cable Commission," *Bell Journal of Economics and Management Science*, v. 4 (Spring 1973).

[332] Lichty, L.W., *World and International Broadcasting: A Bibliography* (Association for Professional Broadcasting Education, 1971).

[333] Lindey, A., *Entertainment, Publishing and the Arts: Agreements and the Law* (Clark Boardman Co., 1963), with updating supplements.

[334] Lippmann, W., *Public Opinion* (Harcourt-Brace, 1922).

[335] Little, A.D., Inc., *Television Program Production, Procurement and Syndication*, An Economic Analysis Relating to the Federal Communication Commission's Proposed Rule in Docket No. 12782, vols. I and II (Cambridge: A.D. Little, Inc. February 1966).

[336] Little, A.D., Inc., *Television Program Production, Procurement, Distribution and Scheduling*, Data Relating to Proposals for Rule Making in FCC Docket No. 12782 (Cambridge: A.D. Little, Inc., April 1969, as corrected).

[337] Litwin, G.H., and W.H. Wroth, *The Effects of Common Ownership on Media Content and Influence: A Research Evaluation of Media Ownership and the Public Interest*, prepared for NAB (July 1969).

[338] Loevinger, L., "The Issues in Program Regulation," *Federal Communications Bar Journal*, v. 20 (1966).

[339] Longley, L.D., "The FCC's Attempt to Regulate Commercial Time," *Journal of Broadcasting*, v. 11 (Winter 1966-67).

[340] Luce, R.D., and H. Raiffa, *Games and Decisions* (Wiley, 1957).

[341] McCombs, M.E., *Mass Media in the Marketplace* (Association for Education in Journalism, 1972).

[342] McCoy, R.E., *Freedom of the Press: An Annotated Bibliography* (Southern Illinois University Press, 1968).

[343] McGowan, J.J., "Competition, Regulation and Performance in Television Broadcasting," *Washington University Law Quarterly* (Fall 1967).

[344] McKay, K.G., "Network," *Science and Technology* (April 1968).

[345] MacLaurin, W.R., "Patents and Technological Progress—A Study of Television," *Journal of Political Economy*, v. 58 (April 1950). Reprinted in S.M. Blumner and D.L. Hefner, eds., *Readings in the Regulation of Business* (International Textbook Co., 1968).

[346] McLuhan, Marshall, *Understanding Media* (McGraw-Hill, 1964).

[347] Machlup, F., *The Production and Distribution of Knowledge in the United States* (Princeton University Press, 1962).

[348] Macy, J.W., Jr., "Public Broadcasting: A Medium in Search of Solutions," *Law and Contemporary Problems*, v. 34 (Summer 1969).

[349] Manning, W.G., Jr., "The Supply of Prime-Time Entertainment Television Programs," Memorandum #152 (Stanford University: Center for Research in Economic Growth, September 1973).

[350] Mathewson, G.F., "A Consumer Theory of Demand for the Media," *Journal of Business*, v. 45 (April 1972).

[351] Mathewson, G.F., "A Note on the Price Effects of Market Power in the Canadian Newspaper Industry," *Canadian Journal of Economics*, v. 5 (May 1972).

[352] Mayer, M., *About Television* (Harper & Row, 1972).

[353] Mayer, M., "Cable and the Arts," report prepared for the Sloan Commission on Cable Communications (March 1971).

[354] Mayer, J.W., "Sanders Brothers Revisited: Protection of Broadcasters from the Consequences of Economic Competition," *Kentucky Law Journal*, v. 49 (Spring 1961).

[355] Mayor's Advisory Task Force on CATV and Telecommunications, "A

Report on Cable Television and Cable Telecommunication in New York City" (September 1968).

[356] Meckling, W.H., "Management of the Frequency Spectrum," *Washington University Law Quarterly*, v. 1968 (Winter 1968).

[357] Meier, R.L., *A Communications Theory of Urban Growth* (MIT Press, 1962).

[358] Melody, W., *Children's TV: The Economics of Exploitation* (Yale University Press, 1973).

[359] Mendelsohn, H., "The Neglected Majority: Mass Communications and the Working Person," report prepared for the Sloan Commission on Cable Communications (March 1971).

[360] Mickelson, S., *The Electric Mirror: Politics in an Age of Television* (Dodd, Mead, 1972).

[361] *Midwest Video Corp., vs. FCC, et al.*, 404 U.S. 1014 (1972).

[362] Milgram, S., and R.L. Shotland, *Television and Antisocial Behavior* (Academic Press, 1974).

[363] Minasian, J.R., "The Political Economy of Broadcasting in the 1920s," *Journal of Law and Economics*, v. 12 (October 1969).

[364] Minasian, J.R., "Television Pricing and the Theory of Public Goods," *Journal of Law and Economics*, v. 7 (October 1964).

[365] Minow, N., *Equal Time: The Private Broadcaster and the Public Interest* (Atheneum, 1964).

[366] Mitchell, B.M., "Cable, Cities and Copyrights," Paper #P-5086, (Santa Monica: RAND Corporation, September 1973).

[367] Mitchell, M.R., "State Regulation of Cable Television," Report R-783-HF (Santa Monica: RAND Corporation, September 1971).

[368] Moore, T., "The Purpose of Licensing," *Journal of Law and Economics*, v. 4 (October 1961).

[369] Moore, T.G., *The Economics of the American Theater* (Duke University Press, 1968).

[370] Mott, F.L., *American Journalism: A History, 1690-1960* (Macmillan, 1962).

[371] Musgrave, Richard A., *The Theory of Public Finance* (McGraw-Hill, 1959).

[372] Myers, K.H., "ABC and SRDS: The Evolution of Two Specialized Advertising Services," *Business History Review*, v. 34 (Autumn 1960).

[373] *NAEB Journal*, (National Association of Educational Broadcasters, semi-monthly, 1941-67).

[374] Nathan, Robert, Associates, *The Social and Economic Benefits of Television Broadcasting* (Washington, D.C.: Robert Nathan Associates, 1968).

[375] National Academy of Engineering, Committee on Telecommunications, "Communications Technology for Urban Improvement" (Washington, D.C.: National Academy of Engineering, 1971).

[376] National Academy of Engineering, Committee on Telecommunications, "Telecommunications for Enhanced Metropolitan Function and Form" (report to DTM under contract OEP-SE-69-101, August 1969).

[377] National Academy of Sciences, *Reports on Selected Topics in Telecommunications* (Washington, D.C.: Printing and Publishing Office, 1969).

[378] National Association of Broadcasters, "Broadcast Self Regulation Manual of the NAB Code Authority (NAB, March 1971).

[379] National Association of Broadcasters, *Dimensions of Radio* (Washington, D.C.: National Association of Broadcasters, annual).

[380] National Association of Broadcasters, *Dimensions of Television* (Washington, D.C.: National Association of Broadcasters, annual).

[381] National Association of Educational Broadcasters, "1971 Directory of Educational Broadcasting," (Washington, D.C.: National Association of Educational Broadcasters, January 1971).

[382] *National Broadcasting Company, Inc., et al. vs. United States, et al.*, 319 U.S. 190 (1943).

[383] The Network Project, "The Fourth Network, A Study" (Columbia University: The Network Project, 1971).

[384] Netzer, D., *Long-Range Financing of Public Broadcasting* (New York: National Citizens' Committee for Broadcasting, April 1969).

[385] *Newspaper Preservation Act*, Pub. Law 91-353, 84 Stat. 466.

[386] Nielson, A.C., Company, *The Television Audience* (Chicago: A.C. Nielson Company, annual).

[387] *Nielson Television Index*, "National Nielson TV Ratings," (various) "What the Ratings Really Mean," (Chicago: A.C. Nielson Company, 1964).

[388] Nixon, R.B., "The Problem of Newspaper Monopoly," in W. Schramm, ed., *Mass Communications* (University of Illinois Press, 1960).

[389] Nixon, R.B., and R.L. Jones, "The Content of Non-Competitive vs. Competitive Newspapers," *Journalism Quarterly*, v. 33 (Summer 1956).

[390] Nixon, R.B., and J. Ward, "Trends in Newspaper Ownership and Inter-Media Competition," *Journalism Quarterly*, v. 38 (Winter 1961).

[391] Noll, R.G., "Broadcast Content and Government Policy," *American University Symposium on Communications*, mimeo (Washington, D.C.: April 1970).

[392] Noll, R.G., "Decentralization of Public Television," in *Conference on Communication Policy Research: Papers and Proceedings* (Office of Telecommunications Policy, November 17-18, 1972).

[393] Noll, R.G., *Reforming Regulation: An Evaluation of the Ash Council Proposals* (Brookings Institution, 1971).

[394] Noll, R.G., M.J. Peck, and J.J. McGowan, *Economic Aspects of Television Regulation* (Brookings Institution, 1973).

[395] Note: "Antitrust Implications of Network Television Quantity Advertising Discounts," *Columbia Law Review*, v. 65 (November 1965).

[396] Note: "Aspects of Pay Television: Regulation, Constitutional Law, Antitrust," *California Law Review*, v. 53 (December 1965).

[397] Note: "CATV and Copyright Liability," *Harvard Law Review*, v. 80 (May 1967).

[398] Note: "CATV and the Copyright Liability: On a Clear Day You Can See Forever," *Virginia Law Review*, v. 52 (December 1966).

[399] Note: "CATV—the Continuing Copyright Controversy," *Fordham Law Review*, v. 37 (May 1969).

[400] Note: "The Crisis in Electromagnetic Frequence Spectrum Allocation: Abatement Through Market Distribution," *Iowa Law Review*, v. 53 (October 1967).

[401] Note: "The Darkened Channels: UHF Television and the FCC," *Harvard Law Review*, v. 75 (June 1962).

[402] Note: "Disk Television: Some Recurring Copyright Problems in the Reproduction and Performance of Motion Pictures," *University of Chicago Law Review*, v. 34 (Spring 1967).

[403] Note: "The FCC's Proposed CATV Regulations," *Stanford Law Review*, v. 21 (June 1969).

[404] Note: "CATV: Liability for the Uncompensated Transmission of Television Programs," *Minnesota Law Review*, v. 50 (1965).

[405] Note: "Professional Football Telecasts and the Blackout Privilege," *Cornell Law Review*, v. 57 (January 1972).

[406] Note: "State Regulation of Radio and Television," *Harvard Law Review*, v. 73 (December 1959).

[407] Note: "The Wire Mire: The FCC and CATV," *Harvard Law Review*, v. 79 (December 1965).

[408] Ohio University Research Center, "Broadcast Stations and Newspapers: The Problems of Information Control: A Content Analysis of Local News Presentations," Study conducted on behalf of the NAB (Ohio University Research Center, June 1971).

[409] Ohls, J.C., "Marginal Cost Pricing Investment Theory and CATV," *Journal of Law and Economics*, v. 13 (October 1970).

[410] Ohls, J.C., "Marginal Cost Pricing, Investment Theory and CATV: A Reply," *Journal of Law and Economics*, v. 14 (October 1971).

[411] Olson, T.B., and N.S. Oberstein, "Aspects of Pay Television: Regulation, Constitutional Law, Antitrust," *California Law Review*, v. 53 (1965).

[412] Owen, B.M., "Diversity and Television" (Washington, D.C.: U.S. Office of Telecommunications Policy, August 1972).

[413] Owen, B.M., "Newspaper and Television Station Joint Ownership," *Antitrust Bulletin*, v. 18 (Winter 1973).

[414] Owen, B.M., "Measuring Violence on Television: The Grebner Index" (Washington, D.C.: U.S. Office of Telecommunications Policy, June 1972).

[415] Owen, B.M., "Public Policy and Emerging Technology in the Media," *Public Policy*, v. 18 (Summer 1970).

[416] Owen, B.M., "Spectrum Allocation: A Survey of Alternative Methodologies" (Washington, D.C.: U.S. Office of Telecommunications Policy, April 1972).

[417] Owen, B.M., "The Regulation of Commercial Radio Stations" (Washington, D.C.: U.S. Office of Telecommunications Policy, December 1971).

[418] Owen, B.M., "The Role of Analysis in the Formation of Cable Television Policy," in R.E. Park, ed., *The Role of Analysis in Regulatory Decisionmaking: The Case of Cable Television* (Lexington Books, D.C. Heath and Company, 1973).

[419] Owen, B.M., "Economics of the First Amendment: Discussion," *American Economic Review*, v. 64 (May 1974).

[420] Owen, B.M., D. Grey, and J.N. Rosse, "A Selected Bibliography in the Economics of the Mass Media," Center for Research in Economic Growth, Memorandum #99 (Stanford University, 1970).

[421] Owen, B.M., and W. Manning, Jr., "The Television Rivalry Grame," (Stanford University: Program in Information Technology and Telecommunications, Center for Interdisciplinary Research, Report #5, July 1973).

[422] Oxenfeldt, A., "A Dynamic Element in Consumption: The TV Industry," in L.H. Clark, ed., *Consumption Behavior: Research on Consumer Reactions* (Harper & Brothers, 1958).

[423] Park, R.E., "Cable Television, UHF Broadcasting, and FCC Regulatory Policy," *Journal of Law and Economics*, v. 15 (April 1972).

[424] Park, R.E., "The Exclusivity Provision of the Federal Communications Commission's Cable Television Regulations," Report R-1057-FF/MF (Santa Monica: RAND Corporation, June 1972).

[425] Park, R.E., "Future Growth of Cable Television," Paper P-4527, (Santa Monica: RAND Corporation, December 1970).

[426] Park, R.E., "The Growth of Cable TV and Its Probable Impact on Over-the-Air Broadcasting," *American Economic Review*, v. 61 (May 1971).

[427] Park, R.E., "Prospects for Cable in the 100 Largest Television Markets," *Bell Journal of Economics and Management Science*, v. 3 (Spring 1972).

[428] Park, R.E., ed., *The Role of Analysis in Regulatory Decisionmaking: The Case of Cable Television* (Lexington Books, D.C. Heath and Company, 1973).

[429] Park, R.E., "Television Station Performance and Revenues," *Educational Broadcasting Review*, v. 5 (June 1971).

[430] Park, R.E., "New Television Networks," RAND Report R-1408-MF (RAND Corporation, December 1973).

[431] Parker, E.B., "The New Communications Media," in C.S. Wallia, ed.,

Toward Century 21: Technology, Society and Human Values (Basic Books, 1970).

[432] Parker, E.B., "Technological Change and the Mass Media," in *Handbook of Communication*, I. de Sola Pool, et al., eds. (Rand-McNally, 1973).

[433] Peacock, A., "Welfare Economics and Public Subsidies to the Arts," *Manchester School*, v. 37 (December 1969).

[434] Pemberton, J., Jr., "Foreseeable Problems in a System of Maximum Access," report prepared for the Sloan Commission on Cable Communications (May 1971).

[435] Perry, R.L., "Current Antitrust Problems in Broadcasting," *Ohio State Law Journal*, v. 27 (Winter 1966).

[436] Peterman, J.L., "The Clorox Case and Television Rate Structure," *Journal of Law and Economics*, v. 11 (October 1968).

[437] Peterman, J.L., "Concentration of Control and the Price of Television Time," *American Economic Review*, v. 61 (May 1971).

[438] Peterman, J.L., "The Structure of National Time Rates in the Television Broadcasting Industry," *Journal of Law and Economics*, v. 8 (October 1965).

[439] Phillips, M.A.M., *CATV: A History of Community Antenna Television* (Northwestern University Press, 1972).

[440] Pike and Fisher, *Radio Regulation* (weekly).

[441] Pilnick, R., "Cable Television: Technical Considerations of Franchising Major Market Systems," Report R-1137-NSF (Santa Monica: RAND Corporation, March 1973).

[442] Pilnick, R., and W.S. Baer, "Cable Television: A Guide in the Technology," Report R-1141-NSF (Santa Monica: RAND Corporation, 1973).

[443] Plant, A., "The Economic Aspects of Copyright in Books," *Economica*, v. 1 (May 1934).

[444] Pontifical Commission for the Means of Social Communication, "Communication: A Pastoral Instruction of the Media, Public Opinion and Human Progress" (Washington, D.C.: United States Catholic Conference, May 1971).

[445] Pool, I. de Sola, et al., eds., *Handbook of Communication* (Rand McNally, 1972).

[446] Posner, R.A., "The Appropriate Scope of Regulation in the Cable Television Industry," *Bell Journal of Economics and Management Science*, v. 3 (Spring 1972).

[447] Posner, R.A., "Cable Television: The Problem of Local Monopoly," Memorandum RM-6309-FF (Santa Monica: RAND Corporation, May 1970).

[448] Posner, R.A., "Natural Monopoly and Its Regulation," *Stanford Law Review*, v. 21 (February 1969).

[449] Posner, R.A., "Taxation by Regulation," *Bell Journal of Economics and Management Science*, v. 2 (Spring 1971).

[450] Powers, K.H., "Diversity of Broadcasting," *Science and Technology* (April 1968).

[451] Price, M., and M. Botein, "Cable Television: Citizen Participation After the Franchise," Report R-1139-NSF (Santa Monica: RAND Corporation, March 1973).

[452] Price, M., and J. Wicklein, *Cable Television: A Guide for Citizen Action* (Pilgrim Press, 1972).

[453] President's Task Force on Communications Policy, "Final Report," (Washington, D.C., 1968).

[454] President's Task Force on Communications Policy, "Staff Papers," #1 to 8, especially #6 ("Future Opportunities for Television") and "Bibliography," (Springfield, Va.: Federal Clearinghouse, June 1969).

[455] *Public Broadcasting Act of 1967*, 47 U.S.C. sec. 396ff.

[456] Quirk, J., and M. El Hodari, "The Economic Theory of a Professional Sports League," pp. 33-80 in R.G. Noll, ed., *Government and the Sports Business* (Brookings Institution, 1974).

[457] Rapaport, A., *N-Person Game Theory* (University of Michigan Press, 1970).

[458] Reddaway, W.B., "The Economics of Newspapers," *Economic Journal*, v. 73 (June 1963).

[459] *Red Lion Broadcasting Co. vs. FCC*, 395 U.S. 367 (1968).

[460] Rivers, W., and W. Schramm, *Responsibility in Mass Communication* (Harper & Row, 1969).

[461] Rivkin, S.R., "Cable Television: A Guide to Federal Regulations," Report R-1138-NSF (Santa Monica: RAND Corporation, March 1973).

[462] Rivkin, S.R., "The Changing Signals of Cable TV," *The Georgetown Law Journal*, v. 60 (June 1972).

[463] Roberts, K., "Antitrust Problems in the Newspaper Industry," *Harvard Law Review*, v. 82 (December 1968).

[464] Robinson, D.E., "The Economics of Fashion Demand," *Quarterly Journal of Economics*, v. 75 (August 1961).

[465] Robinson, G.O., "The FCC and the First Amendment: Observations on 40 Years of Radio and Television Regulation," *Minnesota Law Review*, v. 52 (November 1967).

[466] Robinson, G.O., "Radio Spectrum Regulation: The Administrative Process and the Problems of Institutional Reform," *Minnesota Law Review*, v. 53 (June 1969).

[467] Robinson, J.P., "Television and Leisure Time: Yesterday, Today and (Maybe) Tomorrow" (University of Michigan, Survey Research Center, September 1971).

[468] Robinson, J.P., and P.E. Converse, "The Impact of Television on Mass Media Usage: A Cross-National Comparison" (University of Michigan, Survey Research Center, August 1966).

[469] Rockefeller Panel, *The Performing Arts: Problems and Prospects* (McGraw-Hill, 1965).

[470] Roper Organization, "An Extended View of Public Attitudes Toward Television and Other Mass Media, 1959-1971" (New York: Television Information Office, 1971).

[471] Rose, L.A., "A Comment on Efficiency in the Allocation of the Radio-TV Spectrum," *Journal of Economic Issues*, v. 5 (September 1971).

[472] Rosenblum, V.G., "How to Get Into TV: The Federal Communications Commission and Miami's Channel 10," in A.F. Westin, ed., *The Uses of Power: 7 Cases in American Politics* (Harcourt Brace and World, 1962).

[473] Rosenblum, V.G., "Low Visibility Decision-Making by Administrative Agencies: The Problem of Spectrum Allocation" *Administrative Law Review*, v. 18 (Fall 1965).

[474] Ross, L., "The Copyright Question in CATV," report prepared for the Sloan Commission on Cable Communications (April 1971).

[475] Rosse, J.N., "Credible and Incredible Economic Evidence: Reply Comments in FCC Docket 18110 (Cross Ownership of Newspapers and Television Stations)" Memorandum #109 (Stanford University: Research Center in Economic Growth, April 1971).

[476] Rosse, J.N., "Daily Newspapers, Monopolistic Competition, and Economies of Scale," *American Economic Review*, v. 57 (May 1967).

[477] Rosse, J.N., B.M. Owen, and D.L. Grey, "Economic Issues in the Joint Ownership of Newspaper and Television Media: Comments in Response to 'Further Notice of Proposed Rule-Making,' Federal Communications Commission, Docket 18110," Memorandum No. 97 (Stanford University, Research Center in Economic Growth, May 1970).

[478] Rothenberg, J., "Consumer Sovereignty and the Economics of TV Programming," *Studies in Public Communication*, v. 4 (Fall 1962).

[479] Royal Commission on Broadcasting, *Report of the Royal Commission on Broadcasting* (Ottawa: Queen's Printer, 1965).

[480] Rucker, B.W., *The First Freedom* (Southern Illinois University Press, 1968).

[481] Samuelson, P.A., "The Monopolistic Competition Revolution," chapter 5 in R.E. Kuenne, *Monopolistic Competition Theory: Studies in Impact* (Wiley, 1967).

[482] Samuelson, P.A., "Aspects of Public Expenditure Theories," *Review of Economics and Statistics*, v. 40 (November 1958).

[483] Samuelson, P.A., "Contrast Between Welfare Conditions for Joint Supply and for Public Goods," *Review of Economics and Statistics*, v. 51 (February 1969).

[484] Samuelson, P.A., "Diagrammatic Exposition of a Theory of Public Expenditure," *Review of Economics and Statistics*, v. 37 (November 1955).

[485] Samuelson, P.A., "Public Goods and Subscription TV: A Correction of the Record," *Journal of Law and Economics*, v. 7 (October 1964).

[486] Samuelson, P.A., "The Pure Theory of Public Expenditure," *Review of Economics and Statistics*, v. 36 (November 1954).

[487] Sargent, L.W., and G. Stempel, "Poverty, Alienation, and Mass Media Use," *Journalism Quarterly*, v. 45 (Summer 1968).

[488] Sarner, H., "Assessments for Broadcast Licenses," *Federal Bar Journal*, v. 21 (Spring 1961).

[489] Sarnoff, D., "Communications and the Law," *Antitrust Bulletin*, v. 7, (September-October 1962).

[490] Scanlon, Paul D., "The FTC, The FCC, and The 'Counter-Ad' Controversy," *Antitrust Law and Economics*, v. 5 (Fall 1971).

[491] Schiller, H.I., "Mind Management: Mass Media in the Advanced Industrial State," *Quarterly Review of Economics and Business*, v. 11 (Spring 1971).

[492] Schramm, W., "The Audiences of Educational Television: A Report to NET" (Stanford University: Institute for Communication Research, 1967).

[493] Schramm, W., ed., *Mass Communications: A Book of Readings* (University of Illinois Press, 1960).

[494] Schramm, W., and L. Nelson, *The Financing of Public Television* (Palo Alto, Calif.: Aspen Program on Communications and Society, 1972).

[495] Schramm, W., and D.F. Roberts. eds.. *The Process and Effects of Mass Communication* (University of Illinois Press, 1971).

[496] Schramm, W., et al., *The People Look at Educational Television* (Stanford University Press, 1963).

[497] Schwartz, B., "Antitrust and the FCC: The Problem of Network Dominance," *University of Pennsylvania Law Review*, v. 107 (April 1959).

[498] Seiden, M.H., *Cable Television U.S.A.: An Analysis of Government Policy* (Praeger 1972).

[499] Seiden, M.H., "An Economic Analysis of Community Antenna Television Systems and the Television Broadcasting Industry," Appendix A to the 1965 FCC Progress Report, in *Hearings Before the Subcommittee on Communications of the Senate Committee on Commerce*, 89th Congress, 1st Session (1965).

[500] Seiden, M.H. and Associates, "An Economic Analysis of the Impact of License Forfeiture on the Television and Broadcasting Industry," submitted to the FCC as part of Docket #18110 (Seiden, January 1969).

[501] Shepherd, J.R., "Differences in Demand and Use of Television Programming Variety," *Journal of Broadcasting*, v. 6 (Spring 1962).

[502] Shubik, M., "A Curmudgeon's Guide to Microeconomics," *Journal of Economic Literature*, v. 8 (June 1970).

[503] Simon, H.A., and C.P. Bonini, "The Size Distribution of Business Firms," *American Economic Review*, v. 48 (September 1968).

[504] Simon, J.L., "Are There Economies of Scale in Advertising?" *Journal of Advertising Research*, v. 5 (June 1965).

[505] Simon, J.L., *Issues in Economics of Advertising*, appendix D, "Bibliographical Essay on Some Sources of Data in Advertising" (University of Illinios Press, 1970).

[506] Simon, L.S., and M.R. Marks, "Consumer Behavior During the New York Newspaper Strike," *Journal of Advertising Research*, v. 5 (March 1965).

[507] Skornia, H.J., and J.W. Kitson, eds., *Problems and Controversies in Television and Radio* (Pacific Books, 1968).

[508] Sloan Commission on Cable Communications, *On the Cable: The Television of Abundance* (McGraw-Hill, 1971).

[509] Smead, E., *Freedom of Speech by Radio and Television* (Washington, D.C.: Public Affairs Press, 1959).

[510] Smith, R.L., *The Wired Nation* (Harper & Row, 1972).

[511] Smithies, A., "Optimum Location in Spatial Competition," *Journal of Political Economy*, v. 49 (June 1941).

[512] Sparks, K.R., *A Bibliography of Doctoral Dissertations in Television and Radio*, 3rd edition (Syracuse University School of Journalism, 1971).

[513] Sperry, R., "A Selected Bibliography of Works on the Federal Communications Commission," *Journal of Broadcasting*, v. 12 (Winter 1967-68) and "1967-69 Supplement," *Journal of Broadcasting*, v. 14 (Summer 1970).

[514] Spraos, J., *The Decline of the Cinema: An Economist's Report* (Allen and Unwin, 1962).

[515] Stahle, R.H., "Diversification in Communication: The FCC and its Failing Standards," *Utah Law Review*, v. 1969 (June 1969).

[516] *Standard Rate and Data Service* (Skokie, Illinois: Standard Rate and Data, Inc., various—including daily newspapers, weekly newspapers, consumer magazines and farm publications, business publications, spot radio, spot television and network rates and data).

[517] Stanley, E.R., "Revocation, Renewal of License, and Fines and Forfeiture Cases before the Federal Communications Commission," *Journal of Broadcasting*, v. 8 (Fall 1964).

[518] Statistical Research, Inc., "The Potential Impact of CATV on Television Stations," Appendix E to National Association of Broadcasters, "Comments in FCC Docket #18397-A" (December 1970).

[519] Steiner, G.A., "The People Look at Commercials: A Study of Audience Behavior," *Journal of Business*, v. 39 (April 1966).

[520] Steiner, G.A., *The People Look at Television: A Study of Audience Attitudes* (Knopf 1963).

[521] Steiner, P.O., "Economic and Regulatory Problems of the Broadcasting Industry," *American Economic Review*, v. 44 (May 1954).

[522] Steiner, P.O., "Monopoly and Competition in Television: Some Policy Issues," *Manchester School of Economics and Political Science*, v. 29 (May 1961).

[523] Steiner, P.O., "Program Patterns and Preferences, and the Workability of Competition in Radio Broadcasting," *Quarterly Journal of Economics*, v. 66 (May 1952).

[524] Steiner, P.O., and H.J. Barnett, with the assistance of E. Greenberg and M. Sovereign, "Comments of Economic Consultants Dr. P.O. Steiner and Dr. H.J. Barnett on the MPATI Petition," submitted to the Federal Communications Commission as Exhibit No. 1 of "Comments Submitted by the Midwest Program on Airborne Television Instruction, Inc.," in FCC Dockets 14229 and 15201 (April 1964).

[525] Stempel, G.H., III, "A New Analysis of Monopoly and Competition," *Columbia Journalism Review*, v. 6 (Spring 1967).

[526] Stephenson, W.F., *The Play Theory of Mass Communication* (University of Chicago Press, 1967).

[527] Sterling, C.H., "Newspaper Ownership of Broadcast Stations, 1920-1968," *Journalism Quarterly*, v. 46 (Summer 1969).

[528] Sterling, C.H., *Ownership Characteristics of Broadcasting Stations and Newspapers in the Top 100 Markets: 1922-1967*, an historical analysis prepared for the NAB (Temple University, School of Communications and Theater, March 1971).

[529] Stigler, G., "The Economics of Information," *Journal of Political Economy*, v. 69 (June 1961).

[530] Stigler, G., "A Note on Black Booking," in George Stigler, *The Organization of Industry* (Irwin 1968).

[531] Stigler, G., "A Theory of Oligopoly," *Journal of Political Economy*, v. 72 (February 1964).

[532] Stigler, G., "The Division of Labor Is Limited by the Extent of the Market," *Journal of Political Economy*, v. 59 (June 1951).

[533] Strotz, R., "Two Propositions Related to Public Goods," *Review of Economics and Statistics*, v. 40 (November 1958).

[534] Sucherman, S.P., "Cable TV: The Endangered Revolution," *Columbia Journalism Review*, v. 10 (May/June 1971).

[535] Suelflow, J.E., "Subscription Television, Part I: What Are the Chances of Success?" *Public Utilities Fortnightly*, v. 79 (June 22, 1967).

[536] Suelflow, J.E., "Subscription Television, Part 2: Should Subscription Television Be Regulated?" *Public Utilities Fortnightly*, v. 80 (July 6, 1967).

[537] Tate, C., ed., *Cable Television in the Cities: Community Control, Public Access, and Minority Ownership* (Washington, D.C.: The Urban Institute, 1972).

[538] Teeter, D.L., *The Law of Mass Communications: Freedom and Control of Print and Broadcast Media* (Foundation Press, 1969, with 1971 notes; 2nd edition, 1973, by H.J. Nelson and D.L. Teeter).

[539] *Television Digest with Consumer Electronics* (Television Digest, Inc., weekly).

[540] *Television Factbook* (Television Digest, annual).

[541] *Television Quarterly* (Boston University: School of Public Communication).

[542] Telser, L.G., "On the Regulation of Industry: A Note," *Journal of Political Economy*, v. 77 (November-December 1969).

[543] Thomas, G.L., "The Listener's Right to Hear in Broadcasting," *Stanford Law Review*, v. 22 (April 1970).

[544] Thompson, E.A., "The Perfectly Competitive Production of Collective Goods," *Review of Economics and Statistics*, v. 50 (February 1968). Comments by Bruce M. Owen, James D. Rodgers, and Subrata K. Ganguly, and reply by Thompson, v. 51 (November 1969).

[545] Thompson, E.A., "The Private Production of Public Goods: A Comment," *Journal of Law and Economics*, v. 16 (October 1973).

[546] *Times-Picayune vs. United States*, 345 U.S. 594 (1953).

[547] Toohey, D.W., "Newspaper Ownership of Broadcast Facilities," *Federal Communications Bar Journal*, v. 20 (1966).

[548] Troldahl, V.C., "Studies of Consumption of Mass Media Content," *Journalism Quarterly*, v. 42 (Autumn 1965).

[549] Tuber, R., "An Annotated Bibliography on Broadcast Rights, 1920-1955," *Journal of Broadcasting*, v. 14 (Winter 1969-70).

[550] *TV Pix vs. Taylor*, 304 F. Supp. 549 (D. Nev. 1968), affirmed: 396 US 556 (1970).

[551] *TV Source Books* (Broadcast Information Bureau, Inc., annual) in 3 vols.: *TV "Free" Film Source Book; Series, Serials and Packages; Feature Film Source Book.*

[552] UNESCO, "Communication in the Space Age: The Use of Satellites by the Mass Media" (Paris, 1968).

[553] UNESCO, *Film and Cinema Statistics: A Preliminary Report on Methodology with Tables Giving Current Statistics*, Statistical Reports and Studies #1 (UNESCO Publications Center, 1955).

[554] UNESCO, *Removing Taxes on Knowledge*, Reports and Papers on Mass Communications #58 (UNESCO Publications Center, 1969).

[555] United Research Inc., "The Implications of Limiting Multiple Ownership of Television Stations," 2 vols. Prepared for the Council for Television Development (Cambridge, Mass.: United Research Inc., September 1966).

[556] *United States vs. Citizens Publishing Company*, 394 U.S. 131 (1969).

[557] *United States vs. Paramount Pictures*, 334 U.S. 131 (1948).

[558] *United States vs. Southwestern Cable*, 392 U.S. 390 (1968).

[559] U.S. Congress House of Representatives, Committee on Commerce, *Network Broadcasting*, House Report 1297, 85th Congress, 2d Session (1958) (Barrow Report).

[560] U.S. Congress House of Representatives, Committee on Commerce, *Regulation of Broadcasting: Half A Century of Government Regulation*

of Broadcasting and the Need for Further Legislative Action, a Study, Hearings, 85th Congress, 2d Session (1958).

[561] U.S. Congress House of Representatives, Committee on Commerce, Subcommittee on Communications and Power, *Broadcast Advertisements*, Hearings, 88th Congress, 1st Session (1963).

[562] U.S. Congress House of Representatives, Committee on Commerce, Subcommittee on Communications and Power, *Regulation of Community Antenna Television*, Hearings, 89th Congress, 1st Session (1965) 2d Session (1966).

[563] U.S. Congress, House of Representatives, Committee on Commerce, Subcommittee on Communications and Power, *Financing for Public Broadcasting–1972*, Hearings, 92nd Congress, 2d Session (1972).

[564] U.S. Congress, House of Representatives, Committee on Commerce, Subcommittee on Communications and Power, *Subscription Television*, Hearings, 90th Congress, 1st Session (1967), and 91st Congress, 1st Session (1969).

[565] U.S. Congress House of Representatives, Committee on Commerce, Special Subcommittee on Investigation, *Broadcast Ratings*, parts 1-4, Hearings, 88th Congress, 1st and 2d Sessions (1963 and 1964).

[566] U.S. Congress House of Representatives, Committee on Commerce, Special Subcommittee on Investigations, *Fairness Doctrine*, Hearings, 90th Congress, 2d Session (1968).

[567] U.S. Congress House of Representatives, Committee on the Judiciary, Subcommittee No. 3, *Copyright Law Revision*, Hearings, parts 1, 2, and 3, 89th Congress, 1st Session (1965).

[568] U.S. Congress House of Representatives, Committee on the Judiciary, Antitrust Subcommittee, *Antitrust Consent Decrees and the Television Broadcasting Industry*, Hearings, 87th Congress, 1st Session (1961).

[569] U.S. Congress House of Representatives, Committee on the Judiciary, Antitrust Subcommittee, *Monopoly Problems in Regulated Industries, Part 2, Television*, 4 vols., Hearings, 84th Congress, 2d Session (1956).

[570] U.S. Congress House of Representatives, Committee on the Judiciary, Antitrust Subcommittee, *The Television Broadcasting Industry*, House Report No. 607, 85th Congress, 1st Session (1957) (Celler Committee Report).

[571] U.S. Congress House of Representatives, "Radio Laws of the United States," compiled by G.G. Udell, Superintendent, Document Room (Washington, D.C.: U.S. Government Printing Office, 1972).

[572] U.S. Congress House of Representatives, Select Committee on Small Business, Subcommittee No. 6, *Activities of Regulatory and Enforcement Agencies Relating to Small Business, Federal Communications Commission*, Hearings, parts 1 and 2, 89th Congress, 2d Session (1966).

[573] U.S. Congress House of Representatives, Select Committee on Small

Business, Subcommittee No. 6, *Activities of Regulatory Agencies Relating to Small Business* (Federal Communications Commission), House Report 2344, 89th Congress, 2d Sesssion (1966).

[574] U.S. Congress, Senate Committee on Commerce, *Public Broadcasting Act of 1967*, S. Report 222, 90th Congress, 1st Session (1967).

[575] U.S. Congress, Senate Committee on Commerce, *The Network Monopoly*, a report by J.W. Bricker for the Committee's use, 84th Congress, 2d Session (1956).

[576] U.S. Congress, Senate Committee on Commerce, Subcommittee on Communications, *Federal Communications Commission Policy Matters and Television Programming*, Hearings, Part 1, 91st Congress, 1st Session (1969); Part 2 (March 1969).

[577] U.S. Congress, Senate Committee on Commerce, Subcommittee on Communications, *Hearings on the Ford Foundation Proposal for a Broadcasters Non-Profit Satellite Service*, 89th Congress, 2d Session, Ser. 89-78 (1966).

[578] U.S. Congress, Senate Committee on Commerce, Subcommittee on Communications, *The Public Television Act of 1967*, Hearings, 90th Congress, 1st Session (1967).

[579] U.S. Congress, Senate Committee on Commerce, *Allocation of TV Channels*, report of the Ad Hoc Advisory Committee on Allocations, 85th Congress, 2d Session (March 1958).

[580] U.S. Congress, Senate Committee on Commerce, *Investigation of Television Networks and the UHF-VHF Problem*, report prepared by Robert F. Jones, Special Council, 84th Congress, 1st Session (1955).

[581] U.S. Congress, Senate Committee on Commerce, *Television Inquiry, Part 1, UHF-VHF Allocations Problem: Testimony of Federal Communications Commission*, Hearings, 84th Congress, 2d Session (1956).

[582] U.S. Congress, Senate Committee on Commerce, *Television Inquiry, Part 2, UHF-VHF Allocations Problem: Testimony of Public and Industry Witnesses*, Hearings, 84th Congress, 2d Session (1956).

[583] U.S. Congress, Senate Committee on Commerce, *Television Inquiry, Part 3, Subscription Television*, Hearings, 84th Congress, 2d Session (1956).

[584] U.S. Congress, Senate Committee on Commerce, *Television Inquiry, Part 4, Network Practices*, Hearings, 84th Congress, 2d Session (1956).

[585] U.S. Congress, Senate Committee on Commerce, *The Television Inquiry, Television Network Practices*, staff report, 85th Congress, 1st Session (1957).

[586] U.S. Congress, Senate Committee on Commerce, *Television Inquiry, Part 7, The Television Rating Services*, Hearings, 85th Congress, 2d Session (1958).

[587] U.S. Congress, Senate Committee on Commerce, *The Television Inquiry, The Problem of Television Service for Smaller Communities*, staff report, 85th Congress, 2d Session (1958).

[588] U.S. Congress, Senate Committee on Commerce, *Television Inquiry, Part 8*, Hearings, 86th Congress, 2d Session (1960).

[589] U.S. Congress, Senate Committee on Commerce, *Television Network Regulation and the UHF Problem*, memorandum by H.M. Plotkin, Special Counsel, 84th Congress, 1st Session (1955).

[590] U.S. Congress, Senate Committee on Commerce, Subcommittee on Communications, *Status of UHF and Multiple Ownership of TV Stations*, Hearings, 83rd Congress, 2d Session (1954).

[591] U.S. Congress, Senate Committee on the Judiciary, Subcommittee on Antitrust and Monopoly, *Hearings on the Failing Newspaper Act*, Hearings, 90th Congress, 1st and 2d Sessions (1967-68, 7 vols.).

[592] U.S. Congress, Senate Committee on the Judiciary, Antitrust Subcommittee, *Hearings on the Newspaper Preservation Act (S. 1520)*, 91st Congress, 1st Session (1969).

[593] U.S. Congress, Senate Committee on the Judiciary, Subcommittee on Antitrust and Monopoly, *Possible Anticompetitive Effects of Sale of Network TV Advertising*, parts 1 and 2, Hearings, 89th Congress, 2d Session (1966).

[594] U.S. Congress, Senate Committee on the Judiciary, Subcommittee on Constitutional Rights, *Freedom of the Press*, Hearings, 92nd Congress, 1st and 2d Sessions (1971-72).

[595] U.S. Congress, Senate Committee on the Judiciary, Subcommittee on Patents, Trademarks and Copyrights, *Copyright Law Revision*, Hearings, 89th Congress, 1st Session (1965).

[596] U.S. Congress, Senate Committee on the Judiciary, Subcommittee on Patents, Trademarks and Copyrights, *Copyright Law Revision-CATV*, Hearings, 89th Congress, 2d Session (1966).

[597] U.S. Congress, Senate Committee on the Judiciary, Subcommittee on Patents, Trademarks, and Copyrights, *Copyright Law Revision* parts 1, 2, 3, and 4, Hearings, 90th Congress, 1st Session (1967).

[598] U.S. Department of Commerce, Telecommunication Science Panel, *Electromagnetic Spectrum Utilization—The Silent Crisis* (1966).

[599] U.S. Office of Telecommunications Policy, Executive Office of the President, "Analysis of the Causes and Effects of Increases in Same-Year Rerun Programming and Related Issues in Prime-Time Network Television" (March 1973).

[600] U.S. Office of Telecommunications Policy, Executive Office of the President, "The Radio Frequency Spectrum: United States Use and Management," (January 1973).

[601] U.S. Office of Telecommunications Policy, Executive Office of the President, *Cable Television Bibliography*, staff research paper (February 1972).

[602] U.S. Office of Telecommunications Policy, Executive Office of the

President, *Technical Analysis of VHF Television Broadcasting Frequency Assignment Criteria* (October 1973).

[603] Verrill, C., "CATV's Emerging Role: Cablecaster or Common Carrier?" *Law and Contemporary Problems*, v. 34 (Summer 1969).

[604] Ward, J.E., "Present and Probable CATV/Broadband-Communication Technology," report prepared for the Sloan Commission on Cable Communications (January 1972).

[605] Webbink, D.W., "How Not to Measure the Value of a Scarce Resource," *Federal Communications Bar Journal*, part 1, v. 23 (1969).

[606] Webbink, D.W., "The Impact of UHF Promotion: The All-Channel Television Receiver Law," *Law and Contemporary Problems*, v. 34 (Summer 1969).

[607] Webbink, D.W., "Regulation, Profits and Entry in the Television Broadcasting Industry," *Journal of Industrial Economics*, v. 21 (April 1973).

[608] Wells, W.D., "The Rise and Fall of Television Program Types," *Journal of Advertising Research*, v. 9 (September (1969).

[609] White, S., "Carnegie, Ford and Public Television," *The Public Interest*, No. 9 (Fall 1967).

[610] White, S., "Toward a Modest Experiment in Cable Television," *The Public Interest*, No. 12 (Summer 1968).

[611] Whitehead, Clay T., "Remarks" before the IRTS, October 6, 1971, reprinted as appendix I to *The Politics of Broadcast Regulation*, M. Barrett, ed. (Crowell, 1973).

[612] Whitman, W.F., "Consent Decree in the Motion Picture Industry," *Fordham Law Review*, v. 10 (January 1941).

[613] Whitney, S., *Antitrust Policies: American Experience in Twenty Industries*, v. 2 (Twentieth Century Fund, 1958).

[614] Whitney, S., "Vertical Disintegration in the Motion Picture Industry," *American Economic Review*, v. 45 (May 1955).

[615] Wilcox, C., "Regulation of Broadcasting," Chapter 18 in C. Wilcox, *Public Policies Toward Business*, 3rd edition (Irwin, 1966).

[616] Wilensky, H.L., "Mass Society and Mass Culture: Interdependence or Independence," *American Sociological Review*, v. 29 (April 1964).

[617] Wiles, P., "Pilkington and the Theory of Value," *Economic Journal*, v. 73 (June 1963).

[618] Wolf, F., *Television Programming For News and Public Affairs: A Quantitative Analysis of Networks and Stations* (Praeger, 1972).

[619] Zeuthen, F., "Theoretical Remarks on Price Policy: Hotelling's Case with Variations," *Quarterly Journal of Economics*, v. 47 (February 1933).

Index

Abbott, L., 51n
Access (*see* Fairness doctrine; Prime time access rule)
Adjacency effect, 96, 131, 136
Advertisers, 5, 8, 93-94
Advertising
expenditures, 9, 40-41
prices, 9, 40-41, 75-77, 150-151
Affiliation (*see* Network-affiliate relationship)
Agnew, S., 176
Alexander, S., 161n
All in the Family, 104
American Federation of Radio and Television Artists (AFTRA), 35, 37
American Research Bureau (ARB), 77
Anderson, J., 176n
Antitrust, 100, 138
Archibald, G., 51n
Assumptions
of simulation model, 57-59
of temporal monopoly model, 133
AT&T television tariffs, 176
Aubrey, J, 20
Audience
behavior of, 8, 49-112 *passim*, 95ff
maximization of, 4, 49-90, *passim*

Backman, J., 4
Bailey, E., 147
Baker, R., 169
Ball, S., 169
Barnett, S., 143, 176n
Barnow, E., 10
Barrett, E., 161n
Barron, J., 171
Barton, R., 9
Baumol, W., 25, 30
Beebe, J., 67
BEM case, 172
Bernstein, I., 42
Besen, S., xviii, 86n, 99, 102n, 123, 129, 143, 145
Bias, 112
Blakely, R., 161n
Blank, D., 86n, 126
Bonanza, 40
Bonini, C., 27n
Botein, M., 171
Bowen, W., 25, 30
Bowman, G., 57
Brown, L., 170
Buchanan, J., 81
Budget levels, 165
Burch, D., 177

Cabinet Committee on Cable Communication (*see* Whitehead Report)
Cable television, 141-154
compromise, 143ff
effect on UHF, 143
lease rates, 148f
pay TV, 147-152
prices, 145
revenues, 149ff
structure, 50, 89, 146ff
subscribers, 142
Carnegie Commission, 156ff
Carroll doctrine, 11, 143
Chamberlin, E., 51, 67
Channel capacity, 61, 89, 145ff
Chayes, A., 176
Chazen, L., 4
Children's television, 169ff
Coase, R., 11, 27n, 142, 161n, 172
Comanor, W., 86n
Commercialization, 169
Common carrier networks, 130
and cable, 146ff
Common denominator programs (*see* Programs, common denominator)
Communication satellites, 176
Compensation, of stations by networks, 97-100
Competition, 10, 12ff, 50, 89ff
Comstock, G., 170
Consumer surplus, 88, 127, 145
defined, 56
Copyright, 53, 82n, 143ff
Corporation for Public Broadcasting (CPB), 156ff
Counter-advertising, 172
Cournot, A., 101ff, 110-111
Crandall, R., xviii, 92ff, 167n
Cross-ownership, 175

Deintermixture, 123, 138
Demographics, 4, 77
Demsetz, H., 80, 82
Descramblers, 126
Detent tuning, 123
de Vany, A., 11, 172
Devletoglou, N., 51n
Dirlam, J., 161n
Distant signals, 142ff
Distribution economies, 18ff
Doyle, P., 9
Drop-ins, 125
Du Mont Plan, 124, 125
Dunn, D., xviii

215

About the Authors

Bruce M. Owen is a member of the Economics Department faculty at Stanford University. He was graduated from Williams College in 1965 and received the Ph.D. in economics from Stanford University in 1970. He was formerly a Brookings Economic Policy Fellow and Chief Economist of the White House Office of Telecommunications Policy. In 1974-75, Professor Owen is a national fellow of the Hoover Institution on War, Revolution, and Peace.

Jack H. Beebe has been with the FRS Associates, an economics consulting firm in Menlo Park, California, since 1972. He was graduated from Williams College in 1964, received the M.S. in industrial engineering (operations research) from the University of Texas, Austin in 1966, and the Ph.D. in Economics from Stanford University in 1972. He has taught economics and operations research at California State University, San Luis Obispo.

Willard G. Manning, Jr. has been a member of the faculty of the John F. Kennedy School of Government at Harvard University since receiving the Ph.D. in economics from Stanford University in 1973. He was graduated from the California Institute of Technology in 1968.